...he South of travel tour...
...Thunderbirds. We arrived yeste...
and will be here for about a wee...
14 hours last night, as we had twelve...! ...
...hours to get here. We went into Roxany...
...oncert will be held tonight, and ...
...ay walking around. On the way in ...
...side of the road were field after field ...
...sers. How beautiful they are with their ...
...facing the same direction, like an
audience. We passed a few small
all see ...ingly very old. The buildings were

...through...

...was much ... great reaction. ...
...Houston at ... if ... some in ... there and some ... Dick ... work ...

Happy new year! It's going to be
great year. I feel good... ready to work
...year ... make things happen, get involved.
I'm on my way now to NY to atte...
a seminar at KORG to learn about
...new product they have. I feel real goo...
about my relationship with their
company. I think it could develop in
a long lasting, productive ...

BETWEEN ROCK AND A HOME PLACE

We all do "do, re, mi,"
but you have got to find the other notes yourself.

Louis Armstrong

BETWEEN
ROCK
AND A HOME PLACE

CHUCK LEAVELL

with J. Marshall Craig

Mercer University Press | Macon, Georgia

25th Anniversary

MUP/H694

Published by Evergreen Arts
665 Charlane Drive | Dry Branch, Georgia 31020

*Please note: Some Chuck Leavell Archive photo credits do not assert copyright;
this is in acknowledgement of our not knowing the source of the photos, despite best
efforts to contact copyright holders. Any omissions should be brought to the attention
of the publisher at the above address.*

Distributed by Mercer University Press
1400 Coleman Avenue | Macon, Georgia 31207

Book design by Burt and Burt Studio

Second Printing.

∞The paper used in this publication meets the minimum
requirements of American National Standard for Information
Sciences — Permanence of Paper for Printed Library
Materials, ANSI Z39.48-1992.

Library of Congress Cataloging-in-Publication Data

Leavell, Chuck.
Between rock and a home place / Chuck Leavell;
with J. Marshall Craig.
p. cm.
Includes index.
ISBN 0-86554-975-3 (hardback : alk. paper)
1. Leavell, Chuck. 2. Rock musicians–Biography.
I. Craig, J. Marshall. II. Title.
ML417.L42A3 2004
786'.166'092–dc22

2004025894

Contents

In memory of my parents,
Billy and Frances Leavell,
without whose love and support
this book would never
have been written.

Acknowledgments

Musicians are people who've been touched on the shoulder by God. I don't know who first said that, but if you think about it, there's something so special about musicians from the American South that one can only assume they've been tapped on both shoulders ... doubly blessed with talent.

Chuck Leavell is one of those musicians. The Alabama-born piano player is arguably the best keyboardist to ever grace a rock 'n' roll stage, but don't take my word for it. He's been, at various times in his career, the first choice of keyboardist for the Rolling Stones, Eric Clapton, the Allman Brothers Band, the Black Crowes, Fabulous Thunderbirds, Marshall Tucker Band, the late Beatle George Harrison on his historic final tour of Japan — not to mention the dozen or so other artists you'll read about in this book.

Of all the people I've met, I can honestly say one of the most passionate is Chuck. His piano panache is only a small part of that, however; increasingly, his expertise and knowledge of the world's forests — particularly in his adopted home state of Georgia — has been acknowledged by not only his peers in that field with a long list of awards and honors but by a succession of American presidents. And in the decade I've known Chuck, his passion, commitment, and love for his wife Rose Lane and their daughters Amy and Ashley have asserted themselves too often — and usually too privately — for me to mention here.

Where some celebrity memoirs are exercises in vanity or attempts to mitigate, if not outright abolish, public perceptions, Chuck's story is far more important: he has a lot to teach us and I'm honored he asked me to help him.

Chuck Leavell with co-writer J. Marshall Craig on the Rolling Stones stage at Twickenham, England, September 2003.

His musical career was established but took off meteorically at the age of twenty with the Allman Brothers Band in its early, drug-and-alcohol troubled days, and he has now been with the Rolling Stones for more than two decades. Unavoidably, there are some tales of excess to recount, but if you're looking for a crass tell-all you're not going to find it here. His integrity and loyalty are as ingrained as his musical talent and environmental expertise.

Besides playing piano and keyboards for the Rolling Stones, Chuck is the band's musical navigator, or curator, of sorts. Each show night, he sits down with a pad of paper with the trademark Stones tongue logo emblazed across the top, consults two massive volumes of songs and copies of recent show set lists. Then, depending on the venue, Chuck will write down the first draft of what the fans are going to hear. The list goes on to Mick Jagger and Keith Richards, but it starts with Chuck, and it's always been a blast for me to sit at his side and talk about the music on a number of these occasions.

I'll let you in on at least one secret: Chuck is a fanatical exercise enthusiast which, as you'll read, is one of the many hugely positive traits he was so fortunate to have inherited from his parents. And this is a good thing, since over the years I've been with him on tour with the Rolling Stones in Canada, the United States, England, and

Asia, he's been very quick to find the best restaurants and indulge in a love for food that befits a Southern man. He gets to sweat it out on stage and on his family's 2,200-acre plantation, however, while a civilian like me has to garner the discipline to abandon the computer in feeble attempts to make my gym membership worthwhile.

The list of people in the Stones organization who have extended me graciousness, fun, and friendship over the past decade is long, but I'd especially like to thank Bernard Fowler, as well as Mick, Keith, Charlie, Ronnie, Darryl Jones, Arnold Dunn, Sherry Daly, Jane Rose, the legendary security honcho Jim Callaghan ... well, this could go on for pages. Everyone has always treated me like part of the family. Gregg and his Allman Brothers Band percussionists Butch Trucks and Jaimoe deserve special mention for kindly helping me dig deep into Chuck's past with the aid of their honesty, candor, and deep affection for their former band mate; most of their remembrances of the early Allman Brothers days quoted here came from recent conversations. Capricorn Records founder Phil Walden was also a great asset who generously offered his contemporary perspective on Chuck's early career success, for which he was in no small way responsible. And, indulgently, I have to personally thank Phil for, through the sheer energy of his own inimitable way, making me fifteen years old again when I listen to music. The guy's been through the ringer financially and personally and has had more attempts on the life of his character than Rasputin's worst day. Yet he turns into a little kid when talking about a great album; all the business — the bull — falls away. That, to me, is what music is supposed to be about and it's so nice to be reminded of that.

Most importantly, I thank Chuck for giving me unfettered access to his incredible archive of material and both his written and tape-recorded diaries, the latter of which are deeply personal. I'm honored by the trust he had that I would keep his private life — beyond what he has chosen to share — private. I do joke with him that he's got the goods on me, too, since several of his diary entries mention the two of us embracing the romance of rock 'n' roll excess a little too enthusiastically on a few occasions; not even, well ...

Wild Horses will keep these from getting out of our respective secret vaults!

My endless gratitude goes out to his wife Rose Lane for her arm's-length guidance and insightful advice concerning the book, and her unwavering Southern hospitality and great cooking — my gym is also unwittingly thankful for the latter.

The rest I leave to Chuck — and hope you'll agree that we as music fans, and simply as readers of interesting tales, are lucky he has decided to tell what one hopes is just the first half of a great life story — the first of several glasses of chocolate milk, so to speak. Don't worry, you'll understand what I mean by the time you're done reading this remarkable musician's — this remarkable person's — incredible tale.

J. Marshall Craig
Palm Desert, California

Introduction

People are said to have led — or to lead — double lives. I sometimes wonder how often they're as wildly different as the lives I lead, however. More than half of my life has been spent on the road, playing piano to millions of fans of bands such as the Rolling Stones, the Allman Brothers, the Fabulous Thunderbirds, and artists such as Eric Clapton and the wonderful, late George Harrison. On average I get up at noon or later in some hotel room in some foreign city and start my work in an arena, stadium, or theater sometime in the early evening and rarely make it to bed before 2 a.m., still buzzing from the same excitement of playing music as the fans get hearing it. Or perhaps it begins in a rehearsal room or a recording studio somewhere in the world. Mostly small rooms where I work with my fellow musicians, a few skilled technicians, perhaps a producer, and some sketches of music that we all are trying to create into songs, like making a picture from so many pieces of a puzzle.

My other life — my day job, I guess you'd call it — is wonderfully consumed as the owner, with my wife Rose Lane, of a substantial forest plantation and gaming reserve in central Georgia, which we christened Charlane, historically referred to as the "Home Place," which makes the title of this book pretty accurate! At home I'm up around 5 a.m. and, save for a quick break for lunch, you might find me sitting on a tractor, planting trees, pruning them, or otherwise performing some form of forest management practice or escorting dedicated hunters through the bush. Or I might be somewhere speaking: an elementary or high school, a university, an environmental group, a state legislature, or even before Congress on the importance of family forests or our national forests and how significant they are and how I believe they may be best managed, opportunities I've been afforded after two decades of study and field work.

Rose Lane and me at our home place, Charlane.

Please forgive me if I boast a little, but we are proud of our accomplishments and love being involved in both the world of environmentalism and in music. Rose Lane and I have been honored twice as Georgia Tree Farmers of the Year and in 1999 were recognized as the National Outstanding Tree Farmers. This is an

Playing the National Anthem at the Healthy Forests Restoration Act ceremony in 2003.

Credit: Tina Hager/The White House

I was immensely flattered to be recognized by President George Bush in Washington, D.C. on December 3, 2003 when he signed the bipartisan Healthy Forests Restoration Act.

honor that I hold equally as high or higher than the gold and platinum records I have received through the years from some of the artists I have worked with, or my places in two Music Halls of Fame, Alabama and Georgia. We have also received flattering recognitions from the National Arbor Day Foundation, the Georgia Conservancy, The Georgia Outdoor Writers Association, The Urban Forest Council, and other environmental groups, and I am proud to serve as a spokesman for the Georgia Forestry Association and the American Tree Farm System. I was also flattered to be invited to Washington, D.C. in December of 2003 to perform the National Anthem at a ceremony marking President George W. Bush signing the Healthy Forests Restoration Act into law. And while we don't do the work for the awards — just as I don't play the piano for the applause (but it sure is nice!) — I'm finding it's gradually becoming the more important of my two lives.

Touring with the Rolling Stones, I am fortunate to stay in the finest hotels and to eat in the finest restaurants. But the baby potatoes, hot peppers, fresh tomatoes, Southern greens, and other fare that comes out of Rose Lane's garden; the fresh quail, venison, and other game off our land; as well as the comforting crunch of pine cones and fallen pecans underfoot as we go for walks can't hold a candle to anything even Paris' finest can offer. Besides, no matter where you're from, no matter what your background or how you were raised, I believe there's a deep spiritual nourishment in living someplace where every tree is taller than every building rather than the other way around.

My life on the road can sometimes get weary — I've been doing it intensely since I was sixteen years old — even a few years before the Allman Brothers hired me at the age of twenty in 1972 in the wake of the tragic death of founding guitarist Duane Allman. Now, for more than twenty years, my highest-profile gig has been playing keyboards for the Rolling Stones, in both the studio and on the road. And, if you don't know, when the Rolling Stones go on the road, they don't make it a light affair — when I leave home at the start of every tour I don't see it again for months or even nearly a year a time. Except for the few times I've been fortunate enough to visit some public forests or parks, some forestland owned by a friend somewhere in the world, or a great park or a hiking trail on a day off that means a year of concrete and asphalt instead of the comforting feel of central Georgia's gently rolling hills.

Life's all about balance and I'm not going to give up either extreme.

Recent times have been hugely important for both my "families." The Stones marked their fortieth year in rock 'n' roll while our younger daughter Ashley graduated with honors from Boston University and our oldest daughter Amy got married in a beautiful wedding ceremony, taking the hand of Steve Bransford, a wonderful young man we're so lucky to call a part of our family. Of course, we celebrated the occasion on the graceful grounds of Charlane.

With the end of the latest Forty Licks tour, in which I joined Mick Jagger, Keith Richards, Charlie Watts, Ronnie Wood, and the rest of the band playing to nearly 4 million people in more than a dozen countries on just about every continent over more than a year on the road, I am pausing to reflect. I found myself reflecting not only on that tour, but also on all the events in my life leading up to it.

With this pause came my friend J. Marshall Craig's suggestion that I think about chronicling the fortune of rare opportunities I've had as a musician so far and also to use this reflection to reach out to fans about why my "day job" is just as important to me as those still-thrilling moments when the lights come up and Keith Richards, just a few yards to my left, kicks into the opening chords of *Brown Sugar* or *Start Me Up*.

Some may scoff at the idea of a fifty-two-year-old penning his memoirs in sort of the same way it might be a joke for a star child actor to get a lifetime achievement award. But my life — like everyone's — I like to think of as a work in progress. With good luck, good health, and the grace of the Great Spirit, this is just the first half.

And it wouldn't have been worth living were it not for my beloved wife, Rose Lane. We celebrated our thirtieth wedding anniversary on the road with the Stones in Barcelona in 2003, and every day we celebrate the love and blessing of having two wonderful daughters, Amy and Ashley, and countless friends and relatives around the world.

A lot of this book is based on diaries I've been keeping, both written and taped, for more than two decades. Like most of the good things in my life, it's all Rose Lane's fault: She bought me my first diary notebook for my birthday in 1978. There are gaps, of course, but many of the conversations recalled in this memoir come directly from my diaries, written or recorded within hours of their occurrence. I tried very hard to document my thoughts over the years, less in anticipation of someday writing a book and more as a chronicle for the family that I was so often leaving at home for weeks, or months, at a time.

Here's a funny example, from the summer of 1978, when my band Sea Level was in the studio in New York; I clearly just wanted to go home: "8-12-78. Saturday. Here I am on the 6th floor of the Hit Factory in bathroom #2. They don't have much to read around here, so I figured I'd write a bit. The album is about half done now, mixing that is. And I really want to go *South*." There are some not so funny — I chronicled my thoughts and all the discussions that went on within the Rolling Stones when Princess Diana was killed, and there's also this entry, which still brings a mixture of tears and anger when I'm reminded of it: "12-9-80. John Lennon was shot to death yesterday in New York. The world is in shock. Probably the most influential songwriter of the past 15 years. Was guru to a generation ... I feel so helpless ... I'm just numb."

OK — hardly earth-shattering revelations, but I hope you get the point that I tried to chronicle honestly what was going on in my life, and these diaries have largely made this book possible in the form it has taken. My discipline in keeping the diaries was challenged at times, and there are large gaps of months and even, at one point, several years. I know J. Marshall Craig has done what he could to keep the story straight, and I thank all my family, friends, and fellow musicians who graciously spent time answering all his questions. I need to add a special thanks to journalist John Lynskey, whose interviews with me over the years have provided not only necessary background but in some cases source material and made completing this book a far easier task than it otherwise would have been. Thanks to Keith Richards' manager and our dear friend Jane Rose for her photographs and constant friendship and support over the years I've been with the Stones. I also thank Mary Welch, who helped me write my book on American forestry, *Forever Green*; that book has been another resource for this memoir.

I need to thank Mick Jagger, Keith Richards, Charlie Watts, Bill Wyman and Ronnie Wood for making me a part of their lives these past twenty-odd years; I also wish to thank all the other musicians, producers, and artists I have worked with through my career. There are too many to name them all, but they include Gregg Allman, Dickey Betts, Jaimoe, Butch Trucks, Berry Oakley, Lamar Williams, Eric Clapton, George Harrison, The Black Crowes, Johnny Sandlin, Paul Hornsby, Alex Taylor, Dr. John, Dave Edmunds, Chris Kimsey, Warren Haynes, Randall Bramblett, Jimmy Nalls, Colin James, Russ Titleman, The Fabulous Thunderbirds, Train, The Indigo Girls, and so many more. (You know who you are!)

I'd like to thank tour manager/promoter Michael Cohl, band business advisor Prince Rupert Loewenstein, and tour financial controller Joe Rascoff for all they've done for my family and me.

I wish to say thanks to all of those that have worked with us at Charlane Plantation through the years. And a special thanks to our current stellar team, which includes Mike Hattaway, Marc Smith, Arlinda Height, Jacquie Bryant, Herman Robertson, and Linda McDuffie.

I also wish to thank the following people for making such a profound difference in my life in one way or the other: My wife Rose Lane Leavell, daughters Amy and Ashley, Steve Bransford, my parents Billy and Frances Leavell, my

Credit: © Chuck Leavell Archive

The great Charlane staff (from left): Jacque Bryant, Mike Hattaway, Herman Robertson, Linda McDuffie, Marc Smith, Arlinda Height and Bobby Huellemeier.

brother and sister Billy and Judy Leavell, Rosaline White, Alton White III, Mary Dykes, Buck and Patti Williams, Bill Graham, Phil Walden, Frank Fenter, William Perkins, Twiggs and Skoots Lyndon, Kirk West, Scott Baker, Jewett Tucker, Roy Fickling, Benjy Griffith, Herren and Susan Hickingbotham, Larry Wiseman, Jimmy Carter, Blake Sullivan, all the staff members of the Rolling Stones touring personnel, all the engineers and technicians I've worked with through the years, and all of the musicians who have taught me things directly and indirectly.

My thanks to the following: Dr. Marc Jolley, Marsha Luttrell, and all of the staff at Mercer University Press; Dan Beeson, my publicist extraordinaire at Porter Novelli; Boone Smith, my friend and attorney; Ken Waldron, Fred Whyte, Peter Burton, Anita Gambill, and all at Stihl U.S.A. for their support and friendship; Lynn Lavery for her friendship and being such a great webmistress (www.chuckleavell.com and www.charlane.com); Richard and Natalie Kerris; Kenny Robitzsch at Kenny's Repair for sharp saws and smooth engines; Mike Kovins at Korg U.S.A. for the great keyboards and continued support; Todd Bohon and all at Power Tool and Scagg Mowers for the terrific machines; and a huge thank you to all the fans who have been so good to me through the years.

Thanks to the many photographers whose work appears in this book. I'd especially like to single out Carter Tomassi (messyoptics.com), Gilbert Lee (gilbertlee.com), Sidney Smith (rockstarphotos.net), Dimo Safari (dimosafari.com) as well as the kind permissions from Musidor B.V. and Jane Rose.

I also have a very special thanks to J. Marshall Craig. We have been friends since 1994 when we met in Edmonton, Canada. At the time Jeff was the entertainment editor at the *Edmonton Sun,* the hippest newspaper there. We hit it off straightaway in what would turn out to be a quirk of fate. At his suggestion some of us from the band went to a downtown Edmonton club called the Sidetrack and sat in with a blues group there. We all had a wonderful time, and after we left town Jeff and I stayed in touch. A few years later he soured on the idea of being a journalist reporting on what others were creating and came over to our side, as it were. He went Hollywood and got into the movie and book-writing business in California, and we hooked up backstage at a lot of shows, where he introduced me to people like Nicolas Cage. More recently, we had some great times on the Forty Licks tour in Europe and Hong Kong. If not for his encouragement and talent and for the comfort that I felt in allowing him into the deepest parts of my life, certainly this book would never

Credit: © Edmonton Sun

Sitting in at the Sidetrack Club in Edmonton, in 1994.

have been written. He worked hard to make this book like a song that flows evenly and smoothly from start to finish and to help me find my own voice in the telling of my story. We had many good times during the process, and together we have told my story in a way that makes me happy to share it with others. Our friendship will no doubt continue for the other half of both our lives.

Despite appearances and the sometimes-odd trappings of even moderate fame achieved in conjunction with my work with some of the greatest rock musicians in history, it hasn't always been easy. In fact, it's more often a struggle. Like just about every artist, at times I've been taken advantage of, ripped off, underpaid, underappreciated, and under-acknowledged.

Like all musicians — like everyone in life — I've been screwed more than once. But I've learned to let it all go. My former Allman Brothers Band mate Butch Trucks recently reflected on our mutual past, and he said something that really made me think. "You just have to laugh," said Butch about all the bad times, the bad deals, the rip offs, and missing royalties. "You just have to laugh at the bad stuff — because we got to make magic. We made music. We're the luckiest people alive because we struck like lightning. We're blessed."

He's so right.

As Rose Lane and I toast each other before dinner every night no matter where we are in the world, none of us can forget life is a gift. We all get a few paper cuts along the way, but the Leavell family motto is true — Life is Good!

Chuck Leavell
Charlane Plantation
St. Dunstan's Day, 2004

Music washes away
from the soul
the dust of everyday life.

Red Auerbach

Animals at the Border

It's the Rolling Stones, so what do you expect but a lot of paperwork and trouble with those animals crossing an international border? And I'm not talking about the people in the band or the 250 or so crew members that made the last massive world tour possible; I'm talking about the dogs — the two pups I'd bought just days before.

No matter how rock legend may have informed you, the truth is that for two decades now rock 'n' roll has been as much about business and real life as it has the music and the big dream of stardom, mansions on the hill, and millions in cash stuffed in the mattress. I've now spent half my career — and half their own legendary career — with the Rolling Stones. And while the shows and the fans are spectacular, the travel is grueling, and we do spend a lot of time thinking about how much we miss our homes and our real lives. In the middle of the Stones' Forty Licks tour of 2002–2003 my wife Rose Lane told me that for her birthday, she wanted a border collie to take back to our sprawling Georgian plantation.

Luckily, we were in England at the time, and we had probably the best resource for this kind of thing at close hand — Stones drummer Charlie Watts, who, with his wife Shirley, has an expertly run Arabian horse farm in the south of England; they know their horses, and they know their dogs. With one phone call to an acquaintance, Charlie arranged for us to see some photos of two

Our Welsh border collie pups Molly Mae and Maggie Mae.

collies, which were almost eight weeks old and were available through a breeder on a working farm Charlie and Shirley know in Wales.

If this sounds all a bit surprisingly domestic, believe me, the love of dogs and the Rolling Stones have a fine … well … pedigree. Keith Richards once found a mongrel mutt in Moscow that he immediately fell in love with and insisted — as only Keith can — to have shipped to his home in Connecticut. It was not an easy process, but as you can imagine, when Keith sets his mind on something, it gets done. Throw in his love of animals and there's no stopping him! He wittily named the dog Rasputin. When the Stones were recording an album in Ireland, Keith discovered a kitten that had been abandoned by its mother and was sure to die on its own. The kitten was immediately adopted and moved into the studio with us. Keith called it "Voodoo," and its little corner in the studio became Voodoo's lounge. Now you know where the album got its title.

When we got the photos of the Welsh puppies we were nearing the end of our Forty Licks tour. Just a handful of shows left — and only three in England. The pups, then about seven and a half weeks old, were just beautiful. Both had the typical black and white border collie look, with the medium length coats. We said we still just wanted one, and we chose the one that had nice markings … a little more white than the other, mostly in her face. The other one was also really pretty, with a completely black head save for a snip of white near the nose. We passed the photos around to friends in the Stones entourage and just about everyone predicted we would be unable to make a decision and that we'd end up buying both. They were right. Charlie told us that getting both was better for the pups, too, since they'd be going through the trauma of all that travel together, and if we decided to make them working dogs on our own plantation, they'd be better as a team.

We finished our last two shows at Wembley Arena and a final outdoor concert at Twickenham Stadium and made arrangements for the two puppies to meet us at the end-of-tour show in Zurich before we flew back to Georgia. From the photos alone, Rose Lane decided to call the pups Molly Mae and Maggie Mae.

The trouble was how to get the pups from South Wales to London and then London to Zurich so they could fly with us back to Atlanta. I tried talking to the airlines and various agencies and finally gave up and went to the guy I should have gone to in the first place, Stones road manager Alan Dunn. He's been one of the band's key logisticians for decades and has had to deal with just about every kind of situation and special request you could imagine. We were lucky — pups need to be ten weeks old to fly but less than fifteen weeks before needing shots and a thirty-day quarantine. So all we needed was a single certificate of good health from a veterinarian.

On Oct. 1, 2003, we were in Zurich, Switzerland for our final show. That afternoon, I was at the airport, having paid yet another round of special fees, when a white cap brought out a big kennel container that sported the excited faces of two beautiful little puppies. I leaned down and opened the door, and they were all over me. Forty Licks? Try a couple of hundred! From that moment I didn't regret the extra expense of the second puppy or all the trouble we'd gone through.

An hour later we were back at the hotel. Rose Lane had been pacing the floor in anticipation, but she'd have to wait because we didn't even make it to the elevator before we ran into Alan Dunn, who beamed and insisted the puppies pay a visit to the Stones touring office, which was on the main floor of the hotel. The gals and everyone in the office went crazy for Maggie and Molly. Maybe part of this was that we had been on the road for fifteen months and everybody was missing their homes and pets, but the pair of collies was certainly a hit.

I finally got them upstairs to meet Rose Lane and her reaction alone was worth all the effort. The hotel was very "dog friendly" besides wanting to accommodate any member of the Stones entourage. They sent up blankets, feed and water bowls, and even came up with a room service menu especially for the pups. We then had a constant parade of Stones' folk through the room anxious to meet Maggie and Molly. Keith Richards, who's probably got the biggest heart of anyone I know, hilariously autographed a photo for the pups. If he could have, I know he would have taken them. So would just about everybody in the band. Rose Lane got them accustomed to a dual leash, walking them around outside the hotel, and then took them to the backstage area on our final show day. Man! Talk about the stars arriving: Maggie and Molly were the biggest hit backstage.

Part of the reason for this is that the Rolling Stones are a unique bunch of characters. It's not like most bands that go out for a few weeks, take some time off, record, take some more time off, and then do another short series of shows. The Stones, whether they like it or not, are far too big for that. It takes millions of dollars to set up a Stones stadium show and then takes months before it even recoups its production costs — so hitting the road with the intention of making some serious money — and, let's face it, meeting the expectations of the band's fans all over the world — means a commitment of a year or more.

Because of the SARS health epidemic in Asia in 2003 we were forced to cancel some shows and there was some talk of trying to make them up. But officially, and contractually, Zurich was the end of the Stones' Forty Licks tour. Possibly the last massive Stones tour ever, some people were theorizing.

As I reflected that last day in Switzerland, I thought about what an amazing time it had been. It always is with the Stones. You go in thinking that your life's on hold for the next year or two and in the blink of an eye it's all over. And every time there's magic along the way. On the Forty Licks tour it was our first-ever appearances in India.

And it was also a brief break we had in mid-April, during which we got a chance to attend the graduation of our youngest daughter, Ashley, from Boston University, and then get back to our plantation in Georgia and stage a spectacular wedding of our oldest daughter, Amy, to a wonderful young man named Steve Bransford. It's quite amazing to me to think back when I first joined the Stones in 1982 for the European dates supporting the *Tattoo You* record and realized that Amy was seven years old at the time and Ashley was born during that tour! Now here they were graduating and getting married. Man, how time flies!

Two days later I flew to Washington, D.C. to join Secretary of Agriculture Ann Venneman in presenting an award, the Stihl National Forestry Heroism Award, to a fine young man named Billy Chrimes who helped save some lives in the deadly California forest fires of 2002; it's the kind of honor that I find myself a grateful participant in now after twenty years of serious tree farming, environmental study, and preservation on our own award-winning planta- tion.

Credit: Chuck Leavell Archive

Secretary of Agriculture Ann Venneman, Ken Waldron from Stihl and I present a check to Stihl National Forestry Heroism Award winner Billy Chrimes.

It seemed as if I hardly had time to sleep before I found myself back on another plane for Europe and the final leg of the tour.

I usually go to our gigs early, around 2:30 p.m. But on this final day there was no sound check, and I had things to do at the hotel: some emails, phone calls, and a bit of packing, so I went with most of the other band members at 4 p.m. Not a long drive, so we arrived by 4:30 or so. It was an early show, 8 p.m. start with a 10:30 curfew.

It's the last set list of the tour. One of my great pleasures as a member of the Stones organization is that I come up with each night's set list, submit it to Mick Jagger for review before it goes to Keith Richards for his input. Even though we were all anxious to get home, this was an important show. It needed to rock hard. We hadn't played Zurich in a long time, and it was a stadium show. I suggested a lot of well-known numbers, not too many quirky or weird ones on this night's list. We had about 40,000 folks there, so we wanted them singing along to lyrics they knew. It would be pretty standard, with the icons prevailing. But we wanted to have some fun ourselves, too, so a jam tune needed to be in there. *Midnight Rambler* was a good choice. *Angie* for the ballad, as well as *Can't Always Get What You Want*. For the past few tours, we've had a little stage set up in the middle of the audience, called the B-stage, which we head out to three-quarters through the performance to jam out some more club-oriented material with the stripped-down core band — Charlie, bassist Darryl Jones, Ronnie Wood, Keith Richards, Mick Jagger, and me. Keith likes to have a blues number on the B-stage, and by the time we'd hit Zurich we hadn't done that in a few shows, so I suggested *Mannish Boy*. We'd had *Paint It Black* in there and it had worked well. Here's the set list I came up with and submitted to Mick (opposite page).

Mick quickly agreed with my picks. Then I took it to Arnold Dunn (Alan Dunn's brother. I told you the Stones is one big family!) to take to Keith (who made the choices of his tunes and agreed with the rest), and finally Arnold printed it out and distributed it to all (page 20).

Still, this was a landmark show — the last one of the European tour — number 116 since we began. There were a lot of hugs going around with everyone, band and crew. There was a feeling of relief

CL Set Proposal Zurich   10/2/03

1. B. Sugar
2. Start Me Up
3. You Got Me Rocking
4. Don't Stop
5. Angie
6. Can't Always Get
7. Rambler / Miss You / Rocks Off
8. T. Dice
9. KR
10. KR
11. Sympathy
12. Only R&R / Respectable
13. Rooster / Mantra
14. S F Man
15. Gimmie Shelter
16. Paint It Black
17. Honky Tonk
18. Satisfaction
19. JJ Flash

ROLLING STONES ON THE ROAD / WORLD TOUR 2002-2003

"Rolling Stones" and Tongue and Lip Designs are Trademarks of Musidor B.V.

and gratitude that we got through the whole year plus and that we were all in pretty good shape.

Ronnie Wood's elder brother Ted passed away a couple of days before — not unexpected, as he had liver cancer and been ill a long time, but still a very sad thing. We did our best to support Ronnie in his grief and help him get through those last few days so he could go

THE ROLLING STONES

LICKS WORLD TOUR 2002-2003

THU, OCT 2, 2003	SHOW #	115	ZURICH STADIUM

				KEY	TEMPO
1	BROWN SUGAR*		BOBBY	C	126
2	START ME UP*	BF & LF OFF STAGE		F	120
3	YOU GOT ME ROCKING*	BF & LF OFF STAGE		D	125
4	DON'T STOP*	BF & LF OFF STAGE		A	124
5	ANGIE*	Tim on Keys		Am	73
6	CAN'T ALWAYS GET WHAT YOU WANT*	Tim on Keys	BV's + BONE	C	84
7	MIDNIGHT RAMBLER*			B	120
8	TUMBLIN' DICE*	Band intros after song	BV's + BRASS	B	107
9	SLIPPING AWAY* (KR)	TIM ON KEYS	BV's + BRASS	A	KR
10	HAPPY* (KR)		BV's + BRASS	A	KR
11	SYMPATHY*	Walk to B-Stage	BV's	E	109
12	IT'S ONLY ROCK AND ROLL*	B-STAGE		B	125
13	MANNISH BOY*	B-STAGE		A	68
14	STREET FIGHTING MAN*	B-STAGE	Walk to A-Stage	B	121
15	GIMMIE SHELTER*		BV's	C#m	116
16	PAINT IT BLACK*		Tim on Keys	Em	132
17	HONKY TONK WOMAN*		BV's + BRASS	G	107
18	SATISFACTION*		BV's + BRASS	E	134
19	J J FLASH*	ENCORE	BV's + BRASS	B	135

THANKS TO EVERYONE FOR YOUR EFFORTS DURING THE TOUR,
HAVE A SAFE JOURNEY HOME AND SEE YOU NEXT TIME..

be with his other brother Art and the rest of his family. Ronnie had also gone through a fierce addiction battle before the tour started and had done a magnificent, inspiring job of keeping himself healthy, so we knew the death of a beloved family member would be putting some additional strain on him and everybody was there for him. Ronnie's brother died on Sept. 29 — at roughly the time we were on stage playing the tune *Slippin' Away*, he told me. We hugged and he thanked me for the support.

At the end of a Stones tour a lot of things run through your mind — how can they not? You've spent more time with these people over the past year, year and a half, than you have your own family, and as it winds down it's quite an emotional experience. As I ate dinner before the final show, I real-

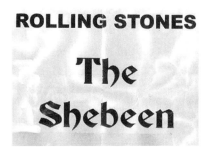

ROLLING STONES

The Shebeen

ized that it would be my last meal in the Shebeen. On each tour someone, usually Keith, comes up with a very cool name for the backstage catering area. It's been the Voodoo Lounge, Bar Babylon, and in this case, Irish slang for an after-hours pub: Shebeen. So just before we all gathered and walked down the hallway, there were all these feelings. But we had one more show to do, and we all wanted it to be a great one. We all had our jobs to do, and there were a lot of folks waiting to hear the Rolling Stones play.

It was a great one to end on.

We could feel the joy on the stage, all of us knowing that we'd be going home soon, but also knowing that we wouldn't get to do this for who knows how long, if ever. We tried to make it rock, and it did, right from the beginning. The sound was good, and when Keith hit the opening riff of *Brown Sugar* and Charlie slammed his snare with that wonderful flam at the intro, we were off and running. I did my "double reverse glissando" on the piano and we were almost into the first verse. Charlie was driving the band, and Keith was playing with the same passion he always does and hitting the right chords and grooves. Mick was totally tuned in to the audience, and they into him. It was probably most difficult for Ronnie, but even with his unfortunate family situation he played great, giving it all he had. Lots of grins all around the stage. Darryl Jones pumped the bass and was locked in with Charlie, raising the stakes. The numbers flowed. The first four were rockers, all tight and strong. Then came *Angie*, and I got to play those wonderful melodic lines one more time, and the tune flowed clear as a mountain stream.

Then *Can't Always Get What You Want* and the whole stadium sang along, Mick directing them. *Midnight Rambler* was our last chance to cut loose with a bit of a jam, and we went to some places we never have before. When we hit the middle section where Mick does the "Oh yeahs," we got into almost a jazz feel with Charlie playfully teasing his symbols and creating a slow easy groove. That one ended with a bang, and we were into *Tumblin' Dice,* which hit its usual

The Rolling Stones rock the B-stage in San Diego on the Forty Licks tour.

groove. Bernard Fowler and Lisa Fischer sang strong as always, pushing things higher, and Blondie Chaplin spiced things up by playing some percussion, singing, too. Tim Ries, Mike Davis, and Kent Smith popped the horns. Bobby Keys, who had been ill and even missed two shows in the previous six, blew the brass off his sax. It grooved and swayed. Keith finally directed the ending and we all saw the pleasure of the fans. Then there were the band intros, the last time to step up front and wave at the crowd. I saw several other familiar faces in the audience. There are a lot of folks that follow this band around the world. Intros finished, it was Keith's turn to take over. *Slippin' Away* paced nicely with some good input from

everyone. *Happy* broke it open again, and the crowd sprung to life, loving Keith's antics and Ronnie's lap-steel soloing. Keith gave the fans his thanks afterward, and there was a short pause before the percussion intro to *Sympathy for the Devil*. Mick appeared back on stage. *Sympathy* spurred the audience on with the ooh oohs,

I love the intimacy of the B-stage portion of the Stones shows — and so do the crowds.

and the pyrotechnics blasted from way above the stage when Mick belted out "pleased to meet you ...." The ending went on a little longer than usual, and we pumped it as hard as we can. Then we went to the B-stage and turned the stadium into a club. *It's Only Rock and Roll* always excites the crowd, and the groove was just right. *Mannish Boy* followed, and we got to play the blues. Then *Street Fighting Man* hit its intense lope, and I got to sing along with Mick for the whole tune. The ending took it up a notch, deeper and tougher than normal. We walked back to the main stage for *Gimmie Shelter*, a great intro, establishing the mood and melody. When we got to Lisa's feature, she set the stadium on fire as she screamed out: "Rape, murder ... is just a shot away!"

In the home run: *Paint It Black* hit the Bolero ending with passion and power. *Honky Tonk Women* lightened things up and everyone got to sing along. It never ceases to amaze me how that song makes everybody so happy and creates a mood of reckless abandonment, especially with the girls. For about four minutes it was if they were all happily working in a bordello in Texas or Louisiana back in the 1800s. Fantastic! A few of them were compelled to show all of us in the band what's under their shirts. It's just incredible the effect that song has on women! I got to play my *Honky Tonk* piano solo, somewhere between boogie and funk with the attitude as if I'd had a few whiskeys.

We had two to go. *Satisfaction* put the stadium into a frenzy, and Keith took full advantage by extending the vamp at the end. Mick found a few new vocal throws in the "hey, heys," the "sat-is-factions," and the "come ons," and of course he ran back and forth across the stage like he always does, looking like he's breaking the 100-yard dash record. The tune ended, and we all felt sort of stunned. Short waves of good night to the audience, and then off the stage for a little breather. The encore remained: *Jumpin' Jack Flash*. Keith hit the riff just as hard as he did the day he wrote it and quickly we were into the chorus: "But it's aaaalllll righhhht now," and it is indeed a gas, gas, gas.

God, this is always so much fun. I've played with this band for twenty-one years now, and it's even more fun now than it was the first time I walked out on stage with them. How is that possible? The final Zurich show Mick made the ultimate end-of-tour gesture and thanked everyone in the band and each crew member, mentioning them by name.

Mick and Darryl did a little high-step, fast-shuffle dance facing each other while Keith went off to the wings to acknowledge the crowd, saying "thanks" with motions of his guitar and his wonderful, dangerous smile. Bernard and Lisa moved and sang, and the horns joined in right at the last few rounds of phrases. Then when Keith got back I looked for his cue, he stared at me and then the rest of the band, and finally he gave the "next one" nod. Ugh, ugh … uh uh HUH … uh … uh … HUHhhhhhh. Long tag … big crescendo by all … I rolled the keys of my Hammond B3 slowly up the register, building up the swell with everything I've got, then the last flam of Charlie's snare and bass drum hit, and Keith's heavy guitar chord. Charlie hurled one of his drum sticks into the audience, then the other one. Keith, Ronnie, and Darryl threw out their guitar pics. We were done. That's it. Only the bows remained. We wandered around the stage for a bit, smiling at each other and to the fans, waving and pointing to some. As we always do, Lisa, Bernard, and I wadded up our copies of the set list and threw them into the crowd. Slowly we all gathered at the front of the stage,

Credit: © 2003 Jane Rose

Coming out to take my bow before yet another sold-out Stones show.

got our arms around each other, and looked down the line knowing this was it. We heard Mick's count — "One, two, three!" — the group bowed, and I looked at thirteen pairs of shoes in a line. Back up for the final waves, and then a last look at a stadium full of people who had come to see if the Rolling Stones were still the "World's Greatest Rock and Roll Band." They weren't disappointed. Even the critics, if you pay close attention, spin all kinds of rubbish about "time not being on their side" and about the Stones being too old to be rocking and rolling, usually about two paragraphs before almost reluctantly admitting that the show was great, the performance terrific, and even something like out of one review I kept: "They may play as well — even better — than before." I see it on every tour.

There's a true Elvis-has-left-the-building protocol with a Stones show. We call it the "Great Escape" and it's a very precisely timed event — more so than the beginning of the shows, in fact. There's no heading back to the dressing rooms — when we leave the stage it's down the back steps of the platform and through heavy black drapes, and there are four black sedans for Mick, Keith, Charlie, and Ronnie and a luxury van for the rest of the band, as well as a full-sized bus for our families and friends, who had to be aboard the bus three or four songs before the end of the show. Security rushes us to the waiting vehicles, which take off just as their doors are closed and the local police fire up their escort, and we're off. The fireworks have barely even begun and to the crowd I'm sure it seems the music is still playing.

In the van with Bobby, Lisa, Darryl, Bernard, Arnold Dunn, and a few other people, there was great relief. We're all healthy, tired, but healthy. And we're headed home. There's a bit of wine and a few beers on the van, and "my Texas Brother" — as I call Bobby (who hails from Buddy Holly's hometown of Lubbock) — jokingly complains about the lack of catering. "Where's the caviar?" he yells out. "This is not like the old days. We should be havin' some fine eats here! I want a damn lobster! And I want more money!" Some smartass passes an American one-dollar bill up to him from the back of the van. Everyone laughs, in part because it's true — being on the road these days is about entertainment but more importantly the business of entertainment. And that means it's unlikely if there's ever going to be champagne and caviar in the vans rushing the band members back to the hotel.

Like after every show, there is a lingering excitement, but this time we were all obviously a bit weary. There were a few final good-byes in the bar, but the reality was we all had a lot of packing to do. We were goin' home.

We had been told there was a possibility of making up the dates in China and Hong Kong cancelled because of the SARS outbreak, but it never really seemed a reality moving this incredibly huge machine halfway across the world for four shows. So it did seem like the end. I had a nice chat with Keith. He said that while they didn't really know what was up, there had been some discussion of possibly more dates in 2005. He also mentioned we still had the stuff in the can left from the Paris sessions, and those could be worked on with some additional tunes as well. However, he was quick to say it was all very speculative and nebulous. I also had a chat with Mick in which he thanked me for the extra work on putting the tunes together for the different venues, doing the set lists, etc.

We talked a bit about some of the funny set lists that Keith and Ronnie had suggested early on in the process and sort of congratu-lated ourselves on working all of this out and giving the fans a broader body of songs on the tour. I chatted with Ronnie and Charlie. Charlie and I talked about the pups, and he also thanked me for the work as the band's "navigator." I made the rounds to as many crew members as I could to say thanks to them. Our daughter Ashley had joined the merchandising team part way through the tour and her boss, Nick Jones, came up and told me what a good job she had done. "That's my girl!" I said.

The party went on late, but I left after a couple of hours. It started around 10 p.m., and some folks stayed until 5 a.m. It was pretty much what you'd expect for that kind of end of tour event. And now it was history. The travel, the shows, all the little experi-ences, the big experiences … fifteen months of my life. It was fun. It was successful — hugely successful — especially for the main guys and for the top business guys. Tons of money made, and tons of press, most all of it extremely positive on the tour. Lots of CD sales on *Forty Licks* and for the catalogue. Ridiculous amounts of merchandise sold. They should be very, very happy. Yet another record-breaking tour for the Rolling Stones.

I think back on the times when we're up there — even fifteen months into tour — and it's all going right. You look around at the smiles on the faces, both the band and the fans, and you know you're doing something very special. People stop you on the streets and thank you for the music. That feels good. I recall some of the frustrations of the past fifteen months, some of the disappointments. Certainly there have been some of both.

But this night is for celebrating the good times, and more importantly, I'm going home! We made a lot of memories on that tour. For ourselves and for a whole lot of people.

Some of those memories are more tangible than others — gifts from friends and fans and things Rose Lane and I have bought on the road over the course of more than a year. We had to send several boxes of things home ahead of us, but we still had our daily staples — clothes, coffee maker, stereo system, computer gadgets, cameras, and all the Stones memorabilia that I keep — things like passes, party invitations, and the famous daily Stones newsletters

Credit: © Chuck Leavell Archive

Rose Lane with our daughter Ashley on the Forty Licks tour.

from the tour office, which are slipped under our doors at night. We'd be lost without them. They tell us what time the vans leave for rehearsals, what time the sound check is, if there's a special event we're invited to, or if Ronnie's got an art show going on in the city we happen to be playing. I remember one warned us that hot water was rationed at our hotel in East Berlin, and another advised us to bring our own toilet paper to South America.

Usually, there's the not-too-veiled reminder that we're crossing an international border and contraband is likely to be discovered by drug dogs — the "puppies," as the tour office jokingly refers to them. And we're always warned not to pack our passports. Either of these situations could result in a delay of a member of the organization and, in theory, threaten the next show.

Or, sometimes, there's more hilarious stuff like this from one of the newsletters in Japan, advising us on some helpful translations of common English expressions:

> GOOD MORNING: Oh-HAH-you goh-zah-ee-maksu
> GOOD NIGHT: oh-yah-soo-mee-nah-sah-ee
> YES: hahh-ee
> NO: ee-eh
> PLEASE: oh-neh-gah-ee shee-mahs
> THANK YOU: doh-moh ah-ree-gah-toh

A few days later the morning newsletter had some additions.

> DO YOU SPEAK ENGLISH: eh-goh oh hah-nah-shee-mahs kah
> EXCUSE ME: goh-mehn-nah-sah-ee
> I DON'T UNDERSTAND: wah-kah-ree-mah-sehn
> I LIKE YOUR UNDERWEAR: so-no sh-ta-gi kawa-ee-ee neh
> YOU'RE A GOOD KISSER: kissu-ga jo-zu-neh (m)
> Kissu-ga jo-zu-dah-na (f)
> DO YOU LIKE TO MAKE LOVE IN THE SHOWER?: SHA-WAH-o abi-nah-gar-a SEK-KI-SU-su-ru no su-key?

They're small touches, but they add to the circus and fun of being on the road with the Stones, which is why I always keep them. Not that I don't carry enough with me on the road — which is why packing up for an end-of-tour journey is always a nightmare. I have two carry-on bags. A Tumi nylon briefcase that holds my Apple iBook and extra battery, necessary papers including set list notes,

PDA, pens, passport, maybe a magazine or two, business cards, my tour laminate, a highlighter, reading and sunglasses, official Rolling Stones guitar pics (which I give to kids and fans from time to time), some aspirin or other such tablets, and a few other ditties. My other carryon has a CD wallet with stuff I might want

A self-portrait of Rose Lane and me on the Rolling Stones jet.

to hear or see during travel, my workout weight gloves, usually a pair of tennis shoes, and a light workout set of clothes, a book or two, wine corks (I like saving them for some reason … memories of great meals or of celebrations. Rosie and I had our twenty-fifth anniversary on the Babylon tour in Amsterdam in the Amstel Hotel and on Forty Licks tour we celebrated our thirtieth in Barcelona. Also, I have this idea that some day I'll have a room, maybe in my studio, where I'll use all those corks on a wall or two).

Rosie and I had reservations on Delta flight 67 departing just after 11 a.m. I woke up at 7 (a half an hour before my 7:30 wake up call). I went to check on the pups, which we had in a small room next to the bathroom. They greeted me with happy faces and wet tongues. I showered quickly and started my final bits of packing, closing up the cases, and getting the kennel ready for Molly and Maggie. We checked out of the room and met John Sampson (one of the security personal) and Dennis Griffin (part security and gig logistics person, the one that always meets us at the venue when we arrive and co-ordinates the "Great Escape" each night) as they had flights that left at about the same time and were traveling with us to the airport. We loaded up all the cases and the pups and headed out. No hitches at the airport, and there we met Ashley who traveled home with us. She had seen the pups for the first time the night before at the show and of course fell in love with them straightaway, showing them off to all her workmates in merchandise and others in

Credit: © Chuck Leavell Archive/Kimberly Smith

Our beautiful daughters Amy and Ashley with the family's number 1 pet, our Jack Russell Terrier, Lilly.

the crew. Finally, we boarded the long-awaited flight and headed home to our little piece of heaven: Charlane Plantation.

I had so many thoughts about home in the forty-eight or so hours before we boarded Delta flight 67. I missed Lilly, our eight-year-old Jack Russell Terrier, and wondered how she would take to the notion of having two border collie pups as new mates. I'd been in touch with Mike Hattaway, our plantation manager, about all sorts of things: the pending hunting season and bookings, working our hunting dogs, planting the fall feed plots for wildlife, the condition of our network of roads in the woods, what shape our grounds and pond are in, how our equipment is holding up (our jeeps, tractors and farm implements). The plan in early 2003 was to plant about 135 acres of trees. And on our first full day back at home, we were expecting about thirty people to show up to tour the plantation, have lunch, and talk about the establishment of an Academy of the Environment for the State of Georgia.

So all of this was going through my head. Above all, I was hoping to get home before the sun went down so I could see a little bit of home in the daylight. Even if it was dark, I would want to take a short look around. I was happy to host the tour group, but I really looked forward to seeing Amy and her new hubby Steve, who came down from Atlanta to spend the night with us. What did I most look forward to? It changed hour by hour on that flight home — but one recurring thought was simply being able to saddle up a horse and take a good long ride around the place on my own, just absorb the surroundings and "decompress."

There was a lot to think about. We started plans for building a new lodge where an old barn once stood to increase our capacity for guests at Charlane. And I wanted to start getting a design in mind for it. We had our young filly Stella with a horse trainer, and I was anxious to see how that was coming along. I also longed to see my mother-in-law Rosaline, my brother-in-law Alton, our Aunt Mary, and all of the family. I wanted to do some work: cut some firewood, plant trees, do some gardening, and such. I was so ready to be away from cities and crowds and couldn't wait for there to be nothing but Georgian soil under my boots rather than concrete and asphalt. I wanted to check out the wildlife situation: look for deer tracks, bear tracks, locate some quail covies, see what's happening with the wild turkeys and the wild hogs. I wanted to breath fresh, clean country air and hear the sound and smell the scent of the wind through the pines. I wanted to look at my stands of trees and see how they were doing. I wanted to take Lilly out on the jeep and let her run in the woods. I wanted to play with Molly and Maggie. I wanted to smell the smells of the barn: the horses, the hay, the leather tack. I wanted to sit by the pond and see ducks and geese coming in. I wanted to sit by the fireplace and do nothing. I wanted to taste the Southern cooking of Rose Lane and Linda (our friend who also works as a professional cook at Charlane, a much-needed asset when we've got a full complement of hungry hunters on the plantation). I wanted to sit on the porch in the evening and watch the sun go down.

On the flight home, I was dreaming of this and other long-term goals like opening a restaurant with all my memorabilia from the Allman Brothers, Eric Clapton, George Harrison, and Rolling Stones tours. I was dreaming of getting myself a new truck and a new shotgun for quail hunting, and I was also thinking of what it was going to be like working on my memoirs — and what I'd gotten myself into with Jeff, who joined the band on the road for a while and whose constant grilling and attention to the development of this book made me realize I was going to have some hard work ahead of me.

After customs and a two-hour drive from Atlanta Rose Lane, Ashley, and I were finally home. The sun was just setting as I grabbed my keys and cranked up the truck and took Lilly for a cruise around the plantation. Ah, my Georgia pines. Beautiful. Each area of the plantation has a tree stand or area that someone in the family has named. Lilly and I rode through the Tall Pines. Looks great. We rode through Longleaf Lane, another area. Over Sandy Hill. Beautiful. Around the Dancing Pines and into what Rose Lane named the Enchanted Forest (and of which she's done a magnificent painting!). Losing daylight … past twilight. Lights on. Now through the Spring tract. I've seen about five deer so far and have let Lilly out to chase them — they're not as fun as squirrels, her favorite, but they're still fun for a little dog. I drove down to the kennels for a quick look at the hunting dogs. I found Mike there, tending to their dinner. We talked for a bit about what we needed to do in the weeks to come.

Lilly and I piled back in the truck and headed home. Rose Lane had taken out some chicken to fire up on the porch where we have a nice brick grill, and I put the pups up in the barn, where a couple of our other employees, Marc and Herman (almost eighty years old and outworks all of us) fixed up a place for them. The pups whined a bit, but settled down. We grilled the chicken, had a cocktail, and talked about how wonderful it was to be home.

After more than a year on the road — late nights and parties and a few near-dawn evenings with Keith in his hotel suite listening to

Credit: © Chuck Leavell Archive

One of our favorite spaces to relax on our plantation ... our "Pondo."

music — I was back into my routine immediately when I got home. Every day, I'm up at 5:30 a.m. Check emails during my first coffee, have a great workout in my small gym that used to be a playhouse when the girls were young, and then head out to inspect the property on foot — giving the Welsh puppies their first introduction to rural Georgia.

Our plantation manager Mike did a great job while we were gone, as did Marc and Herman. But there's only so much they can do. Charlane has grown into quite an operation in the past few years. We've installed a nature trail, water garden, several guest homes, an enclosed, two-story dock on our lake (which my pal Jewett dubbed our "Pondo") and they all need maintenance. Mike and the guys have worked hard during my absence, but there is always much to do ... the truth is that you never get all the work done on a place like this, but we joke that it gives us job security!

My first morning home I was soon hungry, and I knew the pups would be, too. Back at the main house I put some feed in their bowls on the porch and went into the kitchen, which our cook Linda had stocked well in anticipation of our return. Bacon, sausage, eggs, wheat bread, and more! Sausage ... man, it had been a long time since I had some proper country sausage and eggs. As I cooked, Rose Lane woke up and got herself a coffee, we chatted about how wonderful it was to finally be home, and I threw a few extra sausages and eggs on the griddle for her.

Not forgetting that we had a group of conservationalists coming through as part of a plan to set up an Academy of the Environment, Rose Lane and I decided we'd host the lunch but that we'd let Mike and Marc conduct the tour. The rest of the day we spent playing with the pups, checking out the horses, lying out down at the pondo, and just enjoying home. Funny how that while we'd spent much of the year on the road, our home is such a welcoming place that it seems to embrace us as much as we embrace it, and in a matter of only days it seemed like we'd never been away. We'd seen lots of hotel rooms, restaurants, and different cities all over the world, and for the most part Rose Lane had been with me. With a fine meal of smoked ribs and good ol' southern vegetables in my tummy, I went to bed a happy man!

The next day I was almost immediately back into my tree-farmer mode: up early, out to the work shed, and conferring with my plantation manager about the huge amount of work we would be facing. One of the first projects was also a heartbreaker. A huge elm tree that our main house was essentially built around died and had to come down. It was like losing a family member, really. The tree had stood protectively, grandfatherly, over the house for 100 some years. We didn't know whether it was just old age or whether a disease was to blame, but there was no saving the grand old tree. There were tears shed over that one. We left the stump at roof-top level ... we'll turn it into a totem pole or some other sort of carving with the help of a local craftsman named Bobby Hullemier, whom we rely on for much of our fine woodwork on the plantation.

Mike and I discussed the controlled burns we needed to do to prepare some of the land for replanting and for feed plots for the wildlife. We talked about the construction of the new lodge on the property, which we need to accommodate more clients — serious, ethical hunters — who come to Charlane during the quail season.

Rose Lane and me at home just after the final European show on the Forty Licks tour.

We've got an ongoing armadillo infestation leaving holes all over our front lawn and some wild hogs tearing up land down near the pond. The horses needed some lovin' and needed their manes and tails brushed and washed.

I'd just finished playing to nearly four million people over almost a year and a half with the Rolling Stones, but at home, my mind was consumed by other things. And would be — for about three weeks.

Zurich, it turns out, wasn't the last Stones show on the Forty Licks tour. I had to get my butt back on another plane for the nearly 24-hour travel time to Hong Kong. We had two days of rehearsals and then Nov. 7 and 9, the first-ever Stones shows in the former British colony. Keith is wealth of information on just about any subject — he even knew all about these weird birds that circled Hong Kong's Victoria Harbor and their peculiar flight patterns — and has a great memory. He recalled that while the band had never played Hong Kong, it had stopped in the then-British colony way back in 1966 on its way to its first tour of Australia; Keith described how much the place had changed since he'd last seen it. And he told everyone to beware people selling jade products on the street. "All you're gonna end up with is green glass," he warned.

The venue was a temporary festival site set up right on the harbor and while it sat 16,000, a pretty small venue for the Stones to go halfway around the world, the crowds each night were wild.

I was weary from the long flight, but since we had a few days to rest before and between the rehearsals and shows, I did get a chance to get out and see the wonderful, frantic city and — as is my way — take the opportunity to hike up into the steep hills and explore the trees and wildlife.

It was probably the last thing I expected to be doing. But one thing I can never forget about playing piano with the Rolling Stones is to expect ... the unexpected.

There is no feeling,
except the extremes of fear and grief,
that does not find relief in music.

———————————————————

George Eliot

If Not for the Women in My Life

Women. What can I say? They have always been the greatest influence and inspiration in my life. My father, Billy, was an insurance salesman who worked hard to provide for his family and was, of course, a wonderful role model, just as my much-older brother, also named Billy, has been. But there was such an age gap between me and these father figures — my brother is fourteen years older than I, and when you grew up in the 1960s, this kind of age difference was basically a generation gap on its own. Still there was much love in the family.

My sister Judy is only five years older, which made us closer, but also meant that for my first years I was at home alone with my mother during the day. This would prove to be the single greatest formative influence on my life. My mother, Frances, loved music and loved to entertain me by playing the piano we had in our living room in my birthplace of Birmingham, Alabama. In fact, my first memories are of Mom singing church songs and us going to church and singing those hymns *The Old Rugged Cross, Just as I Am, Rock of Ages, I Come to the Garden, Jesus Loves the Little Children,* and others.

Dad was Southern Baptist while Mom went to the Church of Christ. For a while we alternated but mostly ended up attending the Church of Christ, which has a strict interpretation of the phrase in the Bible that says, "Raise your voices unto the Lord" and therefore doesn't have instrumental music during its services. Just singing. There was no choir, just the congregation singing the songs as a whole. The singing could be very beautiful sometimes, but I remember there was this one guy who sang very loud and out of tune — not a shy bone in his body and not an ounce of singing talent. You had to hand it to him for sheer passion, however. We would talk about it after church, laughing about how much he stood out and how funny it was. My mother had a lovely voice. Not neces-

My mother, Frances, and father, Billy, as newlyweds.

sarily the voice of a professional but it was light and pleasant and I loved hearing it. She'd sing church songs during the week at home or in the car if we were going somewhere. What sweet caress for a young son.

What I loved most was when she'd play the piano. Sometimes she did it to amuse herself, but more often it was to entertain me. I loved it so much I'd ask her to stop her housework and play, which she did if she had the time to indulge me. I was transfixed watching her hands move up and down the keyboard, which was right at my eye level.

She played a tune called *The Black Hawk Waltz* that was my favorite. It had a bouncy 3/4 time feel and I just adored that song. I'd make her play it over and over in between hymns and popular tunes of the day. Then she would encourage me to sit up on the bench and try to play it myself. I remember being so intrigued at first but also so afraid and embarrassed to try to play in front of her. She was so encouraging, though, and would sit and let me make up my own little sounds with the keys. Mom would say, "Oh, that was really lovely … it reminded me of watching a sunset." Or she'd tell me that what I'd just played "sounded like you were mad" or "that felt like you had seen a big storm."

Mom was just being Mom and encouraging me, but it had a profound effect, making me equate music with emotion. Sometimes she'd outright ask me to play a "feeling."

"Chuck," she'd say, "what would it sound like if you woke up and it was a beautiful day and you felt wonderful?" And I'd try my best to express that feeling through the keys on the piano. Another one she used was, "What would it sound like if there was a gentle rain outside?"

Me, just after starting to walk … and just before starting to play piano!

She was no music teacher and maybe she didn't really know what she was doing, but the result was that it taught me to think of music in terms of feelings, emotions, colors, and to use my imagination about how to paint pictures with music. It also made me pay closer attention to the way others played, to hear if there was emotion in their hands or if they were just playing notes. It was a very valuable lesson to learn.

I don't have too many other memories of Birmingham — except that I had a toy tractor that I adored and I remember one hot summer there, playing with a garden hose and goofing around on a nearby golf course. I can also remember some of our neighbors, but it's pretty vague. When I was about four, we moved to Montgomery and ended up with three horses — every kid's dream.

They were called Man, Lady, and Ginger. I remember my Dad riding with me on the back of Man one day when he was galloping up the hill to our house. There was a pine tree ahead and Dad said,

"Duck," but it was too late. The needles from the tree hit my forehead and left an impression in red across it. It hurt some, but I got over it pretty quickly, like kids do. I remember Dad plowing a garden with a horse and hand plow. Remember him killing a big king snake in our barn; it was a huge snake. Then he found out how good it was to have one in a barn because they fed on rats. Guess we were learning some things about country living!

I loved playing in the nearby creek with my sister and looking with great bewilderment through my brother's telescope on hot summer nights and listening to him explain constellations and planets to me. He was always taken with astronomy, and Judy once told me that before I was born, Billy really wanted a little brother. He asked God one night to show him a sign if he was to have a brother when mom was pregnant. A shooting star streaked across the sky, and he took that as the sign he was looking for. Judy has made a career as an actor and, like me, showed her passion early by writing little plays and putting them on after Sunday church, using the garage as the stage and usually getting me to join in one way or another. She has always been very inventive and it was a lot of fun. My brother Billy, who has had a long and dedicated career as a minister and missionary for the Church of Christ, is also a self-admitted ham, and I know how much passion he has for his sermons, which have the added flair, as he describes them, of being delivered in American Sign Language.

My brother Billy and I had a very special relationship. Billy was born deaf. Mom had Rubella when she was pregnant, and Billy suffered the consequences. But Billy was always more than a big brother to me. Billy was almost like a second father. By the time I was old enough to play and to remember things, say around four or five years old, he was always looking after me. Often he would put me to bed, telling me stories, often from my favorite comic books at that time — *The Flash*. He says I'd jump up and down with excitement at the great adventures. Billy has a speech impediment because of his deafness, so he's hard to understand unless you've spent a lot of time with him. But I could understand him with no problem and enjoyed the stories he'd read or tell me. Of course, during those years he was going to school, sometimes special schools that Mom and Dad put him in. They were adamant that he be raised as normally as possible and tried their best to get him in regular public schools. They insisted that he learn to lip-read so that he could talk to

Big sister Judy and me.

hearing people. He did quite well in his situation, but they did have to place him in a couple of special schools — one was a military-type academy. Of course, by the time I was six, Billy was off to college, at David Lipscom in Nashville, so we spent less time together. He graduated and went into the ministry of the Church of Christ and has done that ever since. He's been the leader of deaf congregations in Nashville and Memphis and these days does missionary work all over the world. Although we chose two completely different paths in life and these days don't get to spend much time together, I still feel very close to him and have a great love and respect for him and his dedication to his work. I'll always be grateful for the love he showed

me when I was growing up and will always admire the way he overcame his special challenge. As he recalls when asked about those early years, he says, "I can remember the excitement at the thought of having a brother. The large difference in our ages caused a gap in our knowing each other as well as we should have. But I've

Talk about fate – 30 years after this was taken I'd dedicate half my life to a farm.

always loved him and tried to be a big brother to him. I only regret I couldn't hear his music."

Billy recently relayed a funny story about seeing me perform in the early days in some band in Nashville. He says he and his wife, Marilyn, and their three young children were standing in the wings during the show — and that, in fact, he did sort of hear it.

"It is rare for a deaf person to be completely deaf," he explained. "And the playing was so loud in the wings it must have been painful for my family's ears, but I definitely could hear it! I enjoyed the basic rock 'n' roll melody, but I couldn't pick out the notes nor identify the tunes. Nor could I tell when Chuck was playing."

Not long after we'd moved back to Birmingham from Montgomery, my parents realized I had a talent for the piano and asked me if I'd like to take lessons. I agreed and started meeting once a week with a lady named Mrs. Jeeter. I remember her being a big woman who was nice, but very firm about practicing and reading music. This was my first encounter with sheet music, as I had played entirely by ear. In fact, my ear was remarkably good for such a young boy, and I quickly learned how to trick the woman. She'd put down a piece of music for me to play, and I'd ask her to play it first for me. It was usually a breeze for me to play it back, pretending to read the sheet while in fact starting blankly at it.

Eventually, Mrs. Jeeter caught on and made me buckle down to learn to read music properly. I tried for a while, but it was taking the fun out of it for me and I dropped the lessons, which were also keeping me from playing baseball or other games with my neighborhood pals.

To this day, I kind of regret not having stuck with it because I never did learn how to read music properly. But my Mom never interfered, other than to encourage me. She never insisted I resume the lessons and never chastised me for not learning to read, which quite possibly could

Credit: © Chuck Leavell Archive

My only distraction from music as a child was baseball.

have altered the experience for me. Forced learning all too often exacts the sad toll of destroying natural passion.

My sister remembers that I certainly had an ear for music, recalling recently that when she was trying to learn piano, she'd struggled so hard to learn a number from one of the music books and was so proud the night she finally performed it for the whole family. After Mom and Dad congratulated

Credit: © Chuck Leavell Archive

Me, with my brother Billy, sister Judy, and our Mom, Frances.

her on her hard work, she says, she went off to her room to read only to hear me climb up on the piano stool and play the same piece off the top of my head, having learned it by ear.

But we didn't always get along that well. I remember us fighting a lot, once so fiercely that Mom cried. I'd never seen her cry before, and it made a profound impression on me. Judy and I both stopped and tried to comfort Mom. It was a heavy moment for a little kid. I also remember Granny, our grandmother on Mom's side. She lived with us in Montgomery. We loved her very much, and Judy and I would sometimes fight to see who would get to sleep in Granny's room.

Then came my epiphany. So many people go through life not knowing what they want to do or become, while I was blessed at a very early age. It came like a lightning bolt. Judy had a date and free tickets to a Ray Charles concert and invited me to go along. Talk about fate! Ray was so brilliant, playing such cool and sophisticated licks and phrases on the piano and singing with that wonderful big soulful voice. The band was so tight and the arrangements so swingin'. The Rayletts were singing great harmonies in just the right places. Billy Preston was in the band at that time and while Ray played an incredible show, I was mesmerized by Preston, the guy behind the star, sharing the spotlight but being given lots of space to play. It seemed to me that he was having a better time than anyone else there, and it was truly a life-changing experience. I decided that night, at the age of ten or whatever it was, that I was going to spend my life as a piano player. I wasn't going to be an insurance salesman, a scientist, racecar driver, preacher — the path my brother took — or anything else. It seemed to me that I didn't even have a choice. Ray Charles has remained a huge influence on me my entire career. When he passed away in June 2004 at age seventy-three, it felt as if I had lost a close relative. It hit me like a ton of bricks. If not for that incredible man — his voice, his playing, and his many contributions to music through the years — I would never have followed the path I did. I'll always be more than grateful that I went to that concert with my sister; it changed my life. As you'll read later, I did get to play with him once and was able to tell him briefly how important he was to my career. I'm so glad I had that chance, but if I could tell him a thousand times it wouldn't be enough. Ray was simply "The Man."

Just as I was about to graduate from elementary school, a teacher from the junior high school came in and showed us all the different

Credit: © Chuck Leavell Archive

The proud son takes his mom backstage in the 1970s.

band instruments we'd be able to chose from when we moved on to his school. Like most of the boys, I wanted to try the drums first. The teacher encouraged us to wander around the room and give each instrument a try. I had blown on my Dad's old bugle — said to be from the Civil War — that had always been around the house. So I was able to make a few sounds as I tried the sax, clarinet, flute, and trumpet. I tried the trombone and then the tuba, which, for some reason, I had a real success with. The teacher said that I should consider it as my instrument if I joined the school concert band when I got to junior high. And I did! For two years I blew into that thing, and it was a lot of fun, teaching me for the first time about ensemble playing, how to listen to all the other instruments while playing my part, a little music theory, and — more tangibly this time — the importance of practicing. The Tuscaloosa Junior High bandmaster, Mr. Jones, was a pretty tough cookie, very strict. But I learned quite a lot under his teaching, and I'm forever grateful for the experience.

But the keyboard was my first love, and at home I had also begun to teach myself how to play guitar. My cousin Winston (who we called Windy) was a pretty good guitar player and taught me some chords. We loved playing and singing harmony. Ultimately, I just didn't have time for it all and still be a kid out having fun, so I gave up the school concert band and the tuba.

Credit: © Chuck Leavell Archive

Of course, Mom wasn't the only musical inspiration in my family. My father's side was forever having great get-togethers. Now, this was long before I was born, but my paternal grandmother, whom the family called Mama Leavell, performed at Vaudeville shows and did jokes. Billy remembers being eight or nine years old and being asked to help out in one of her

"Mama Leavell," my Dad's mother, doing her Vaudeville act.

shows, wearing blackface (offensive in today's enlightened times, but consider the time and social climate of the day) and carrying her bags onto the stage. She'd give Billy a tip and he'd wander off the stage. Uncle Jay played clarinet quite well, while Uncle Emory played banjo. Dad would join in on spoons. Cousin Windy, his sister Candy, and I along with everyone would laugh and join in the fun. In later years, there were two more cousins, Wiley and Tracy, born into the family. But Windy and I were the closest, in part because we both played the guitar and we talked a lot about music.

At home during these days, my mom and dad listened to the popular big-band stuff like the Dorsey Brothers, Benny Goodman, Al Hurt, and others. My folks loved Lawrence Welk and we watched his show every week. I didn't care for him, as I thought he was so square, but Mom and Dad loved that show. Roger Williams was also played on the turntable. Mom loved his piano playing. Ferrante and Teicher were in the collection. There was a little bit of Duke Ellington and Count Basie, but not a lot of black music in the record collection at home. The things that I heard on the radio and TV during those early years in Alabama were varied. Gospel was a huge influence, both black and white. Hearing the black programs on the radio on Sunday was amazing to me. The way the preacher performed his sermons, the way they sang and played. It was all really exciting and moving for me.

Country music was big. We had several Chet Atkins records, and I loved them. Floyd Cramer and Boots Randolph as well. There was a weekly program locally out of Birmingham that we got on TV down in Tuscaloosa on Saturday mornings that had local country bands and artists. I enjoyed watching that.

Suddenly in the early 1960s, however, for me, folk music became the big thing and there was a show called *Hootenanny* on every Saturday night, which we watched religiously. Sort of an early MTV *Unplugged*, it was hosted by Art Linkletter's eldest son, Jack. The Kingston Trio, Chad and Jeremy, Peter, Paul and Mary were typical artists on the show. I liked the harmonies and the playing, which was mostly acoustic string instruments: acoustic guitar, banjo, fiddle, maybe an Autoharp occasionally. So Windy taught me some of these songs and we'd have fun playing them together. Another influence was — and is — Bob Dylan. He was relatively new on the scene then and certainly was one of the leaders especially in the "protest" songs of the day. Little did I know then that I'd play with him when the Stones would do his great song *Like a Rolling Stone* and he would sit in with us.

Hootenanny broke some important ground early on, allowing some protest song performances — such as Chad Mitchell Trio's *John Birch Society*, which had been largely banned by radio. *Hootenanny* also broadcast a few all-black folk and blues acts and with a band called The Tarriers, crossed another line by broadcasting a performance by an interracial band.

But it was short lasting, as the protest movement of the 1960s grew and artists such as Dylan and Pete Seeger were blacklisted and other up-and-coming artists boycotted appearances and the show soon lost our interest. *American Bandstand* became our favorite. As well, I remember watching Paul Revere and the Raiders every week on a show called *Where the Action Is*, which was produced by Dick Clark.

As my sister Judy and I got older, we became a lot closer and when I was about twelve — she was seventeen — Judy became my main source material for the newest, hippest music. She turned me on to a lot of the greats, especially the Beatles, Stones, Animals, Dave Clark Five, and all the British Invasion groups. For a time, Judy had a job in the local record store and remembers spending most of her earnings on new LPs. I looked to her to know what was hip, and she would "educate" me. Being Southern, we also listened to soul music: Aretha, Wilson Pickett, Sam Cooke, Otis Redding, Johnny Taylor, Major Lance and so forth. Instrumental bands also intrigued me. Especially The Ventures. I loved their stuff, and would try to learn it on guitar. *Walk, Don't Run* was one of their big ones as well as *Telstar* and *The Lonely Bull*.

Still more of my influence came, as it did for most people of my generation, from the radio, where we were first exposed to Simon and Garfunkel, Dylan; I soaked it all up: Ray Charles, Little Richard, Jerry Lee Lewis, Floyd Cramer, Chet Atkins, Leon Russell, Elton John, Billy Preston; later blues greats like Otis Span, Memphis Slim, Little Walter, Pinetop Perkins; and later still, I started listening to some of the jazz guys, like Earl Hines, Monk, Oscar Peterson, Art Tatum. Keith Jarrett is one of my favorites of all times. I'll never be in their league, but listening to them remains an influence and inspiration.

Like so many others I also fell under the spell of the Motown acts such as Stevie Wonder, The Temptations, Four Tops, Supremes, and the list goes on and on. I also had the fortune of exposure to English keyboardist Ian (Stu) Stewart, who was to become a great friend and influence in my life many years later. But I was also quite simply born in the right place at the right time — the American South, ground zero for the soul and R&B of such greats as Otis Redding and Wilson Pickett. Some of my success and career, I know, has been due to the fact that I'm a Southern musician. It's in my blood, in my veins. In interviews, Keith Richards has been very flattering, saying, "Chuck is our direct link to Stu. Without that continuity, the Stones would not be the Stones."

By the time I was in my early teens, I was playing in a little neighborhood band in Tuscaloosa. Electronic keyboards were rare back then, at least where I lived, so I was playing mostly guitar. I still played the piano in the house on my own, but when we'd get together to play, it was the guitar that was in my hands. Back then I didn't even own a guitar, but borrowed one from Marc Clements, a guy a couple of years older than me who lived across the street in The Downs, where we lived. He also played a bit, and we'd trade off. He played guitar, and owned a bass, I think. Kenny Catrino, who lived a couple of doors down from Marc, played drums. There were a couple of other kids who would occasionally come by, but because we lived so close together it was mostly us. We played for our own enjoyment, no real gigs. Then one day the father of a little girl who lived in a close by neighborhood told us he'd pay us two dollars apiece to play for her birthday party. Wow, that was great! I think it wound up just being two of us, and I can't remember exactly who else played with me, but it was a real eye-opener to be paid to play! I remember distinctly, too, that I wasn't nervous. I've never really had stage fright. Even then, I always tried to focus on what I was supposed to be doing. Certainly there have been times when I've been in a band and it all fell apart mid-song, which can be quite embarrassing, but I learned from the Stones attitude about it not to worry when that happens. You fall down; you pick yourself up and keep going.

Eventually I got more serious about this stuff and began to seek out other kids who could play. This led to my first real band, the Misfitz. By then I was maybe thirteen or fourteen. The Misfitz consisted of me on guitar (but by then I had seen a Farfisa organ and had talked my parents into

My Misfitz entry into a battle of the bands.

helping me get one, so I played that on a few tunes as well) and vocals, Jonathan McAllister on bass and vocals, Rodney Etheridge on guitar (he sang one song, *Long Tall Texan*, which was very funny because he was a short guy), and Bill Johnson on drums. We practiced at our house in The Downs. Mom let us move her furniture around and set up and play. We got pretty good and started playing in public. It didn't take long before we had a steady gig every Friday night at the YMCA. A much better player named Ronnie Brown eventually replaced Rodney. Ronnie was a great addition, and that took the group to a higher level. When Tuscaloosa finally got its own local TV station, WCFT, one of the producers asked us to be the

MISFITZ RONNIE Brown (l.-r., standing) and Chuck Leavell; (l.-r., kneeling), Bill Johnson and Jonathan McAllister.

Local Rock'n Roll Singers Make Swinging Sounds

Meet the Misfitz, one of Tucaloosa's liveliest entertain-

Johnson on the drums. Believing that fads make life a bit more colorful the rock

My first bit of press.

house band of a Saturday morning show. It was a half-hour show based on *American Bandstand*, called, well, *Tuscaloosa Bandstand*. The host was a DJ from the local radio station named Tiger Jack Garrett; he'd introduce us, and we'd play some tunes. Back then there were very limited graphics for TV, and I remember the station had these really corny placards made up with little slogans on them like, "Gut pluckin' Ronnie" or "Go get 'em Chuck!" when we were featured. We were in heaven, playing the Y on Friday nights and the show on Saturday mornings. The chicks loved us and the guys thought we were cool. Man, was that a great time!

And what did we play? Well, Rolling Stones tunes, among others. I remember the first Stones song I ever played in public was on guitar; it was *The Last Time*. It has a great riff, and when I learned it I played it over and over until my fingers hurt. We also did *Satisfaction*, *Nineteenth Nervous Breakdown*, and a couple of others.

Of course, by then I had to have my own guitar and a keyboard. Mom and Dad eventually agreed to get me both, but I had to pay for some of it. The guitar was a relatively cheap model, a Kingston. It had four pickups, which was the main feature. The keyboard was a red Farfisa Combo Compact. There was another band called the Gents that played on Saturday nights. Jim Coleman on guitar and vocals, Court Pickett on bass and vocals, Lou Mullenix on drums — those guys were all really talented players — and there was a fourth guy that played guitar named Jimmy Romaine. He wasn't very good, but because he came from a well-to-do family, he had great equipment, including a PA system. They were a couple of years older than us and at least in the beginning were a much better and hipper band.

The Misfitz: me, Jonathan McAllister, Bill Johnson and Rodney Etheridge.

We were sort of rivals, but not too much because of the age difference. As time went by I became better friends with them and even played with them in different bands later after the Misfitz and Gents broke up. Court, Lou, and I wound up in one of the first bands I recorded with, Sundown.

When I saw the Beatlemania on TV, I thought it was silly and didn't fantasize about that kind of success for myself. All the screaming kept me from hearing what they were doing. It was the music that I was interested in, not the idea of a few thousand girls screaming their heads off and fainting at the sight of me. The sheer excitement of four guys playing some simple tunes being a world-changing event wasn't lost on me, though; the fact was they were moving people with their music, and that had a huge effect on me.

All the British Invasion groups were big influences on the Misfitz, and as they all began their quick climb to success we were pretty happy with where we were going at a much younger age. The Y gig paid us $50 a week, $12.50 each, and the TV gig paid us $100, $25 each; we thought we were rich. And we were! This made me realize that there were both financial and professional sides to

THE MISFITZ *Channel* **33**
— SATURDAYS 10:30-11:00 —

An advertisment for the Misfitz on local television.

playing music, and was a valuable lesson for a young teenager. I started to believe that I could indeed make a pretty good living playing music. After the Misfitz, we had other bands later, the South Camp, Care, and a couple of others. We'd play fraternity parties at the University of Alabama and make $400 for a night, with a four-piece band, we were making a $100 each. If we played a couple of gigs a week, that was $200, quite a respectable sum of money for kids back in the 1960s.

Dad would have been very happy if I'd chosen to follow his lead and be a businessman and get into selling insurance. He had a passion for it and was very good at it, even if he never made a whole lot of money. He'd get all excited about a new product. I remember him writing a lot of letters and such to promote his business. He could type pretty well, but he pecked with two fingers and never learned proper typing technique. He'd work for hours typing stuff, coming up with new ideas and such. He was also very civic minded

My Dad, Billy, leaving his office.

and was heavily involved with the Exchange Club, and eventually became state president. He loved going to the conventions, having meetings, and so forth. I remember him practicing speeches on a tape recorder, trying out phrases, listening back, changing them. He was quite good at it and very dedicated.

His work ethic was a clear influence on me, but so too was his dedication to health. He worked out fairly regularly at the YMCA and always encouraged me to stay in good shape. In my teenage years this may not have taken so well, but later it did, and from my early twenties to this day I always take time to stay in shape, mostly nowadays in the gym with weight resistance, but also doing a bit of cardio or playing tennis, and a little Yoga and stretching thrown in. Of course, running a 2,200-acre plantation when I'm not on the road has its own physical challenges, and I love the work. Tree farmers sleep very well at the end of the day!

Dad was never thrilled at the idea of me being a musician, especially a rock 'n' roll musician, but I can say without hesitation that he never discouraged me. He supported me even if he didn't think it was a wise career choice. He wanted me to go to college, get "smart," and go into business. Mom was somewhat the same way. I remember her saying things like, "Well, you've got talent, and that's a great thing, but you might want to think about something else to fall back on if music doesn't work out."

Like most teenagers, I didn't listen. In fact, I dove deeper and deeper into the wonderful world of music, discovering American black music next. Some of my musician friends turned me on to cats like Mississippi Fred McDowell, who sometimes played a coffee house in Tuscaloosa. Johnny Shines would come through, too. Shines had worked with the legendary Robert Johnson and had become a legend himself. We used to sneak into a black club called the Blue Moon in Northport to hear some of the blues artists. Of course, we were the only white faces in there — underage to boot — but we were playing at the time with Charlie Hayward, a great bass player and good friend, who lived in Northport and was a familiar character to the club's owners.

It seems like a world away when I look back but here's the truth: it was Alabama in the 1950s and early 1960s and was of course very segregated. I didn't have a lot of interaction with black people until I really got into music. It was simply the way life was in the South. When we lived in Birmingham and Montgomery, we lived in white middle-class neighborhoods and went to white churches. It wasn't a conscious choice, but it was simply the way. It was Deep South, and at that time segregation was the order of the day. There were "White" restrooms and "Colored" restrooms. "White" water fountains and "Colored" water fountains. White and Colored churches, schools, restaurants, everything. Very little interaction between races. I never thought much about this as a child. It was just the way it was and I was too little to understand. But I do remember my mother making sure that all of us children understood that the Bible taught that we were all equal. The little Sunday school song called

Jesus Loves the Little Children of the World — "Red and yellow, black and white … they are precious in His sight, Jesus loves the little children of the world." — was something we sang often, and Mom always pointed out how important it was for us to understand this. I even remember a picture in a children's Bible songbook that went along with the song; it showed kids from all around the world sitting by Jesus. Still, when it came to everyday life whites and blacks didn't mix. By the time we'd moved to Tuscaloosa in the early and mid 1960s, integration became a huge issue. The KKK held marches, Martin Luther King had begun his crusade, and there was the Selma march and George Wallace standing on the steps of the University of Alabama and blocking entrance to Vivian Malone and James Hood, the first black students to seek entry to the school. In those days things were really tough. My Mom's teachings had held strong for her children. I remember the first black kid to come into our high school, a guy named Willie. None of the kids wanted to talk to or play with him. He was in my PE class, and the other kids sometimes refused to let him work out or would ignore him despite the coach's orders. I liked Willie a lot and we became friends of sorts. I didn't care what anyone else thought, though I can't imagine how it must have been for him.

This was also the time of the so-called Beatle burnings in Birmingham — which followed John Lennon's off-the-cuff remark that the Beatles had sold so many albums they were more popular than Jesus. In the Baptist South, this was a hard thing for a lot of people to swallow, no matter how lightly they tried to take Lennon's quip. I remember a lot of people being upset, but it was really not as big a deal as it's been made out to be. There were about two weeks of hoopla and it died down. I certainly wasn't about to burn my Beatles records!

Around this time I began hanging out with a mix of musicians and nonmusicians from school. One was a fellow named Glen Butts. Glen was a good guitar player, and we did play together for a short time, but mostly we were just good friends who got along well and kept each other laughing, doing crazy kid stuff. There was Walter

Phillips, Glen, me and a guy named Wayne Bryant. We were all about the same age, around fifteen. We all had our learner's permits and had begun driving, but were underage to drive without an adult in the car. My parents had recently bought a new ride, a 1966 Mercury Monterey. It was a four-door sedan, painted sky blue, and one of the unusual features of the car was that it had a rear window slanted backwards that could be opened via an electric switch on the dashboard, allowing for better air flow. Mercury called it the "Monterey Breezeway Sedan" model. Being mischievous young teenagers, anxious for good times and some action, we always wanted to go out carousing. Sometimes it was hard to find an older friend of driving age who would let us tag along, so we'd often be stranded. The remedy we came up with was to sneak out of the house at night after our parents had gone to bed and meet in our driveway. I had taken the spare key that stayed in a desk drawer in our house and had another key made from it. So one of us would quietly open the door on the driver's side and put the car in neutral while the others pushed the car out of the driveway and into the street. After getting it down the street about a block away, we'd crank it up and head out. We usually just drove around, or maybe we would hook up with some other friends somewhere. We did this about once a week for a long time and never once got caught. We called ourselves the "Monterey Men." Many years later I told my mother about this, thinking that she'd see the humor in it. She didn't. "Chuck, no! You didn't really do that, did you? I can't believe my sweet little boy was stealing our car!" The Monterey Men had some wonderful times, I must admit. We never got into any bad trouble, thank God. Of course it was a wrong thing to do and the potential for disaster was certainly there, but we sure did have fun!

After my experience with The Misfitz, I sort of hit the wall with the guitar. I just didn't have the same love or feel for it as I had for keyboards, and the local guitar players were beginning to eclipse what talent I had for the six-string so I had to concentrate on my strengths, which lay in the keyboards. After the Farfisa I got a Wurlitzer electric piano, and loved that ax. What I like about the piano is that it's an organic instrument. The touch and personality of the player comes through. I always loved one of Thelonious Monk's quotes about piano playing: "There's no such thing as a mistake, it depends on what you do afterwards."

As time went on the tension of racism escalated in Tuscaloosa, there were KKK rallies and parades in town, and things got very tough. Despite the racial temper of the times, I wound up playing in a band called the Jades, which was an all-black group that was going to Stillman College, a black college in Tuscaloosa. They were a Temptations/Four Tops kind of group: five guys, four of whom were out front singing and dancing, and one of them playing keyboards. They would use different musicians for a back-up band. I got the gig because their keyboard player, a guy named Freddie, wanted to be out in front with the rest of the guys singing and dancing. So he taught me a lot about playing soul and R&B-type keyboard styles. I caught a lot of flack for playing with them, and I was lucky to never have been beaten up, though there were lots of times when I thought it would come to that. I was very fortunate, but I remember a few instances of having to drive away from a gig at lightning speed to keep from being attacked by kids angry that I was playing with blacks. I was called a lot of names, and you can imagine what they were. But I loved that band, and while the gig lasted less than a year, it was a great learning experience, and the guys treated me like a little brother.

Not long after, I hooked up with a guy named Paul Hornsby, who became a life-long friend and mentor. He was in the South Camp band I was in after the Misfitz. Paul was the leader, he played a Wurlitzer electric piano, a Hammond B3 organ, and guitar. So he invited me into the group, getting me to play the Wurly, and he'd play the B or his guitar. He called all the songs, and we were learning Moby Grape, Ray Charles, Beatles, all kinds of stuff. Paul also encouraged me to sing, and while I was reluctant, he pushed me to do it and I did. He was like a big brother pushing me to step out and backing me up. I learned a great deal from Paul, and we're still very good friends today. It was a real education playing in that band.

There was Bill Stewart on drums, Charlie Hayward on bass, and Joe Rudd on guitar. Other musicians floated in and out of South Camp. It's interesting how many people out of that time who went on to become famous in their own right. Charlie went on to eventually play bass with the Charlie Daniels Band, and Paul became a top-notch producer working with the CDB, Marshall Tucker Band, and many others, with lots of gold and platinum records to his credit. Lou worked with us with Alex Taylor and Dr. John. Ol' T-Town produced some very good musicians.

Like all the bands at the time, the experience didn't last for all that long, but it was a terrific education, and Paul Hornsby would be back in my life very shortly. In the meantime, I moved back to

Birmingham and worked with Joe Rudd, Charlie Hayward, and Louis Mullenix in my third band, called Care, which ended up being my introduction to the recording studio. Back then we were just happy to have music to play, but we had the fortune of hooking up with a black guy named Sam Dees who was doing sessions in town. We'd get paid twenty-five bucks a day to sit in working on the demos. Sam was a talented songwriter and had a pretty good head for arrangements. We also chimed in with ideas, and Sam was always receptive. Mostly these demos were to encourage other artists with bigger names to record his songs, and some of those sessions made it onto released records, but I couldn't say which ones now. We were just happy to be playing and to be making the twenty-five bucks!

Credit: © Chuck Leavell Archive

Paul Hornsby around the time I met him.

I don't know if I really had a career-launching moment, but certainly one of my initial breaks was playing on my first album, by John Buck Wilkins. He is the son of Mary John Wilkins, a prolific

Credit: © Chuck Leavell Archive

Take a high school kid, add rock'n roll and here's what you get …

country songwriter (who co-wrote *Long Black Veil* with Bill Dill). Bucky had lived in Nashville and was a roommate of Kris Kristofferson. Kris had written *Me and Bobby McGee* when they were roommates. Bucky played it for us along with all the other tunes he had written, and we recorded it. There's some trivia for you — I was in the first band ever to record *Me and Bobby McGee*. Roger Miller had a hit with it before ours could get circulated, however, which is why it's a matter for trivia buffs and nothing else — while of course Janis Joplin's later version became the standard. The session was at the now-legendary Muscle Shoals Sound Studios — the place Aretha Franklin, Wilson Pickett, and countless others made their most revered recordings.

I met another guy named Johnny Wyker from up there. He was a really interesting and intriguing songwriter/visionary. He gave me the first self-help book I ever read, *Three Magic Words*. I found it very inspiring, and that whole summer was just incredible for me. We finished the basic tracks in Shoals and then we went up to Nashville where the string parts were added and the record was mixed. It was the first session like that I'd ever been to, lots of string players, all the Nashville cats hanging out. We actually moved there for about three months in mid-1969. The idea was that we were going to start as a three-piece band, add some other players, and call ourselves the The American Eagles. This concept didn't last long, and because Bucky was writing and singing most all the songs, it rightfully became his solo project. The three of us — Wilkins, Wyker, and I — had a rented house on Richland Drive in Nashville. We never did do any gigs, though; we just wound up hanging out and playing songs. It was an exciting summer, though. One day, Wilkins burst through the door saying, "I've got it!"

"Got what?" we asked.

"The new Stones record. I heard it on the radio and pulled over to listen to it, then went straight to the store to buy it and here it is."

And there it was. *Honky Tonk Women*. Fantastic. We played it over and over, learning every note and every harmony.

Only a few weeks later Neil Armstrong walked on the moon. We were just dumb-founded. Bucky wrote on one of the walls of the house in huge letters: "July 20, 1969: Man on Moon. Good God!"

Like I said, the band was going to be called The American Eagles, but of course it wound up just being Bucky's LP. I didn't care. I was so excited to be on a real album, and to be living with talented and creative guys. It never got off the ground, and at the end of the summer of 1969 I went back to Alabama and transferred to Birmingham for my senior year of high school.

Then the coolest thing happened. The owner of a local recording studio, a guy named Bob Grove, talked with my parents about what was then called DE (diversified education), which meant that you had a job and got out of school around noon each day. For most guys, of course, this meant working at a garage or something. For me, it was working as a session piano and keyboard player.

I was recording mostly demos for people. I did a couple of tracks for myself; one was the Beatles song *For No One*, and it was sort of a soul arrangement. It never came out, but it was a thrill to do it. I found the studio just fascinating. Back then it was all four track machines, and eventually the eight track machines. I learned about overdubbing, ping-ponging tracks to open up other tracks, mixing, getting good sounds, and trying to figure out what made a great record. Of course, I learned that could be so many things: the song itself, the arrangement, a great solo, a great vocal, the right harmonies, or a great mix. These were the years when I was figuring it all out, experimenting with different instruments, like the tack piano they had in Muscle Shoals that had tacks on the hammers so that when it struck the strings it sounded very metallic and "honky tonk" like. Also I began to learn more about mic techniques and more about the organ. It was a wonderful learning ground for how to make a record. I admired the Muscle Shoals Rhythm section very much, as many musicians did. They had a magic sound, a really great collaboration of musicians: Roger Hawkins on drums, David Hood on bass, Jimmy Johnson on guitar, Eddie Hinton was around there, as well as Pete Carr. Barry Beckett on piano. Clayton Ivy was also a great piano player who worked around Muscle Shoals back then. A guy named Marlin Greene was a fantastic engineer as well as songwriter/musician. Lots of talent hanging out, and I just was hoping some of it would rub off on me!

There were other studios up there, as well — Quinvy, Fame and some others — just so much going on musically. I had no illusions — I was so young and inexperienced that I figured it would take me a long time to get anywhere in Shoals. Beckett and Ivy were much older than I, were much more experienced, and had most of the work; there were other keyboard players in line in front of me.

Credit: Chuck Leavell Archive

Still, I enjoyed some very early success as my career was beginning. Of all the sessions I did as a teenager, I suppose my playing on the Freddie North *She's All I Got* was the most successful. It went gold — the first gold record I played on, and the biggest hit of Freddie's career.

Freddie North's *She's All I Got* ... the first gold record I played on.

I wasn't content just doing the session work and kept busy with live performances as well, in a band called Care, with Joe Rudd, Charlie Hayward and Lou Mullenix. We were good enough that word spread and we soon found ourselves actually on the road. This meant missing school days, since we'd leave on a Friday and drive to, say, New Orleans, play that night, Saturday, and Sunday, and not make it back until Monday. I was doing pretty well with my grades, but a three-day school week just didn't cut it. The principal called me into the office at mid-term and told me that there was a law requiring me to attend a certain amount of days to graduate, and that I couldn't miss any more school for the rest of the year even though I had good grades. I didn't want to drop out, but I was enjoying playing music and was making a pretty good living at it. Also, if I quit the band that meant I was letting down my friends. So I decided to quit school. That was tough on my parents, who at first tried to talk me out of it. Eventually they accepted my decision. My brother Billy was also alarmed. "Remember, it was the 1960s," he recalls, "when rebellion was in the air. Young people questioned our role in Vietnam and started rejecting the moral standards we had been adhering to, engaging in live-ins, hippie communities, drug use, LSD, nude streaks, and all that stuff. Being a conservative family we naturally were concerned. Through the years we did see that Chuck never really seemed to get into that rebellious stuff — although he might wear long hair and a beard, he didn't get deeply involved in the drug culture. We did see Chuck on TV when my wife and I came down to Tuscaloosa to visit my family from time to time. I even used my movie camera to capture the TV image of Chuck playing, though regrettably, camcorders weren't available at the time so we could capture the music being played."

It was at this time that Paul Hornsby came back into my life — and changed it forever. Before I'd met him, Paul's first big break came with a short-lived band called Hour Glass with a couple of Nashville-born brothers named Gregg and Duane Allman. I'd seen Gregg and Duane Allman play in their previous band the Allman Joys. They often played the local Ft. Brandon Armory in Tuscaloosa.

I loved seeing them and hearing them. Gregg and Duane were really strong on stage — the way they looked, the way they played. They were one of the first bands I had heard that had the element of psychadelia in them. They dressed cool; they looked cool; they *were* cool! Duane's guitar playing was stellar. I remember he was the first guy I heard that used a "fuzz tone" on his guitar. Actually, the product was called a "Fuzz Face," a small round device that was on the floor, and when he kicked it in it distorted the sound of the guitar through the amp. It made an amazing sound. Of course, Gregg had this incredible voice and was playing a Vox Continental organ, which blew my mind. I'd seen them on TV with groups like Paul Revere and others, but never had seen one live. He also played guitar on a couple of songs, but it was the organ that I liked. The Joys was really a fantastic band but, like a lot of the groups back then, didn't stay together all that long.

Hour Glass did a couple of LPs on Liberty Records out in California, including a brilliant B. B. King medley, but the record company hated it. The band split up after a couple of years. Gregg stayed in California, while Duane went to Alabama and started doing a lot of session work at Shoals, participating in lots of hits with artists like Aretha Franklin (*The Weight*), Wilson Pickett (*Hey Jude*), and many others, in the process making quite a name for himself as a session musician.

Jerry Wexler of Atlantic Records first heard Duane on Pickett's version of *Hey Jude*

Credit: © Bob Gruen/Star File

Gregg Allman and his maverick older brother Duane in the very early days.

and signed him, but soon turned a maverick Macon native named Phil Walden onto him. Walden had discovered a young Otis Redding in a Macon high school some years before and had steered him — as well as Sam and Dave and Percy Sledge — to world success. Otis' death in a plane crash in 1967 had devastated Phil, he was still trying to put the pieces back together, and the first step of that was signing Duane to his Capricorn Records label. Through his growing success, Phil had concentrated on black players, and Duane was the first white musician he signed.

"Everybody said," Phil recalled recently, "that there was no way I could have any luck with a white musician."

Phil signed Duane, and Duane began to think about a band. Walden had offered Duane carte blanche to start up Hour Glass again, but the plan failed. Undeterred, Duane started putting a new band together. He found bassist Berry Oakley and guitarist Dickey Betts in the Jacksonville psychedelic band The Second Coming; drummer Johnny Lee Johnson was an R&B veteran who had toured with Otis Redding, Joe Tex, and Percy Sledge (Johnny's name

Credit: © 1975 Sidney Smith

Phil Walden (left) with his pal Bill Graham at one of the annual Capricorn Records picnics.

evolved into Jai Johanny Johanson, which gave way to the nickname, which became the name by which he is now, and for 30 years, has been known — Jaimoe); and drummer Butch Trucks who played with the Jacksonville folk-rock band The 31st of February. They all hit it off, and Duane had the makings of the band — except for a lead vocalist.

Walden suggested Duane's brother Gregg, who was always such a great white blues singer. There was talk about Gregg being mired down in California, and they had tried it with the Hour Glass, which had broken up. I've heard that Gregg didn't want to leave California, as he was going to do a solo album. All I know is what we all know — Gregg did, in fact, move to Macon. The Allman Brothers Band was born. They did that first album, just called *The Allman Brothers Band*. Phil put them on the road, and they went for it. Paul told me he was skeptical of the name, believing perhaps that it was a bit pretentious, but he also told me that they were all remarkable players and that something was bound to come from the new group.

Credit: © 2004 Carter Tomassi

ABB: Gregg and Duane tearing toward stardom.

I heard the album for the first time in 1969. It shook us all up: the two drummers, Duane's great playing, the twin guitar leads and harmonies, Berry's unique style of bass playing and, of course, Gregg's blue-eyed soulful singing. Not to mention great arrangements and tunes. It was an epiphany for the times, and for all of us struggling Southern musicians looking for something new, they were it. They immediately became regional heroes.

Duane called Paul Hornsby to tell him of the new activities going on, and Paul quickly moved to Macon, signing on as part of the studio band at Capricorn — a band that included Johnny Sandlin on drums, Pete Carr on guitar, and Robert "Pops" Popwell on bass.

After a couple of months, Paul called me and told me that I needed to check out all these goings-on in Macon. There was Capricorn, which was a record company, Paragon, which was a booking agency, Phil Walden and Associates management, and of course the studio, which was at the time state of the art, and all of this was rolled into one little town, Macon, Georgia. It all seemed

Credit: © 2004 Carter Tomassi

The original Allman Brothers band.

very attractive and very new, and not as impenetrable as Muscle Shoals and Nashville. I smelled opportunity — and a place where I'd find less competition for session work.

One day Charlie Hayward and I loaded up my 1965 Oldsmobile Cutlass station wagon with some equipment and drove to Macon. Immediately, we met Phil at Capricorn. He greeted us readily, walking out from behind his desk offering his hand. I thought he had an air of coolness, confidence (definitely ego — something you want in a guy like that). He spoke with almost a sort of soft stutter. He was boasting about his accomplishments, touting his successes, and talking about his plans for more bands, more albums, a great future. I must admit that I was taken in by it all. Immediately I felt like I was in a good place, but also had a slight wariness of Phil.

He had that "manager" thing — talking tall, talking about changing the world of music. But I could tell he was passionate about his work and had a lot of confidence in himself and the company. He asked me a few questions about what we had done in Alabama, about Paul, and so forth. It ended by him saying that he thought there would be a place for us there, that there was a lot

The original, historical Capricorn Studios in downtown Macon.

Credit: © Chuck Leavell Archive

Like the studios, the Capricorn Records office in Macon remains empty after all these years, but still offers a glimpse of its famous past.

going on and while he didn't know exactly what we might be doing, he just thought we'd add to the mix there and something would happen. I left there thinking that this was a pretty darn good situation — lots of opportunities. I felt like here I could move up the ladder more swiftly, not have to be waiting too long in the wings to do records and get dates to play.

We saw the studio, the offices, the booking agency. It was all very impressive. This was just after I had dropped out of high school. I was sixteen. As you can imagine, my parents were very concerned about this. I found out years later that my Dad called over there to talk to the executives about me. He talked to a guy named Bunky Odom, who was working for Walden. He was checking up on his son, making sure I wasn't getting into some kind of mess. I was very young, and he knew how much music meant to me. He didn't want

Credit: © Allman Brothers Band Archive

The Allman Brothers in Capricorn studios working on their Idlewild South album.

me to quit school and was very concerned about my leaving Alabama. Anyway, they convinced him that it was OK, that they would look after me there, and that I'd have work. Immediately, I did. It was a band called Sundown, a mixture of us Alabama boys — Lou Mullenix, Charlie Hayward, Court Pickett and me — and some Georgia guys — Asa Howard on vocals, Ronnie Chambley on bass, and Bobby Cornlius on guitar and vocals and who wrote most of the songs.

We cut a record at Capricorn, which Paul produced, and then hit the road, playing around the South for about a year. The record didn't sell and we were constantly broke; I had thoughts of returning to Alabama but the road experience was good for me and certainly put me in a good spot for what was to come next which was, quite simply, the birth of Southern Rock.

The Allmans had minor success with the first record and had toured for several months. Then they went in and did a second LP, *Idlewild South*. That was another great record, taking the band to the next level. They continued to tour, by this time making a name for themselves. One thing that helped to broaden their popularity in the South was a series of free concerts they held in Piedmont Park in Atlanta. Hippiedom was in full, long-haired swing and the free shows were huge hits. The ABB toured endlessly, honing their chops in the best clubs and opening for some of the biggest acts of the day. For us musicians back in Macon, we caught them live whenever we could. The band's performances were simply dumbfounding and had a huge impact on every one of us. So strong. So different.

Then came *Live At the Fillmore East*. The first permanent recording of just how great the band was live — and an introduction to all kinds of music fans who had never had a chance to see them in person. Hailed by critics and the public alike, it made the band, quite simply, famous almost overnight. It was a defining moment. Rock from the American South went international.

During the rise of the ABB, Alex Taylor — James Taylor's elder brother — recorded a very good album on Capricorn with Paul, Johnny Sandlin, Joe Rudd, and Bill Stewart, the steady studio

Credit: © Chuck Leavell Archive

Alex Taylor's Friends and Neighbors band.

session guys. The record was called *Alex Taylor with Friends and Neighbors*. When it came time for him to go on tour, he needed a band and Charlie, Lou, and I were instantly in the mix. We recruited a guitar player we'd met from the Washington D.C. area named Jimmy Nalls, and hit the road for about two years. We toured in a Ford LTD station wagon, with a van for the gear and two roadies. The road manager was a guy named Earl Simms, nicknamed Speedo. He did most of the driving. So with Alex, there were six of us in the LTD. I learned to sleep in just about any position, as there was not much choice. We went everywhere in the United States, playing mostly clubs, colleges, and some concert venues. In the middle of it we recorded Alex's second record, *Dinnertime*, with Johnny Sandlin producing. Alex was a wonderful man — he had such a great laugh and spirit about him and was truly one of the band and made us all feel welcome and valued as musi-

cians. A very jovial man, he was nevertheless always harder-edged musically than his brother James — a lot more rock 'n' roll and blues. I loved it. It was a very exciting time for me, the first time I toured across the entire United States, the first of many. We had such fun, playing all those places. The Troubadour in Los Angeles, as well as the Whiskey A Go-Go on the Sunset Strip. In New York, it was the Gaslight in the Village. We played the Cellar Door in D.C., The Boston Tea Party in Boston as well as Paul's Mall and the Jazz Workshop there, and there was a club near Philly called The Main Point we used to do all the time. We did My Father's Place on Long Island. We played lots of college dates across the United States. We were on the road most all the time, either playing or traveling or rehearsing. Sometimes we'd just play for fun, up on the Vineyard for friends of Alex or in Macon at a couple of the really cool black hangouts. One was Le Carousel, run by this black guy named Hodges. He didn't open until about 1 or 2 a.m. and sold extremely hot BBQ chicken and extremely cold beer. He had a couple of pool tables in there, and we'd go there after jamming at another local black establishment that would become legendary in the Macon and Southern music scene, Grant's Lounge.

Macon's legendary Grant's Lounge.

And of course, one of the most important things to all us musicians back in these early days in Macon was a good meal — something that we often couldn't afford. But never fail: if one of us wandered into the non-descript H&H Restaurant in the heart of the downtown, we could count on the occasional freebie from the wonderful owner, Mama Louise. We all ate there — the Allman Brothers, Alex Taylor's band, Dr. John. Most of the area musicians were pals with Mama Louise. Best fried chicken, black-eye peas, cornbread, and greens to be had anywhere. It was so cool a few years later when the Allman Brothers hit it big — as a way of saying thanks to Mama Louise they would send the plane to get her and fly her in to wherever the band was playing so that she could cook up a feast for the guys and crew. Talk about sweet payback! Allman Brothers drummer Butch Trucks remembers that Mama Louise's favorite trip for the band was when they had her flown from Los Angeles to San Francisco by helicopter.

"She just thought that was the best thing," Butch recalls.

Me in the kitchen of the H&H Resaurant in downtown Macon in early 2004 with one of the dearest souls I've known — and best southern cooks — Mama Louise.

Mama Louise is still going strong, nearly fifty years after she first opened a restaurant in an old gas station across the street from where she's now been for decades. The restaurant is covered with autographed photos from all of us and a great Capricorn Records platinum album award that Phil Walden gave her for her support over the years. Gregg Allman still drops in, as do the guys from Gov't Mule and, of course, tons of locals.

"She's somethin' else. I've set out to eat my weight in her greens," Gregg laughs. "Collards are the No. 1 cancer fighter, I've heard. Every time I play anywhere near Macon, I send a limo for her. A Cadillac — she don't go for no Lincoln shit. And it's gotta be a stretch."

Butch recalls that in the earliest days of the Brothers, the only money they had was roadie Red Dog's Vietnam pension split evenly between all the band members.

"We were living on $2 a day," Butch says. "Lunch at the H & H was $1.35. That left 65 cents for some Ripple … and people were always bringing (magic) mushrooms around."

The original Allman Brothers Band in the H & H.

I still drop in when I figure my waistline can afford it — hey, we're talking down-home, don't-even-think-about-the-calories cookin' here. Sure brings back great memories every time I go in the place.

God, those were great times. With Alex Taylor we opened a lot of shows for everyone from the Brothers to Jefferson Airplane, Yes, Mahavishnu Orchestra and many others. I probably played nearly 400 shows with Taylor, and we must have crossed the country five times. But it was also a time that was shattered by some personal tragedy for me. Alex lived on Martha's Vineyard, which I loved. We used to spend quite of bit of our off-time there rehearsing. And it was at Taylor's place that my Mom called one day. Dad was very sick. While there was some irony in the fact that he was a top salesman of insurance policies for cancer, Dad was a heavy smoker of Taryton cigarettes, which proudly advertised their special "charcoal filter." Eventually that caught up with him and he contracted lung cancer. It hit him pretty quickly. Mom said on the phone that if I wanted to see my father I'd better get home. Devastating news. It was too much for me to take, and I went out and got totally drunk. I barely made it home to where I was staying. I was trying to run away from the news.

But the next day I had to face reality. So I booked a flight home to go watch my father die in a hospital. It was a hard thing to take. Dad and I were just becoming friends. While he had a hard time accepting my career choice, he was still supportive of his son. When I'd come home to visit before he got sick, he did his best to be my friend as well as my father. He'd offer me a beer or a drink and try to get me just to talk to him, so we were beginning a new relationship as friends as well as father/son. Now he was dying of lung cancer in a hospital. He was conscious for the first day or two when I got there, but very weak and couldn't talk much. He went downhill very quickly and went into a coma. I can remember that one of the last things he requested was that I shave my beard. I had grown a beard as soon as I could, and it had been a while since he'd seen my face. I didn't want to shave, but I did it for him. I remember him opening his eyes and looking at me when I tapped him to see. He was pretty far gone, but he turned his head a bit toward me and smiled. It was a very tough moment for me. He died on 26 April, two days before my eighteenth birthday. I don't know why, exactly, but it was about ten years later, when I was firmly ensconced in my chosen career — married with a child — that I think I missed him the most. All I wanted to do was to be able to sit down with him and to have a conversation as a grown man. There were so many things I wanted to ask him, things that only a father can tell a son. He would have loved Rose Lane and, of course, the girls. And I think he would have been proud of my career. But it was not to be that he would see these things. Such is life, and we must learn to accept the things we cannot change.

After my father died I started worrying about my mother a lot and checked on her all the time after I went back to work with Alex. But she did fine, and after she moved to a new house, all of us children felt better. She had found a nice small house to live in, just right for her. She wasn't interested in remarrying, but she had lots of friends and the new house was only a couple of blocks from her church. So we all felt better about her situation. Mom was a huge inspiration to her kids. She had a severe case of rheumatoid arthritis that had developed when she was in her fifties; it may have even started before, but it was becoming worse. However, she never complained. She'd just go on about her business. She loved flowers and loved to garden. That became difficult for her, but she'd do what she could. At that time the treatments for her disease weren't nearly as good as they are today, but she did get help. One thing I remember was gold shots. They injected her with low levels of gold, which had become one of the modern treatments.

She also took a lot of aspirin, which thinned her blood and eventually caused problems if she cut herself, as her blood wouldn't coagulate properly. Judy, Billy, and I sort of did "shifts" looking in on Mom. We all lived away from Tuscaloosa, and it required us coming to see her, so we'd sort of check with each other as to when we could go visit her. This worked out pretty well, as we all got to spend time with Mom during those years, and I think she liked mixing it up.

On the career front, things were going great, even though Capricorn was still a pretty small company in terms of personnel. There was Phil, the owner and president; his personal assistant Carolyn Brown; Phil's brother Blue, who looked after the books; and Frank Fenter, the company's executive vice president. Frank was great — another father figure to a lot of us, especially in the early days. In fact, he's one of the reasons I stuck out the hard times when the band Sundown just wasn't catching on. Capricorn was built around the Allman Brothers, and we were the lowest guys on the totem pole, living in a rundown apartment stuck in a less-than-desirable area. When times got really tough, though, we could go into the Capricorn office and Frank was always there, always encouraging and sympathetic. If we needed $250 to make it through the next month, he'd wander off and come back with a check. He was fascinating for a Southern boy like me who'd never seen much of the world. Frank was a tall, slim white man born in South Africa and had wonderful stories — told in his fascinating English-sounding accent. In later years he was a huge supporter of my post-Allman

Brothers band Sea Level and landed us the coveted gig of playing the Montreux Jazz Festival.

Frank was also the boss of the first thing I set my eyes on the first time I walked into the offices of Capricorn records, a long-legged and extremely attractive girl behind a desk. She had on hot pants, and you could see her shapely long legs under the desk. She had a beautiful face and a wonderful smile. My first thought was "Wow! What a fox!" I smiled back at her, and she introduced herself as Rose Lane White. She was the

Capricorn executive Frank Fenter.

personal assistant of Frank. She did a lot of work, including the royalty statements for all the bands and other functions.

Rose Lane came from Twiggs County, twenty-five miles southeast of Macon, but so rural and beautiful it seemed hundreds of miles from the city. She had grown up the daughter of a farming family, had excelled in school, and was looking to broaden her horizons in the world. She had been to the University of Georgia for a few terms, but decided that she wanted to work a while and had left there. She had jobs in Macon at a car dealership, and some other places. But she was not quite satisfied and had found out about the record company. There was an opening, and she interviewed and got the position.

As time went on and I began to get settled in Macon, I got to know Rose Lane and all the folks at Capricorn better. I was impressed and certainly had the hots for her. But I was far too shy to do anything about it, thinking that surely she already had a boyfriend, or that even if she didn't she wouldn't be interested in a kid from Alabama. I was seventeen and she was twenty-one. As she recalls these days, I was right! She sort of noticed me around the office but didn't pay too much attention because I was so much younger. That age difference isn't a big deal now, but when you're that young ....

She was a striking figure — tall, slim and carried herself with an air of confidence and dignity, but was friendly. I thought she was absolutely beautiful, and all of us guys had a crush on her.

But I was intimidated and afraid to hit on her for a date.

It's easy to play any musical instrument:
all you have to do is touch the right key
at the right time and the instrument will play itself.

———————————————————————

J.S. Bach

Becoming a Brother ... and a Husband

```
029194    EVENT   728    WATKINS GLEN  WATKINS GLEN NEW YORK
          CODE
          20G.A.         SHELLY FINKEL JIM KOPLIK          20G.A.
                                      PRESENTS
                         TO BE HELD RAIN OR SHINE
                              SUMMER JAM            $10.00
          10.00                                  EST. PRICE
                                            NO REFUNDS /EXCHANGES
                         SAT JUL 28 1973   12:00P    $10.00
                                                     TOTAL
```

As I was coming to terms with the death of my father, I felt secure in my career — the two years in the studio and on the road all over America with Alex Taylor had been more than I'd dreamed — and I wasn't even twenty years old!

Then, overnight, Alex and Capricorn Records owner Phil Walden had a falling out and Alex refused to do any more touring. I was out of a job.

Thankfully, not for long. Dr. John had just recorded *Right Place, Wrong Time*, which was to become a big hit from his LP *In the Right Place*, and he signed a management contract with Phil Walden. Best of all was that he didn't have a band to tour with so, just like that, Alex Taylor's touring band became the backup band for one Malcolm John Rebennack Jr.

OK — it wasn't "just like that."

We had to audition first.

This took place in what we called the Barber Shop, which was adjacent to Capricorn Studios, an old barber shop that had been made into a rehearsal space. So we went there, set up, and waited. Mac finally came in and all I can remember thinking was that this was one weird cat. I was still innocent enough that I had no idea that Mac was a heroin addict and, most of the time, was very high.

This had no effect on his music, however, and once he was there it was all business. Thankfully, he liked me right from the start. I say thankfully because Mac is tough when it comes to the band he's playing with. He was always on the drummer's case. We had a few different drummers with him: Lou Mullenix, Bill Stewart, Sammy Creason and others. Mac would drill them on "second line," a particular style of New Orleans drum playing. He'd say, "Y'all ain't got that second line thang down … you gotta listen, now! Listen to dem records and get dat rhythm. Man, y'all is playin' square!" He also would get on all of our cases about that and other points of the music. I learned so much from him. I played mostly organ in the band, as he would play the piano. But occasionally he liked to play the guitar, and I'd get to play the piano. I would watch his hands when he played the piano as much as possible to try and get what he was doing. One thing I realized was that his hands are so big — like bear paws — that he could make these amazing stretches, creating fantastic chords that I'd never been able to figure out before. I tried to do it and did learn a lot but my hands are so much smaller I just physically couldn't do some things he would do. I learned to cheat a little by rolling the chords when I couldn't hit them straight on, and that helped my playing and let me at least project Mac's feel. But there was so much more I learned from Mac. He just has this amazing sense of rhythm and knew how to voice chords. He was — and still is — my Guru. And I'm sure just about everyone who's ever worked with him would say the same thing.

After a couple of days auditioning, I wanted to get to know him better. He was staying at a Holiday Inn in Macon, so I went over there and knocked on his door one day. He answered, and said, "Aw … Chuckie … c'mon in, man … good ta see ya." So I went in and we hung out for a bit, talking about the music, mostly. Well, truth be known, it was more the parched, eager student begging the teacher for some of his quenching elixir of knowledge. He was more than happy to oblige. Over the years I've seen time and again that when musicians aren't playing music, they'll settle for talking about it.

About an hour into my visit, Mac excused himself and glided gently into the bathroom. Time passed. Then time seriously passed. In the moment I innocently didn't realize that the cat was in there sitting on the toilet fixing. Maybe he'd even nodded off but was at least enjoying the ride while I waited. Only trouble was that I got bored, curiosity got the best of me, and I started poking around the room.

On the desk I saw a book that looked like sort of a notebook or diary. Fighting my better manners and simple common courtesy, I opened the cover and started stealthily turning the pages. I was shocked. I saw all the names of

Mac "Dr. John" Rebennack

us in the band and beside all the names were these weird voodoo symbols! I had no idea what they meant — and still don't. I had mixed emotions about it. On one hand, I felt guilty about looking at a private notebook. On the other hand, I wondered what all that stuff meant. Was it good? Bad? Anyway, I figured in the end it must have been good because we got the gig.

So we hit the road with Mac. It was all the same cats that had played with Alex Taylor: Lou Mullenix on drums, Charlie Hayward on bass, Jimmy Nalls on guitar, me on the keys, and of course Mac. We were also joined by two great backing vocalists, Jessie and Robbie, who had worked with Mac before. While *Right Place Wrong*

Time, a pretty mainstream funk tune was climbing the charts, Mac was still very much into his "gris-gris" phase. We did songs off the great early records like *Dr. John, The Night Tripper*, and *Moon, Sun and Herbs*. Mac had us all dressed up in costumes, sort of "wizard rock" duds, and with glitter put on our faces held there with Vasoline petroleum jelly. We'd start the show off with an instrumental tune, *Croker Courtbullion*, and he'd come out in all his regalia and his big staff, throwing glitter out into the audience and waving to them. He looked amazing and really did look like a Voodoo King or something. I think I still have some of that glitter inside my Hammond B3 organ from those days! But the band cooked, and I loved every minute with Mac. I liked playing those weird tunes like *Where Ya at Mule?*, *Black John The Conquoror* as well as the songs off of the *Right Place*. I was soaking it all up like a sponge and loving every minute. We also played with some other interesting acts in those days: Ike and Tina Turner, Sun Ra, Mahavishnu Orchestra, and the Allmans, which only made sense, since both bands were being managed by Phil Walden.

Every time, I loved being around the Allmans. I was always mesmerized by the dual drums, twin-guitar leads, Gregg's vocals, and the overall sound. I always insisted on an acoustic piano in our set, and when we would finish, the roadies would pull the piano backstage while they set up the Allman's gear. Some of the rest of our band would go back to the hotel after our set, but if it was possible and we didn't have a schedule to meet, I would stay and listen to the ABB. Many times I would go back to where the piano was and would play along with them, hidden backstage, playing for my own enjoyment. I'd play along with songs like *Statesboro Blues, Don't Want You No More, In Memory of Elizabeth Reed*, and more. I remember some of the road crew watching me and coming over to sort of listen in on what I was doing. I got smiles from them and nods of approval, which was pretty gratifying, since during the nightly drum solo, everyone but Butch Trucks and Jaimoe would come off stage and see me. Gregg Allman recently remarked that he'd noticed me jamming along and thought it was pretty cool.

"I remember him playing along backstage and thinking 'Who the hell is this kid with Dr. John?' "

Butch himself recently commented, "I heard about this kid back there playing along with us. I was on stage every moment of the show, so I never saw or heard him, but I'd hear about him all the time."

Little did I know that this was a rehearsal for what was to come.

The only time I met Duane was sort of a prophetic moment. Some of the Capricorn crowd was up in Muscle Shoals working on an album by the group Cowboy, which was led by Tommy Talton and Scott Boyer. Cowboy was a great band and another rung in the ladder of Southern music, yet was distinct. Sort of a Southern version of Poco or Buffalo Springfield. A few years later I found myself on stage with them backing up Gregg Allman on his acclaimed 1974 solo tour.

When their first album was being recorded and produced by Johnny Sandlin, whom I'd befriended, I was asked to come in to play on some of the sessions. Johnny

Credit: © Allman Brothers Band Archive

Duane Allman, whom Eric Clapton says was perhaps the finest electric guitar player ever.

also convinced Duane to participate and add some Dobro on the track *Please Be With Me*.

He had finished his session and I was just arriving to do my part. When I came into the studio, I went down a hallway that let to the control room, out of which popped Duane. I had never met him and was reluctant to just stop him and get into a whole conversation, so

Credit: © Allman Brothers Band Archive

Duane Allman

when we passed each other I just smiled and nodded to him saying, "Hey, man."

He smiled back with a nod as well, and that was it. Still there was something special about it, at least for me. It's the only time Duane and I were alone. He was an amazing musician and had a fantastic persona. He had this sort of glow about him. When he played it was hard not to look at him. He was so into his music, just in a zone. Eric Clapton told me years later that Duane made such an entrance when he walked into a room he made the place glow. He was usually beaming, very intense, but if he was angry you damn well knew it, Eric said.

The last time Duane played was on Oct. 17, 1971 at the Painters Mill Music Fair in Ownings Mills, Maryland. Twelve days later he was dead at the age of twenty-four. It was a huge blow to all of us. He was the leader. Not only of the Allmans but the whole scene in Macon and Southern rock in general. His loss was huge because Duane was a real figurehead, we all looked up to him. Like some music fans remember where they were and what they were doing when John Lennon was killed or when they first heard Kurt Cobain was dead, I remember very clearly Duane's death.

Credit: © Chuck Leavell Archive

Johnny Sandlin and me in the summer of 2004.

I was at Johnny Sandlin's house. Johnny and I hung out a lot. His girlfriend at the time, Dottie, was a great cook. She always had lots of cold iced tea as well, and we would just hang at Johnny's house and eat Southern cooking, drink cold iced tea, and talk about music. I remember Tommy Talton, the guitarist from Cowboy, being

there that day along with a couple of
other guys. The phone rang and it was
for Johnny. He talked for a moment,
looking very concerned. When he got
off, he gave us the news that Duane
had been in an accident on his motorcycle. The details were sketchy, but we
knew that he had serious injuries. It
was all so surreal, so unbelievable. We
talked, waiting for further news. Time
passed so slowly, and we were all sort
of in a mist of not knowing what to do
or what to say. Time plays tricks with

Credit: © Allman Brothers Band Archive

Berry on his beloved Harley.

the mind, as does tragedy, so I could be wrong, but it seemed like two
or three hours before the phone rang again.

We were all looking at Johnny, and he began to cry. We all knew
what it meant. He got off the phone, and we were all just dumb-
founded. No one knew what to say; it was all so unreal. So we all
huddled together and told each other how much we loved each
other. It was definitely a moment of realizing how precious and
fragile life is.

There was a memorial service three days later, Nov. 1, at the
Snow's Memorial Chapel in Macon, featuring the Brothers and
guests Dr. John, Bobby Caldwell, Thom Doucette, Delaney
Bramblett, and others going emotionally through a few tunes,
including *Stormy Monday*, *In Memory of Elizabeth Reed*, *Will the
Circle Be Unbroken*, and a couple of others. Atlantic Records honcho
Jerry Wexler, who first had Duane under contract before Phil
Walden came into the picture, gave the eulogy.

When Duane was killed, the band was in the middle of making
the album *Eat A Peach* and had to go back into the studio to finish it
without him, which was very intense. To watch the Brothers go
through that and decide to carry on, and to do so without a replacement, was a very emotional time for all of us — even those on the
outside of the band. There was a lot of speculation about the

Credit: © Allman Brothers Band Archive

Duane's service, at which Dr. John (left) joined the surviving band members in honoring the much-loved guitarist.

Credit: © Allman Brothers Band Archive

Berry and Jaimoe in the studio working on *Eat a Peach* after Duane's death.

situation at the time. Would they replace Duane? If so, with whom? Rumors ran rampant. Some said that Eric Clapton would take his place, or perhaps some other well-known guitar slinger. Maybe they would just break up. But in the end they decided to carry on with just the five of them, and this was a really bold move. We all had a great admiration for the Allmans for doing what they did, knowing that Duane had cut only three tracks before his death and they had a whole album to fill. Once they were done, they went out on tour and came back to Macon to consider their future.

Duane's death knocked the wind out of all of us. And yet another tragedy was to occur. Our long-time drummer from the Alex Taylor/Dr. John band and close friend Lou Mullenix died from an overdose of methadone. Lou was one of the cats that just loved to get high and had a hard time knowing when to shut it off. He was a brilliant drummer, probably the most natural drummer I've ever worked with. I remember way back in the Tuscaloosa days even before my bands the Misfitz or the Gents, Lou used to play at the YMCA by himself with a jukebox. The first time I saw him do it I was just amazed. Anyone could punch up any song on the jukebox and Lou would play along, sounding as good or sometimes better than the drummer on the record. Later after the Gents broke up and I began to play with him, he took my musicianship to another level. I never realized before how that could happen, how when you play with someone that inspires you it pushes you to be better. I became a much better player because of him. We all loved Lou so much. He was always happy, witty, fun, and funny. He loved a good joke and could keep us laughing. He was also the epitome of cool. He was a slender guy, very handsome with dark hair and skin and wore the coolest clothes of anyone around. Mac loved him, too. But as I said, Lou loved to be in an "altered state" and took quite a lot of drugs. One time he took too much, and we lost him. We had to go back to Tuscaloosa and bury him, which was a very emotional affair. His mother had been good to us in the early days, letting us hang out at her house, feeding us, and not minding if we drank a beer or two, and we dreaded seeing her in this terrible situation. But she didn't hold anything against us about it. She knew her son and knew that he lived on the edge. Still, it was one of the hardest things I ever had to do — to face her with Lou in a casket. We were all devastated, sad, depressed, and — for me — angry. I was mad at Lou for leaving us. We needed him in the band. There was no drummer as good as Lou, and we had to find a way to carry on without him.

We carried on without him with Mac for a while, but after a time we were all pretty burnt out. Dr. John decided to take an extended break from the road, so adding to the general feeling of uneasiness, I also found myself suddenly unemployed. Again.

I decided to go back home to see my mom for a bit and to think about what my next move would be. I enjoyed her home cooking for a couple of weeks or so and was just hanging out visiting old friends, pondering over my situation when the phone rang. It was Johnny Sandlin on the line, asking me if I'd be interested and available to work on Gregg Allman's first solo record, which he was producing. I jumped at the opportunity — for the music and, honestly, for the money — I needed the work. I was coming close to being broke and was grateful to have the chance to play some fun music with a great artist and also to make some bucks. So I loaded up my Olds Cutlass station wagon once again and headed back to Macon.

I had met Gregg, of course, but only briefly. I didn't really know the guys in the ABB very well and had never really hung out with them, since I was either in the band opening for them or off touring America with Alex Taylor or Dr. John. When I got back to Macon, Johnny had me over to his place to give me the general concept of Gregg's record. Scott Boyer and Tommy Talton were to be involved, not only playing guitar and doing harmonies, but also writing some of the material.

"When I decided to cut my solo record *Laid Back*," Gregg said recently, "I was really trying not to sound like the Brothers. It was just kind of accidental. Someone came down and said 'There's a hell of a piano player y'all might want to think about.' That was Chuck. Chuck made it a lot easier for me to do what I wanted with the record."

Gregg had written several tunes that didn't fit the ABB, and there were a couple of other outside tunes like Jackson Browne's *These Days*, a cover of *Don't Mess up a Good Thing* by Fontella Bass and Bobby McClure, and the traditional *Will the Circle Be Unbroken*.

Johnny, who also played some bass on the album, was looking for a different sound from the ABB, a more "laid back" sound. Strings and horns were overdubbed later with Ed Freeman providing some beautiful arrangements. Jaimoe and Butch, the two ABB drummers, helped out, and my old pal Paul Hornsby made an appearance, as did many of the Macon musicians of the time.

Idlewild South about the time I moved in when I joined the Allman Brothers Band.

I had been chipping in on the rent on a place right in Macon, but in yet another quirk of fate a cool place outside of town became available, so Scott and Cowboy bassist David Brown and I jumped for it. Turned out it was Idlewild — the same place some of the Allman Brothers had lived a few years earlier, and the place that gave their second album its title.

The three of us decided we'd take it over, and we did. It was great for us at the time, a cabin located right on a nice twenty-acre lake. The cabin was pretty sparse, and the only heat was from the fireplace. It could get really cold in there, and we'd all huddle up to the fireplace to stay warm. Still, for me it was wonderful. I had this really small bedroom, barely big enough for a double bed. The back porch was actually over the water, built on stilts. I loved being there and would take long walks around the woods that surrounded the property, walk around the lake, or just sit on the back porch or by the fireplace and enjoy the space. Scott would play the guitar, and there was an old piano that someone had given to us. It was in terrible shape, but I'd play it anyway, and we'd play all sorts of tunes.

Scott was a talented writer and singer, and we spent many hours there playing and talking about life and our dreams.

As plans for Gregg's solo album slowly gelled, we began having great jam sessions at the Capricorn Studios as a sort of warm-up. One night all the Allmans showed up, and there was lots of interaction. It was the first time I played with the band, jamming late into the night on blues and country tunes, some ABB originals, even some jazzy-sounding things. God, it sounded great! And every one of us was having a blast.

I think in some small way it also served a little bit like a healing process for the guys in the Allmans, getting their minds off the terrible loss of Duane and just cutting loose. It also provided me with some healing after the loss of Lou. These jams went on a few days, and then we started Gregg's album. Those sessions went well, too. The combination seemed to be working out, and Gregg was very happy with the outcome. Every few days, we'd take a night off and one of those jams would occur again — with Dickey Betts, Berry Oakley, Jaimoe and Butch on drums — or perhaps things would shuffle and Charlie might play bass for a bit or Bill might get on a jam. It was nothing but fun at first. It slowly grew into something a little more serious as the jams I was having with Butch, Jaimoe, Dickey, Gregg, and Berry started to sound really good — I mean seriously good — and we were all getting along wonderfully well.

Gregg's record was coming along nicely. Everything was clicking. The Allmans had a few dates here and there between all of this, and so we'd break for a bit while they went on the road to play a select few shows. But when they would come back and we'd jam again. They seemed happy to have me there. Finally, it became obvious that this formula was taking shape, and there was talk about their next record. By then we had finished the basic tracks for Gregg's record and it was going into the overdub phase.

"He was just what I needed," Gregg recalls. "Oh, God, Chuck was just perfect. Some of the bros came down for some of the sessions and everyone thought he was a hell of a piano player."

Then one day I got a call from Capricorn asking me to attend a meeting. I didn't quite know what to expect. I was called into Phil Walden's office, and the entire Allman band was there.

"*Laid Back* is a beautiful album," Phil recalls today. "And Chuck is quite prominent on that. I remember I recommended to the Brothers that they add him as a member. Chuck simply shone."

After some short pleasantries, the penny dropped, and I was asked to join the band. Man, you could have knocked me over with a feather. While I knew we had something going, I really thought it

Gregg Allman

was just for fun and had no idea they wanted me in the group. I had thought that maybe they would ask me to play a tune or two on the next record, but I really had no idea that they were considering adding me in as a member. I tried to maintain some sort of calm about it, but of course I accepted right away. I was in the Allman Brothers Band! A group that had sold gold and platinum records, was now a huge live draw, and had gained the respect of not only their large audience but by critics as well. Finally, I had been handed the big break, as they say. I had just turned twenty, and was on top of the world!

Immediately, we started sessions for the next Allman Brothers Band album, which was to be called *Brothers and Sisters*. During breaks from those sessions I helped on the finishing touches on Gregg's record. I was in heaven. We were in the studio just about all the time. The tunes were coming along well for both, and it was so much fun for me to be involved with the arrangements and the whole process. We spent hour upon hour playing, listening back, overdubbing, and putting it all together. Even at the time there was a feeling that we were doing something very special. I was just trying to focus on the music and to make the best contribution I could, and when we would listen to the playbacks, it became evident that the music was indeed clicking and that things were going in a very interesting direction.

Butch said recently that my addition to the band came at a crucial time. "We'd gone eight or ten months without Duane and playing with Chuck took the pressure off me, so I could focus on the groove again. People talk about there being a curse on the band, but there's always an upside. And the best upside we ever had was Chuck. He was by far the best musician on the stage. Unschooled — but simply born with an innate talent. Chuck cuts a groove five miles wide. Nobody like him. Having Chuck laying a groove meant I could wander off and have no idea what I was doing and when I came back it was all still there! He always amazed me."

At the time there were tunes that stood out, and they continue to, not just for me as a musician but for the band's fans, who regard them as classics. From *Brothers and Sisters, Wasted Words*, Dickey Betts' brilliant *Ramblin' Man*, and *Jessica* — where I really got to cut loose — continue to be my favorites. From Gregg's solo album, I always thought *Midnight Rider, Multi Colored Lady* and *Queen of Hearts* were standouts. I was on a high, doing both of these landmark records, joining the Brothers band and knowing that we'd be going on a major tour after *Brothers and Sisters* came out.

Bassist Berry Oakley was the first guy to welcome me into the group. He was so nice to me and went out of his way to make me feel at home, feel comfortable. Berry had a real elegant persona — he looked graceful, and I liked that. When I started playing with him and getting to know him I learned what a sweet person he was, a genuine human being who cared about others. In the studio, he would always come over and say, "Hey man, how you feel? You OK? You want something to drink? Everything all right? What do you think — is this going OK?" He would always compliment me — Berry was the first one to compliment me. He would say, "Chuck —

damn, that was just great, man."
He made me feel good, and I
think that was one of his talents
— he made people feel good. He
had a way about him, but it went
one way or the other: there was
no in between with Berry. He had
a very strong opinion, one way or
the other. I saw him a couple of
times get upset about things, and
he would be just as passionate
about why something was wrong
or why it was a waste of time.

Berry on stage at the Warehouse in New Orleans.

Credit: © 1971 Sidney Smith

Duane's death had taken a huge toll on Berry, though. He had
lost his best friend and the undisputed leader of the band. Berry was
following him that day, but took a wrong turn and ended up driving
around the crash scene, which was perhaps the only small blessing
to come out of it. Berry tried to bury his pain in drink and drugs. In
those days there were always things to get high on, and while we all
did our share, Berry was in pretty tough shape, drinking about two
fifths of vodka a day and doing a lot of cocaine and other drugs. In
fact, Jaimoe once told a reporter, shortly before I was asked to join
the band, that there was secret talk — though I have no firsthand
knowledge of this — of replacing Berry after he'd fallen off the stage
in Chicago and a roadie had to finish playing bass in the set.

Berry was in such bad shape, such horrible emotional pain, that
even today, more than thirty years later, Butch says he thinks the
poor soul's death "came almost as a blessing. I've never seen a man
in so much pain and trying so hard to drown it out."

"He wasn't himself during that time," Jaimoe said. "He had lost
all interest. Then we got Chuck in the band, it was like seeing the
light. He was back being the old Berry again, playing his ass off."

I sure remember him playing his ass off. He was so sweet and so
into the music, even though he was in rapidly declining health and
losing weight he couldn't afford to lose — he was tall and lanky to

begin with. I remember him saying sometimes, "Alls I want to do is to play, man." And play he could. He had such a unique approach to the bass. He used it more like a counterpoint instrument. While most bass players look at the role in terms of "holding down the band" or working in tandem with the drums, Berry had this style of floating around the melodies. His bass would intertwine within the guitar riffs, the piano, or even the vocals. It was an approach that I'd never heard before, and it worked perfectly with the Allman Brothers. Absolutely unique. Berry was individualistic, with his own style — he danced to his own beat. He played what you could call a lead bass, very melodic. He would follow the lines that Dickey was playing, the lines that Duane had played, and he followed the lines that I played. That was the thing about Berry — he was listening to everyone in the band and paying great attention to what was going down musically. He had a great gift for listening — he really had it. Berry was all the time listening; the cat was right with you. He didn't wander. Whatever you were playing, you had his attention, and he would flow with you. If you made a little side step in a certain direction, he was right there with you. His tone was another unique feature of his playing. It was very powerful and clear, and because of his melodic playing, he required a rather big rig to handle the clarity of what he was doing. His rig was really powerful sounding — when you played on stage with him, you felt it — it was an inspiring sound. I would call it a "leadership role" style of bass playing.

Credit: © Allman Brothers Band Archive

Berry Oakley — one of the most original bass players in rock.

I thought Berry's vocal on *Hoochie Coochie Man* was tremendous, too. Berry was tops in my book and I regret that I didn't get to play with him more. I was nineteen going on twenty, and I remember at the time that some people were obsessed with my age, and I did my best to ignore it. It was a defense mechanism because I felt that if I let that become an issue, I'd get distracted, and I didn't want that. I felt that my age wasn't important — what was important was that I was there working with these people. I wanted to find out what they were about, and I wanted them to know what I was about.

Butch jokes that the band wasn't just worried about getting busted for all the dope it was carrying — the guys were concerned that they'd also get pinched for contributing to the delinquency of a minor since I was under age! Well, I just decided to ignore my age. It was just a number.

It sure was an unforgettable time for me. I remember traveling with Berry in a limousine — one of my early rides in a limo! Berry was just so cool. I remember him dressing hip. He looked fantastic, he talked cool, and he made me proud to be with him. It was exciting just to be around him. He was the Baddest of the Bad, man. He had the look, but he had the vibe as well. With Berry, it just wasn't talk; it was walk. We jammed a lot, but as fate would have it I played only one Allman Brothers show with Berry. I count my blessings that I got to play with him at all. Only a year after Duane had died — the sad incident that landed me in the Allman Brothers to begin with — Berry also crashed his bike. Like the day Duane died, I'll never forget it. Berry came out to Idlewild with band employees Tuffy Phillips and Kim Payne to invite the rest of us down to a place called the Ad Lib in Macon for a jam session. They were all pretty high and having a great time.

"We're going to have the 'BO Jam' tonight," Berry said as he came through the door. "We want y'all to come." That's what he called it, the "BO Jam." But before that, he told me, the band was going to have a rehearsal at what was called the Big House — an old mansion in Macon where the rest of the band lived.

"We'll be there in a couple of hours, so if you want to come, we'll be there."

This was exciting for us, and to me especially, so I said, "OK, I'm ready," and a couple of hours later, we got in the car. I still had my old burgundy 1965 Olds Cutlass station wagon, and we drove over to the Big House for the rehearsal. What I didn't know was that in the

The Big House — where the ABB lived — as it appears today in Macon.

meantime, Berry had crashed his Triumph into the side of a Macon City bus after taking a corner too fast — a corner, as rock historians know, is just a few blocks from where Duane had been killed a year earlier. The cops and paramedics had tried to get him to go to the hospital, but Berry told them he was fine — a little banged up but fine. The bleeding from his ears and nose had stopped. He just wanted to go home to the Big House.

Turned out he wasn't fine. He'd suffered severe internal injuries, though no one knew it at the time. Scott Boyer and I arrived at the Big House that afternoon just after the accident occurred, but unaware of it as Berry wasn't there yet. There were a few folks in the house. I can't remember exactly who, but I seem to recall some of the girlfriends of the guys and maybe a friend or two were there hanging out. We waited a short time, talking with each other about what tunes we might get together for the gig in what was a little music room on one side of the house where we were going to rehearse. Berry arrived soon with the others that were with him and he saw Scott and I waiting in the music room. He greeted us, looking shaken, clothes torn from the accident, but nevertheless coherent.

He said something like, "Man, I just had a little spill on my bike, but I'm ok. I'm going up to the room to change and we'll get started." Kim Payne and the others that had witnessed the accident didn't seem so sure, but Berry had said he was fine. As he was upstairs getting changed, it hit him. He started convulsing and collapsed on his bed. Then Scott and I heard crying and all kinds of commotion coming from up the stairs.

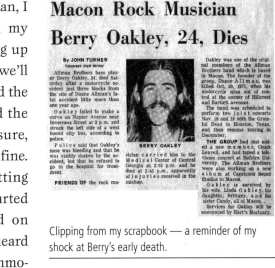

Macon Rock Musician
Berry Oakley, 24, Dies

By JOHN TURNER
Telegraph Staff Writer

Allman Brothers bass player Berry Oakley, 24, died Saturday after a motorcycle accident just three blocks from the site of Duane Allman's fatal accident little more than one year ago.

Oakley failed to make a curve on Napier Avenue near Inverness Street at 2 p.m. and struck the left side of a west bound city bus, according to police.

Police said that Oakley's nose was bleeding and that he was visibly shaken by the accident, but that he refused to go to the hospital for treatment.

FRIENDS OF the rock mu-

BERRY OAKLEY

sician carried him to the Medical Center of Central Georgia at 2:55 p.m. and he died at 3:45 p.m. apparently of injuries received in the mishap.

Oakley was one of the original members of the Allman Brothers band which is based in Macon. The founder of the group, Duane Allman, was killed Oct. 29, 1971, when his motorcycle spun out of control at the corner of Hillcrest and Bartlett avenues.

The band was scheduled to perform two joint concerts Nov. 18 and 19 with the Grateful Dead in Houston, Texas, and then resume touring in December.

THE GROUP had just added a new member, Chuck Leavell, and had taped a television concert at Hofstra University. The Allman Brothers were also working on a new album at Capricorn Sound Studios in Macon.

Oakley is survived by his wife, Linda Oakley, his daughter, Brittany, and his sister Candy, all of Macon.

Services for Oakley will be announced by Hart's Mortuary.

Clipping from my scrapbook — a reminder of my shock at Berry's early death.

By the time we got to the staircase, Red Dog (one of the now-legendary ABB roadies) and Kim Payne and some of the others were bringing Berry down the stairs. Blood was coming out of his ears. He was in obvious pain and was writhing in agony … his eyes rolling back in his head. Out of it. The girls were all crying and there was general confusion. Everyone knew it was serious and that we had to get him to the hospital. We loaded him in one of the cars and got him to the hospital as quickly as we could. The nurses or a doctor or someone came out and told us that Berry had suffered severe internal head trauma and that he was in very grave shape but that they were going to operate and hope for the best.

About half an hour later, a doctor came out and told us that Berry had died on the operating table. Like Duane, he was only twenty-four. The doctor said that even if Berry had gone straight to the hospital after the crash, they probably wouldn't have been able to save his life.

I had been in the band for about three months. We'd done lots of jamming and had just begun recording and had two tracks finished, *Wasted Words* and *Ramblin' Man* and another partial track that came to be called *Berry's Tune* or the *BO Jam*, which I hear may soon

Berry Oakely and Duane Allman … the two Allman Brothers whe died so tragically and so young.

finally have some sort of official release. It was just a wandering jam, but with a great feel.

At the time of his death, I hadn't yet met many of the large group of family and friends of the ABB and, sadly, the first time I met Berry's mother was at his funeral. Just like the band had done for Duane, they'd set up to play a short service. The poor, devastated woman came up to me and begged me to get the band to play *Hoochie Coochie Man*, which Berry had sung on the record. I didn't know what to say to her, since I'd never played the tune with the band and, besides, was the last guy she should be asking. I mentioned her request but as I recall the band did *Elizabeth Reed* and a couple of others, but we did not play *Hoochie Coochie*. I always thought that was a little extra sadness for Berry's mother. Berry was laid to rest in Macon's Rose Hill Cemetery right next to Duane.

For ABB fans who don't know the full irony of this, Rose Hill Cemetery played muse, in a way, for the band's early success. It's close to the Big House, where most of the band lived, and often Duane, Gregg, and Dickey would wander down to the area, spark up a few joints or cruise on some 'shrooms and find inspiration in the peaceful surroundings. In fact, the classic tune *In Memory of Elizabeth Reed* is a song that Dickey had already written but didn't have a name for — he simply saw her name, Elizabeth Reed, on a tombstone in Rose Hill when he was there one night misbehaving and used it for the title. Same with Duane's tune *Little Martha* — there is a grave with a statue of a little girl on it, which was the inspiration for the song, Dickey told a reporter once.

James Dean, Buddy Holly, Big Bopper, Ritchie Valens, and other maverick artists just managed to make the world aware of the

The graves of Berry and Duane, side by side, in Rose Hill Cemetery in Macon. Like Jim Morrison's grave, the site's become a tourist attraction for devotees of the dead musicians.

promise of their genius when they died tragically — and so it was the same with Duane and Berry. And similarly, a cult of rumor and urban legend begins to swirl around their deaths because, I believe, people refuse to believe that greatness can be so easily, senselessly lost.

About two weeks after we said our final goodbyes to Berry, a new TV series premiered, called *In Concert*. Produced by Don Kirshner, it was the film of the only show I played with Berry, just nine days before his death. The show was at Hofstra University in Hempstead, New York, and also featured Chuck Berry, Blood, Sweat & Tears, and Poco. I thought it was a ballsy move, but the band decided to unleash *Ramblin' Man* on the world during that show — the first time it was ever played in public, and the crowd went nuts. What a drag it was the last time Berry was on a stage.

My only gig with Berry Oakley (right) was November 2, 1972, three months after I'd joined the band — and just nine days before his death.

I'm going take this opportunity to dispel a long-standing rumor about the ABB and the *Eat A Peach* album, which I'm in a position to do even though it was released before I joined the band. Some fans believe the LP was so titled because Duane — who was killed three months before its release — slammed his Harley into a peach truck. This is not true, but it is true the album was renamed after his death. After I joined the band, Butch told me the story of where the *Eat a Peach* line came from. It was in a *Rolling Stone* magazine interview that Duane did. The interviewer asked him something like: "So why do you live down there in some small Georgia town? What in the heck do you do down there?" To which he responded something like: "Man, it's great down there ... every time I'm in Georgia I eat a peach for peace."

It was Butch who suggested to Phil Walden that the LP be called *Eat a Peach for Peace.*

"I walked into Phil's office," Butch recalls, "and he pulls out this great art work for the record. The cover has this giant peach on it and the title they had was *The Kind We Grow in Dixie.* I told Phil the artwork was great but the title sucks and suggested using the quote from the interview that Duane had done just before his death."

It's sad that urban legends kind of spin off like they do and graves like Duane's and Berry's are treated as shrines inappropriately — though, in their cases, thankfully, not as dreadfully as Jim Morrison's.

In the midst of the shock and sadness of Berry's death we still, of course, had to come to terms with the reality that we were in the middle of recording a new album. Dates we had booked to play with the Grateful Dead were immediately cancelled. Dickey Betts once told a reporter that it all could have ended right there.

"When Berry was killed," Dickey said, "it wasn't a matter of some guys in the band moving forward to cover that. We had to bring in outside influences. We were very lucky to have Chuck on hand. I think that if we'd made any other move besides Chuck at that point, it would have ended just like that. Because he is so powerful a lot of people accepted the change."

Thankfully, the show went on. Everybody pulled together and said, "We're in the middle of a project and we're not going to stop. Berry wouldn't want us to stop."

The first thing the band had to do was find a new bass player. A few guys came in and auditioned, I recall, and there was some thought that the band needed to hire an established, "name" player. So two names popped up: Mark Andes (who later wound up being the bass player for Heart) and Kenny Gradney (who played with Little Feat, and at the time they weren't working). There was also a guy named Stray that Dickey had been playing with. We auditioned all three, and all of them did quite well. But Jaimoe said, "Listen man, there's this guy I really want to audition. His name is Lamar Williams."

Lamar had grown up with Jaimoe in Mississippi, and they'd been best friends and had played together off and on since they got into music as young teens. Lamar came into the studio that day, and he didn't seem nervous or concerned about who the Allman Brothers were and while respectful, wasn't freaked out at the prospect of replacing the much-loved Berry. Lamar just played music. No more, no less. It was that air of confidence and professional atti-

Butch Trucks, me, Gregg Allman, and Dickey Betts in our Macon rehearsal hall, planning the first tour after Berry Oakley's tragic death.

tude that helped land him the gig. He was presented with an opportunity, and he made the most of it. Believe me, it was a very brief audition. Lamar had an incredible ear and was very quick to understand what was needed in a particular song. I was so impressed by his ability to remember complex melodic lines after hearing them once and then hum them back to me. If somebody played a note wrong, it was Lamar who was always able to pick out where the mistake had been made. He just had an innate gift for music and, truth be told, was a more melodic player than most people realize. In that way he was very similar to Berry. He played much more with the drums than Berry did, but he was also willing to explore and experiment. Like the tentacles of an octopus, he was always searching for the limits of a song. One of the cool things I remember him doing was making his own hand-cut guitar pics — out of Clorox bottles.

With Lamar in place but still stinging from the loss of Berry, we continued on with the recording of *Brothers and Sisters*. It went very well, and the music acted as a healing agent to all of us. We had finished most of the tracks for Gregg's solo project by then and were concentrating on the ABB record. We also played a few shows with the band in between the recordings … some of which had been booked before Berry died. In December we played the University of Michigan; concerts in Hollywood, Florida; the Spectrum in Philadelphia; and two dates at The Warehouse in New Orleans on New Year's Eve and New Year's Day. In January 1973 we played Jacksonville and Tampa, Florida; Athens, Georgia at the University; Knoxville, Tennessee; Cincinnati, Ohio; and Madison, Wisconsin. As main thing was to finish the album, we only did these few dates. The only other show we did around then was in Macon, an annual benefit that the band did for the city. The money was spread around to several local charities, one of which was connected to the police and sheriff's department. Billed as "A Benefit for Better Quality of Life in Macon," we called it the "Get Out of Jail Free" gig, because it put us in good standing with the police, and if any of us got into trouble, we could call our goodwill into play. This came in handy for me in short order due to an unfortunate driving violation. It was fairly harmless. I was stopped for speeding while driving home to Idlewild one evening. I had been living in Macon for a couple of years by then but still had an Alabama driver's license. Unbeknownst to me, it had expired a few days before. Plus my tag had expired. So the cop hauled me into the station under arrest, took my fingerprints, all that good stuff. Embarrassed, I called the Capricorn offices for help. They sent down Bunky Odom, a good guy who helped the organization run smoothly despite its rather small size and skeleton staff.

Bunky got me out of jail, but I had a court date to meet about a month later. A few days after the incident, some phone calls were made by the Capricorn folks to the police authorities. I was told to go with Bunky to see one of the head policemen. We rode down there and met in his office. After some cordial talk about music, and a little reminder of the money the band had raised for the department, Bunky said something like, "So what about Chuck's situation?" The guy smiled and said, "Well, what situation?" That was the last I heard of it, and the court date was erased from the docket.

Not ignoring this blessing, I immediately set out to get my Georgia driver's license. I went to the Capricorn offices to ask Bunky where I should go to get a driver's license. He said, "Oh, you need a liquor license." I said, "No, man ... a driver's license." Bunky smiled. "Chuck, here's what you do: get a fifth of Jack Daniels and put it in a plain brown paper bag. Go to the license bureau and ask for (so-and-so). Give him the liquor and he'll give you a driver's license." I did exactly as he told me, and I had my new license.

Time seemed to be flying by at double speed and there was a whirlwind of activity. After the Allman Brothers' highly successful tour in 1973 following the release of *Brothers and Sisters*, I went out with Gregg on two solo tours, one of which was a stripped-down band and the other of which hit Carnegie Hall and many other legendary theater venues with a full orchestra. The latter we recorded and released, to much acclaim, as *The Gregg Allman Tour*. The core band consisted of me on keys, Tommy Talton and Scott Boyer on guitars, Bill Stewart on drums, Jaimoe on drums and percussion, Kenney Tibbets on bass, and of course Gregg on organ, vocals, and guitar. Randall Bramblett headed up a fine horn section, and we had three female vocalists and a thirteen-piece orchestra, arranged and conducted by Ed Freeman, who had done the arrangements on the *Laid Back* record. Including the orchestra there was a total of twenty-eight musicians. It was a challenge to put it all together and make it work, and the rehearsals were tough going with so many players. But when the dust settled and we got it all worked out, it was truly an amazing band. Cowboy, which of course was Boyer and Talton's band, was the opening act. Randall, Bill Stewart, and I joined in along with bassist David Brown to round out the group. Sometimes Jaimoe or some of the horn players would sit in on Cowboy's set. The whole thing was one big groove, and we had so many good gigs and good times together.

That tour was a great experience, but there was nothing like the success of the first Allman Brothers album after Berry's death,

Brothers and Sisters. Not only did it feature Berry's final recordings but it also featured the instrumental *Jessica*, which I think was the first tune Lamar recorded with the band. This is probably the song for which I'll always be most known. I'm forever indebted to Dickey for writing it. As I recall, Dickey first played it to us on acoustic guitar. It was written for, and named after, his young daughter. Dickey had been listening to Django Reinhardt and watching Jessica play around the house, and he developed the song from the rhythm of her play. We sort of toyed with it at first, just getting comfortable with the changes and getting the harmony parts between the guitar, piano, and organ. Then we ran through it like, once a night for a few nights in a row until we felt confident about all the twists and turns, and slowly developing some of the transitions that occurred. I don't know how many takes it was, but not many after we learned the song. I guess not more than three. As far as my piano part, it just came to me. I try not to think too much or "organize" a part too much, other than to learn the harmony and other necessary aspects of the arrangement. I was just trying to keep up with those guys, and the notes I played on the solo just fell off my fingers. The solo just sort of played itself. It felt very natural and I was just thrilled, and continue to be grateful, to have a song like that with such a strong role for my instrument.

Reminiscing recently, Gregg was very flattering remembering our first instrumental recordings together.

> Those instrumentals would get out there. And Chuck would go right out there with you ... you couldn't get too far out there that Chuck wasn't right there with you. Made it a lot easier for me because, no pun intended, I always searched for some simplicity in the band.[1] It's jazz and blues and of course rock and roll surrounds, but if it gets too much over to the jazz I try to take it back to the blues; if it speeds up too much you gotta get back in there and rehearse every song back down. Chuck's always had that versatility. I know some good piano players, man, but as far as it goes, Chuck smokes 'em. And that's

---

[1] *Searching for Simplicity* was one of Gregg's solo LPs.

saying something. He is one accomplished man on the keys. I mean, he enriches the Stones thing — I've seen it. He's the most professional of the bunch.

I've been pretty blown away by Gregg's kind words, but the root of it all was in that music we created all those years ago, and it wouldn't have happened without Gregg. He has always put his heart and soul — and, believe me, he's got a lot of both — into his singing and playing. He was very good to a young aspiring piano player and remains an inspiration and a friend to this day.

Jessica has always been a fan favorite, too, but the Allman Brothers were pretty much ignored throughout their history by the Grammys until 1996, when they won their first trophy for a live version of the song. I was a little bewildered, I have to admit, that the studio version was ignored by the same academy. But Butch recently put it all in perspective, as only Butch can.

> *Jessica* — it's Dickey's name on it but that's Chuck's song. The fact that it won a Grammy for a live version all those years later, well, it's ludicrous. I use that fucking thing for a doorstop. Those fuckers ignored us for all those years. I don't want to sound too arrogant but we were the most influential band, the most popular draw with the No. 1 album at that time. Innovative. Original. These assholes just ignored us. To get something 20 years later is pretty silly. It's almost an insult.

While I am happy for the band finally getting some well-deserved recognition from all the years of great music, I must admit that it made me feel a little better to hear Butch say that. But the best compliment I've probably ever had was from Dickey himself. In 2000, the longtime Brothers' guitar tech, Joe Dan Petty, was killed in the crash of his private plane. I joined the ABB playing his memorial service at the Grand Opera House in Macon. Afterward we went back to the Big House, which is now owned by tour "magician" (as he likes to be called) and band archivist and photographer Kirk West, and Dickey said to me, "Chuck, it was so good to hear that

One of the first promo shots of the ABB after the addition of bassist Lamar Williams.

piano in *Jessica* again. You know, it's just not *Jessica* without it." I had to hold back the tears, I was so touched by this.

In late 2003, Dickey graciously gave me permission to rerecord the song on my next solo CD, which I did in 2004 with Michael Rhodes on bass and Chad Cromwell on drums. "Tell Chuck," Dickey said to our mutual friend John Lynskey, "that *Jessica* is as much his song as mine." I'll always be honored away by that gesture and kind sentiment.

Of all the gigs I did with the ABB, though, I have to say that the one that stands out most prominently was at the Watkins Glen race-track in New York on July 28, 1973. The Grateful Dead and The Band opened. The promoters were expecting 80,000 to 100,000 people to show up, but we ended up with a crowd of roughly 600,000 — for a one-day event. That topped the Woodstock festival by over 100,000 people. The players had to fly in by helicopter because the roads were all blocked. People had abandoned their cars and were walking to the site, reminiscent of Woodstock.

It was incredible. I'll never forget looking out on that crowd, a mass of bodies that looked to me like a forest (that's how I described

The stage at the Watkins Glen show.

it in my diary; talk about foreshadowing!) And the show was simply amazing. The Dead played for almost five hours, the Band for three hours, and we played for four hours. Then everyone got on stage for a ninety-minute jam. It should have been, in Butch's words, the greatest jam in rock history. But I must say that in reality it was a train wreck.

"It was a disaster," Butch recalls with some laughter, describing the jam as a case of rock and roll pharmacy gone bad. "The drugs didn't mix. The Band was fucked up on drink, the Dead were all tripping (on LSD), and the Brothers were all coked out of our minds. There's no way that jam was going to come together."

I remember it rained a lot and the crowd got pretty muddy, but it was a terrific time. The only weird incident I ever heard about was of some parachutist jumping out of a plane over the track hoping to put on a bit of a show of his own by setting off an explosive of some kind, forgetting the very basic law of physics that he and the explosive would fall at the same rate. As he opened his parachute, I've heard, he was blown to bits. I was backstage or somewhere but photographer Mark Spaulding, whose shots from Watkins Glen appear in these pages, says he saw it happen from the moment the guy stepped out of the plane until the explosion and grizzly fallout. I was probably too busy making sure I didn't get dosed

Watkins Glen. The crowd was so huge the bands had to fly in by helicopter.

with LSD. Back in those days, when the Grateful Dead were around, it was a real and present danger. You had to watch yourself; never leave a drink sitting on a table or accept a drink that you didn't pour yourself into a glass that you knew was clean. Augustus Owsley Stanley III, nicknamed "Bear" or simply "Owsley," had been the Dead's soundman since 1966, but his fame really came from his experience as a cook. Well, not a cook — *the* cook of the best LSD

A view of the stage at the Watkins Glen show from the crowd.

ever made, the hits made for the now-legendary Acid Tests. And he was pretty efficient at making sure everyone within arm's reach was tripping most of the time.

We played a big gig at the Cow Palace in San Francisco on a New Year's Eve with some of the Dead sitting in with us, and I remember being on my toes then, too. Butch wasn't so lucky, despite trying his best.

Butch recalls:

> God, that was awful. I remember we were playing to like, 50,000 people and it was being broadcast coast to coast. I was trying so hard not to get dosed by those guys. Owsley would dump a vial of liquid acid into the ice chest the beer was in ... and it was enough that if you took a can out and opened it and drank from it, you were dosed. You really had to be so careful. I had my bottle of Mateus and never let it out of my hands. I set it down between my tom-toms on stage. We were playing a three-hour set and I thought I was fine — if I'd been dosed I would have started tripping a half hour in ... then came my drum solo and it hit. I couldn't understand how I'd been dosed. But all of a sudden my drums started drifting away from me. They then turned into marshmallows. It happened at the worst possible time. I couldn't play and had to stand at the side of the stage and watch with a stupid grin on my face as Bill Stewart played my solo. Turned out Owsley was at the side of the stage with a water gun filled with acid and was shooting it at my bottle of wine. That's how he dosed me.

Joining the Brothers was a bit like being admitted into some elite club. They were already successful, and their whole lifestyle had changed from struggling musicians to a band that had made it. When I joined, they were playing to large crowds — 10,000 and more. There were limos, a private plane, unlimited expense accounts; whatever you wanted, it would be there. But this was so foreign to me, and really my main concern was the music. I found all the glamour somewhat distracting. Certainly interesting and eye-opening, but what did all the "stardom" have to do with the music? I remember Jaimoe saying, "Chuck, you know there are musicians, and there are rock stars. Some rock stars are musicians, but not all of them." That hit home to me. I think the Allmans had both things going. Gregg was a rock star, no doubt. He had the looks, the swagger, the persona. He was also a great singer, a great songwriter, and a damn good B3 player, too. Dickey had a certain rock-star

The Cow Palace gig with the Grateful dead: Jerry Garcia and Dickey Betts. This was the night Butch got badly dosed with LSD.

charisma, too — paired with incredible talent as a songwriter and guitarist.

I thought that the Allmans were one of the coolest bands around, and it was a real honor to be a part of it all. Being so young, there was a lot I didn't know. I had never traveled in these kind of circles before, and I was just a naive kid, really. In the beginning, Gregg took me under his wing. He'd ask me to ride in his limo and hang out with him. He called me the "boy wonder," which was uncomfortable for me, but flattering nonetheless. During the first year I was with the band, he was dating Jenny Arnez (among many other girls). Jenny was the daughter of James Arnez who played the great cowboy sheriff Matt Dillon on the TV series *Gunsmoke*. Gregg took me to her house once, just letting me tag along. Jenny was a really sweet but troubled girl. Very attractive, as well. I can remember going over there and thinking to myself, "Good

The famous "Starship" that the Allman Brothers used, as did Led Zeppelin and the Rolling Stones.

Credit: © 1973 Sidney Smith

Credit: Chuck Leavell Archive

heavens, you're at Matt Dillon's house!" It was one of those really fancy Beverly Hills homes, and I'd never been to a TV or movie star's place before. The sad thing is that eventually Jenny committed suicide. There was speculation that she might have done it because of her love for Gregg and that he wouldn't commit to any type of serious relationship with her. I don't know if that's true or not, but it was certainly a tragedy. I know that Jenny was deeply in love with Gregg. She told me so. Gregg was good to her, I believe, but he just didn't want to go too deep into a relationship at the time.

In my personal life, I had gained a lot more self-confidence and — now being a member of the Allman Brothers Band — had a much higher profile both in public and within the offices of Capricorn Records. On our first tour that took us through San Francisco, Gregg joked that it was time for me and Lamar to get our tattoos. All the members of the ABB had a small tattoo of a magic mushroom on the calf of their right legs, and they got them from the premiere tattoo artist of the day, Lyle Tuttle, in San Fran. So Lamar and I, as well as roadie Scooter Herring, went in and got the marks that literally branded us Allman Brothers.

At one point out on the road with the Brothers, I was pleasantly surprised to find that Dr. John had decided to go on tour himself again after his hiatus and he opened for us. It's always so cool when I run into him. He stayed and watched the whole Brothers gig. At the time I had an unusual piece of equipment for my Steinway grand piano that was custom-made by ABB

The New York debut of the new ABB.

Credit: © Allman Brother Band Archive

Atlanta Braves Stadium, June 1, 1974: The ABB play to the largest crowd in Southern history … 61,232 people.

roadie Twiggs Lyndon (more on him in a second), that we called the piano mute. It allowed me to mute the strings and create some interesting sounds. Mac had witnessed this during the show and was fascinated by it. After the show, he asked me to come back to his hotel room for a chat. He was so encouraging and so sweet, complimenting me on my playing and telling me he was proud that I'd landed the gig with the Allmans. And he loved the piano mute; he liked weird stuff like that. "Man, dat mute thang was the bomb, Chuckie!" We reminisced about my time on the road with him, talked about poor Lou Mullenix and how much we missed him, talked about music, and had a great time. A few hours later, I decided I'd better head back to my hotel. As I bid Mac farewell, he said, "Wait a minute, my Chuckie," and went to a bag he had in the room. He got an envelope and fooled around in the bag for a while, then brought it to me. He said, "Listen, bro, I want you to take this and get yo' self a little bag to put it in and keep it around ya as much as ya can, but don't never show it to nobody else, ya hear?" I accepted gratefully and left. While, obviously, I can't reveal what is in that bag — even Rose Lane doesn't know its secrets — I can say that it was a special Voodoo mix of things that would help keep me safe and healthy and bring me good fortune. I have to say that I think it's worked! Mac is still one of my true friends, and I will always look up to him. I'm definitely a protégé of his, still his student. And that's the best way to describe it because playing with Mac was like going to the University of Funkology. I learned so much from him and still do today just by listening to his latest recordings. He is "The Man" as far as I'm concerned.

This was an exciting time in the development of Southern music. The great setup of Capricorn and the Brothers' schedule allowed me — and some of the other guys — to stretch out and play on a long list of other artist's projects. Among many of the records I made appearances on, I've always been fond of my contributions to records by Livingston Taylor, Kitty Wells, Don McLean, Marcia Waldorf, Bobby Whitlock and Tim Weisberg. One of the bands that Phil Walden latched onto early on was a new group out of Spartanburg, South Carolina, called The Marshall Tucker Band, and he signed them right around the time that I joined the ABB. We all hung out a lot together, and Marshall Tucker opened quite a few shows for the Brothers. Marshall Tucker wasn't one of the band members, of course — the band was composed of brothers Tommy and Toy Caldwell, Doug Gray, Paul T. Riddle, George McCorkle, and Jerry Eubanks. The name Marshall Tucker, if you don't know the story, came from the key ring of a blind piano tuner in Spartanburg, who had dropped it in the band's rehearsal space. Just another one of those cool rock 'n' roll trivia stories. Their debut album sported the huge hit *Can't You See*, and several years later Jaimoe, Paul Hornsby, and I appeared on their biggest album, *Carolina Dreams*, with its terrific songs *Fly Like an Eagle* and *Heard It in a Love Song*.

They were a good group adding to the whole Southern music movement, but like all the big bands of the era, seemed to suffer tragedy. The ABB lost Duane and Berry, while Lynyrd Skynyrd was nearly wiped out in a 1977 plane crash. The Caldwell brothers lost their younger brother Tim and then shortly after Tommy was killed in a car crash. Toy, with whom I was closest, never got over his brothers' deaths and he died in his sleep in 1993.

It was so sad. I saw Toy shortly before he died. He was on a small solo tour and came to Macon, playing in a little club called Flaming Sally's. I dropped in and hung out a bit and talked, which was sweet. It sure brought back memories of the early ABB days.

Speaking of which, I have to tell you about Twiggs. He had a profound effect on me from those days. He was the Brothers' first road manager — Phil Walden sent him out with most of the Capricorn acts. There was no one — and probably never will be anyone else — like Twiggs. He was a technical genius. He could make anything work. I mentioned the piano mute earlier. The story is that I used to mute the strings of my piano with my left hand, leaving only my right hand to play

Twiggs Lyndon, the great roadie and technical whiz.

the notes. Twiggs loved the sound but saw that I could only play with one hand. This bothered him and he came to me saying, "I think I can build you something that will let you play with both hands." The next thing I know Twiggs designed, welded, and delivered a device to do just that. The mute was controlled by a foot pedal, and through a system of hydraulic mechanisms the apparatus would push down a bar of felt on the strings of the piano, making a "plucking" sound. I only used it a little bit, mostly in the long instrumental songs like *Les Brers in A Minor*, when we would all stretch out our solos. Another clever idea that came from him was when I expressed concern over the safe transport my grand piano on rickety old tour trucks. Twiggs invented a 100 percent-effective protective case. He built it sort of like a "frame inside a frame." The inside frame held the piano, and that frame was connected to some small shock absorbers he had bought from an auto parts place and connected to the larger frame. This allowed the piano to take the rough hits of the highways, absorbing them with his special system.

He was also a wild man with an insatiable appetite for girls and was responsible for arranging some outrageous orgies, which are probably better left under-described, for some music stars who are better left un-named.

Curiously, I'd heard all about Twiggs before I met him. That's because when I first moved to Macon people would stop me on the street and ask me what I was doing out of jail. This kind of thing just can't help but freak you out a bit. I soon learned that Twiggs and I looked a lot alike, same build, curly long hair, and beards. The big difference was that at the time, Twiggs was in jail for stabbing a nightclub owner to death after he'd refused to pay the Brothers after an appearance in Buffalo. The story I always heard was that the club owner was mob connected and probably never planned on paying the band to begin with — a volatile situation made far worse by the fact that Twiggs and a lot of the other guys were pretty strung out as they worked days at a time with little sleep and sometimes relied on speed trying to deal with a grueling tour. Twiggs just lost it and attacked the guy with a fishing knife and stabbed him three times.

Phil Walden recalls that he spent the next afternoon making frantic calls to find out what was going on and to get Twiggs some legal protection.

"I finally got Twiggs on the phone," Walden recalled recently, "and told him not to say anything until the lawyer got there."

Walden, he says, would have done anything for Twiggs. "He was Road Manager Number One — a very special person, one of a kind."

"I called a lawyer I knew in Buffalo," Walden says, "who was one of the best criminal defense attorneys in the country, a guy named John Connor. I asked him what it was going to take to get Twiggs off and he told me $25,000 — which is about $100,000 in today's money. I went to the band and they said they'd pay for it. Well, at the time the Brothers owed me a couple of hundred thousand dollars but I went ahead and paid it. I think they eventually paid me back a few years later."

The money was certainly worth it. The lawyer managed to convince a judge that being the road manager for the Allman Brothers Band was enough to drive anyone insane. Berry Oakley, as I understand it, was called to the stand to testify and had to leave the courtroom several times to vomit because he'd been using heroin. The lawyers asked him if he'd been taking drugs. He said yes. In the last month? Yes. In the last week? Yeah. In the last hour? You bet.

Twiggs beat the murder rap.

Instead of spending the rest of his life in jail, he got six months or so in a mental hospital. "He was home by Christmas," Walden recalls. "He brought me a candleholder he'd made in the hospital shop!"

But Twiggs was still in custody when I moved to town, which, considering we looked so much alike, explained why quite a few people were a little freaked out when they first saw me.

Twiggs worked with most of the Capricorn acts after the Brothers broke up. In November 1979, he was on the road with Steve Morse's Dixie Dregs band. At a show in upstate New York, Twiggs — a veteran skydiver — told everyone he was going to make a jump before the gig. He did, but something went wrong and his chute didn't deploy and he was killed instantly. Rumors have abounded ever since. Many people in Macon have always believed Twiggs never even tried to open the chute, and it was his way of checking out, a rumor fueled further by the fact that the incident happened in a place called Duanesburg, and Twiggs, like a lot of people, hadn't really come to terms with Duane Allman's death.

Walden said recently that he'd heard Twiggs had slept with the jumpmaster's wife the night before, and the jumpmaster — the guy who packed Twiggs' chute — got the ultimate revenge. Others insist Twiggs always packed his own chute.

"I don't know where the truth ends and the bullshit begins," Walden said. "He was an unusual guy and I remember he always used to say things like 'I don't want to live past thirty-nine. I don't want to be forty years old. I want to do all the things I want to do in life before I'm forty years old.' And Twiggs certainly never wasted a waking moment, let me tell you! But I hate to think that he did it deliberately."

Of course, I wasn't there. Walden wasn't there. In fact, there weren't very many people who actually witnessed the event. But Steve Morse was one of them, and he says simply that "anybody who said it wasn't an accident wasn't there and is just trying to romanticize this crap. I spent a lot of time with him right before he went into the plane." Morse is a pilot himself and Twiggs had done jumps from his plane. He says the day of the jump was freezing cold and very windy, and he suspects Twiggs — who was jumping from 8,500 feet — suffered a heart attack from the shock of the elevation and cold and was unable to save himself on the way down.

We'll never know, and it doesn't really matter. Everybody who was lucky enough to call Twiggs a friend will always treasure his memory. And Twiggs' younger brother Skoots, who followed in his rock 'n' roll footsteps as a hugely respected technician, is also one of my closest pals today. As a matter of interest, Skoots has worked for Steve Morse for many years and as of this writing is still with him, touring with both Deep Purple and The Steve Morse Band, and the occasional Dixie Dregs reunions.

Thinking about Twiggs brings back great memories. But the best memory of that time of my life in the early days was New Year's Eve 1972. The Allman Brothers were given the chance to make a bit of history with the first nationwide, live simulcast of a rock concert, from a place called the Warehouse in New Orleans, which the band played every year for several years.

The beautiful Rose Lane White had come down from the Capricorn office in Macon to work on the show, since she'd been involved with it from the beginning. She was as beautiful as ever and, as always, everyone in the office had a crush on her. By now I had gained a good bit of confidence, having landed the ABB gig. There was a big dinner being given by the promoters to the band, and as I was checking into the hotel and was told about this, I noticed Rose Lane there. On a quick whim, I decided I'd ask her for a date. Much to my surprise, she accepted. We went to dinner and just had a great time. There was an immediate connection between us, and I thought to myself, "Wow, this is cool. Don't blow it, Chuck!" I tried to be on my best behavior and to be careful to mind my manners, like my Mom and Dad had taught me.

We did the show, and I asked her to hang with me for it, which she did. When we got back to Macon, I called her right away to ask her out again. She accepted — and we've been together ever since. Very little time passed before I knew I wanted to spend the rest of my life with her. But before I could marry the farmer's daughter, I had to go meet the farmer and his family.

I was the most nervous guy on the planet that day. Here I was, a long-haired, bearded musician in a rock band with a reputation intent on asking a traditional Georgian farmer for his daughter's hand in marriage. Of course, I didn't do this all in one day — this was the first meeting, just to get to know the family and settle in. Rose Lane's father was a wonderful man named Alton White, Jr. He was a tall, slender man, hardened by years of farming. While he was a traditional country farmer, he was also knowledgeable in other outdoor issues. He tended the family's forestlands and had also been a timber cruiser and procurement agent for several local timber companies. He served as a county commissioner as well. Mr. Al was certainly a gentleman and loved his daughter very much, and he equally loved his son, Rose Lane's younger brother, Alton III.

Credit: © Chuck Leavell Archive

Years later I was told a story by Baby Joe Falulk, a family member. Baby Joe was a wonderful guy — about six feet tall and just as wide with a wonderful jolly round face. He was built solid as a rock. He almost always had a big cigar

Rose Lane and me (center) with her father and mother shortly before we were married.

with him, but didn't really smoke it much. He'd just keep it in his hand or his mouth. He'd had a hunting accident many years before when he was crossing a fence with a shotgun. The shotgun went off and he lost three fingers. So he'd hold that cigar between the remaining ones, his thumb and his little finger. Baby Joe had an easy smile and a hearty laugh. And here's what Baby Joe told me: Before I arrived to meet the family, Mr. Al. gathered all the boys together. He said to them: "Now listen. Rose Lane is bringing a boy home with her this evening. And I understand he's a little … well … different. He's got long hair, and he plays in a band. Not a country band. Some kind of modern stuff, she calls it rock music. So he looks different, not only got long hair, but a beard, too. And may have a tattoo or somthin'. But her mom thinks that they are getting pretty serious. So now listen to me … I don't want y'all makin' fun of him, hear?"

Sure wish I'd known that then! Before meeting her family I was so nervous I didn't know what to do. I had even asked her a couple of days before if she thought I should cut my hair. She had said no, of course not. Rose Lane tried to calm me down, telling me not to worry, to just be myself and relax.

Relax? Impossible. Finally, we arrived. I sucked it in and put a smile on my face as we got out of the car and were greeted by the family. Of course, they did indeed put me at ease straightaway. Her mother, Rosaline, was just as sweet as she could be, asking me about the music and my past in Alabama. Her Dad was equally as gracious, prying some history out of me and getting a sense of who I was. Baby Joe was there, and Alton, Rose Lane's brother. There were some other cousins and a neighbor there as well. The dinner was fantastic — traditional Southern fare: a couple of different meats and lots of cooked vegetables like black eye peas, butter beans, greens. Of course, there were homemade biscuits, which were amazing. The deserts were awesome, a couple of pies, cakes, and such. Sweet iced tea to drink.

After dinner the boys went outside to smoke cigarettes (or in Baby Joe's case, his cigar) and chat. They asked me if I'd ever hunted. I told them the truth, that only once had my Dad ever carried me to a deer stand, and we didn't see anything. I was very young at the time and fell asleep in the stand waiting. They asked me if I'd ever shot doves, and I said no. They invited me to the opening day of dove season, which was a few months away; I said if I wasn't on the road I'd come. The evening ended well, and I was much at ease, although they were yet to know I was going to be a part of the family!

Rose Lane and I spent more time in the country with her relatives — almost every weekend when I wasn't on tour. The next major family member I was to meet was Miss Julia, Rose Lane's grandmother. She lived not too far away on a separate farm they called the "Home Place." Miss Julia was quite a remarkable woman. A true Southern matriarch, a grand dame of the South. She was a very attractive lady in her seventies at the time.

Not long after I asked Rose Lane to marry me — and I became the luckiest guy in the world when she said yes. It was with great

Credit: © Chuck Leavell Archive

Me with the girl of my dreams … Rose Lane White, who on July 26, 1973, became Rose Lane Leavell. In this photo, she's pregnant with our first daughter, Amy.

pride and love that I married into the family when Rose Lane and I took our vows on Jul. 26, 1973, in a really beautiful ceremony just around the corner from the Big House in Macon. We were married — like a Gregg and his second wife Janice, and a lot of our gang, in fact — by this funky cat named Reverend Gerald Buffalo Evans, who was licensed to conduct weddings by the Church of Universal Truth. I know, it sounds pretty hippy-dippy these days, but at the time it was the coolest way to go and was a blast. Wouldn't have had it any other way!

Like my mother, Rose Lane's mother has been a major influence on me, though I've always been saddened that her father passed away only about six months after our marriage, just as Mr. Al and I were really getting to know each other. He had been very good to me in a short time, but his cancer came on quickly and swept him away. It was devastating to everyone. Rosaline had lost her husband, Miss Julia had lost her only son, while Rose Lane and her brother Alton had lost their father. And I lost the new father figure that I had hoped would be a big part of my life for many years.

Credit: © 1973 Sidney Smith

Sandy Blue Sky with hubby Dickey Betts.

I found I had some support from friends in the band. Dickey warmed up to me. At the time Rose Lane and I were newlyweds, Dickey was married to a Native American girl, Sandy Blue Sky (thus the song *Blue Sky*). Dickey had some Indian blood in him as well, and had become very interested in Native American issues, befriending many tribal chiefs, mostly from the Creek Nation.

We were all sympathetic to this subject, and we all were willing and wanting to help. After consulting with an attorney, we set up the North American Indian Foundation and did several benefit concerts that raised quite a lot of money for this cause.

The ABB was on tour and had a stop in Oklahoma City with a few days off. Dickey invited Rose Lane and me to visit a reservation and to meet some of the chiefs and others in Tulsa. We stayed with a Medicine Man named Stanley Smith. With him we met Chief Daniel Beaver. Beaver spoke only in Creek language and told us, with Stanley interpreting, the story of the Trail of Tears. It was so moving and magical to be there and to hear all of this. We went to church with them. It was a Christian service, very modest, held in a small white church way out in the middle of nowhere on the Creek reservation. We drank peanut coffee, which was served before the ceremony, and it was truly a memorable and moving journey for Rose Lane and me. Dickey was gracious to take us along, and it helped me a great deal with my relationship with him. Prior to that, Dickey had been a bit aloof, and while we had a great musical bond, I wasn't sure if we had much of a personal relationship. That all changed with this experience, and from then on we were friends. I'll always be grateful to him for that eye-opening experience.

In the short run, the NAIF did quite a lot of good. We not only raised awareness, but also a great deal of money for the foundation. I think it made a positive difference, and it was a good feeling to be doing something to help those folks who had been so taken advantage of. In the long run, the foundation fizzled and dried up. Still, it was something I know we're all still proud to have been involved in.

It was the start of my political awareness, I guess. The ABB was a big supporter of Georgia governor Jimmy Carter, who showed a genuine interest in the Macon and Atlanta music scenes and would appear at Capricorn Records once and a while, especially for the company's annual BBQ and jam. He liked seeing what was going on and asked lots of intelligent questions about the recording process. He saw music as an art form, but also realized it was good for the state and offered us moral support in return, despite the danger cavorting with the country's most popular, hard-playing, and hard-partying band sympathetic to his political aspirations. Back then the band's drug use was universally known, and it was certainly a risk

To my good friend Chuck Leavell – Jimmy Carter 1975

Me with Jimmy Carter, Dickey Betts and Don Johnson.

he took, but he did it because he was genuinely interested and believed in us and, generally, in the power of music.

When Carter decided to make a run for the presidency, all the Capricorn artists got on board and helped raise money for his campaign. I've developed a special acquaintanceship with the President over the years, based largely on our shared interest and goals concerning Georgia forestry. Rose Lane and I had some wonderful moments at White House events. Carter himself has an impressive plantation, and I've known his forester, an excellent man by the name of Blake Sullivan, for years. One day Blake called and told me that he was putting together a quail hunt for the President and

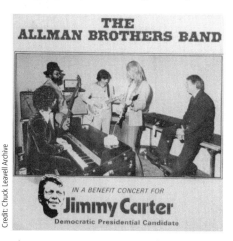

THE ALLMAN BROTHERS BAND

IN A BENEFIT CONCERT FOR

Jimmy Carter

Democratic Presidential Candidate

The ABB came out to support our fellow Georgian in his bid for the White House.

some other interesting people and extended an invitation for me to join them — I jumped at the chance and we had a wonderful time.

I've always been so impressed with President Carter's knowledge, intelligence, and altruistic nature. A couple of years later I enjoyed another hunt with him and then, in March 2004 we reunited yet again out on a Southern Georgia plantation hunting quail. And I have to tell you that the seventy-nine-year-old former President simply embarrassed me with his excellent shooting skills, and I ain't that bad myself!

I am constantly impressed by Carter and his intelligence and his concern for the problems in the world. During lunch that day we talked about world affairs in countries like Venezuela, Africa, the Middle East, Haiti, and of course we talked about forestry and hunting and, as always with Jimmy Carter, I came away feeling like I'd been through an excellent college course.

Phil Walden, Gregg Allman, and Jimmy Carter at a fundraiser for Carter's presidential bid.

Credit: © 1975 Sidney Smith

Quail hunting with President Carter in early 2004.

Credit: Chuck Leavell Archive

Like most of my career and the way my life has gone, it's due largely to the fact that I was lucky enough to land the gig with the Allman Brothers Band. Which isn't to say it was all roses filled with summer rain. It was the early 1970s, after all, the heady, druggy days for all rock bands. We certainly had our own dark moments — many of which have been chronicled in various accounts of the band and the time and which I feel no need to repeat. But I can't deny it was going on, plenty of it going on. We all experimented with this and that, some more than others, perhaps, but all of us were trying things, me included. Gregg as well as other members of the band fell victim to heroin addiction and struggled through several rehabs, but blessedly he finally beat the habit long ago and is now healthier than he's been in thirty years. There was pot, cocaine, acid, speed, heroin, magic mushrooms, hash, and hash oil going around at one time or another. While I have always been relatively moderate in these things, I certainly did my share, which of course I wouldn't recommend to anyone. I was born, thankfully, with some kind of built-in governor that would kick in and, for the most part, keep me from doing too much of anything. Hey, I had my moments, like everyone, but fortunately heavy drug and alcohol use honestly didn't hold the glamour, appeal, or a deeply needed emotional relief for me as it did with some others. Maybe I'm just lucky and not quite — however marginally — as susceptible to addiction. Like Gregg and most others I know that are survivors of the times, I simply don't have the desire to go there any more. It's sad that some people suffer such emotional pain that they're willing to do just about anything to get anywhere but where they are in the moment. How horrific. I am so glad that in later life Gregg has found happiness and conquered his demons. There are so many people — a few famous, most not — who are not that fortunate and don't survive. I can only feel that I luckily dodged a bullet there. I like to believe a loving mother, father, and wife had a lot to do with my survival as well. For me, the music came first. It didn't always come first for some of the bands I played with in those days, however, and there were times when drugs definitely affected not only our playing and writing but also the relationships between all of us. I remember times when I was just about the only one sitting around practicing, wanting to play, while the rest of the gang was partying it up.

Don't get me wrong — there were some great, high times. Drugs almost ruled rock 'n' roll for a long time. There was a lot of erratic behavior going on in just about every band, much of it fueled by dope and drink. That's a simple fact, and it was rampant with many of us. Part of it was the cliché of success. Our *Brothers and Sisters* album came at a time the whole music business was in a slump, Phil Walden has always maintained, and got people into the stores to buy lots of everyone's product when it went to number one within days of its release.

"That album and tour afterward was probably the peak of their success," Phil says. "And Chuck was a very visible and audible part of that whole thing. But success, as it so often does, tends to bring with it a whole lot of problems. And to be honest with you the narcotics, the drugs, it was just a nightmare."

Dickey was known for trashing hotel rooms, and while it didn't happen at every place, it would happen once in a while. He might have a fight with his wife, Sandy, or be upset with someone for one reason or another and just go off on his hotel room, smashing everything. One such occasion was in New York at the Essex House hotel. Rose Lane and I were staying in a suite next door to Dickey and Sandy. They had a big fight over Waylon Jennings, who was in town playing and with whom Dickey believed Sandy was having an affair. He tore up the room — smashing lamps, the TV, and his guitar, a beautiful Les Paul that he bashed into tables and the wall. Finally, I got up to see what was going on. I went next door to find Dickey huffing and puffing and ranting and raging. Sandy was fine, but the room was trashed. Dickey wandered out into the hallway stomping around, still hyped up. He was like a little bull, breathing heavy and snorting. The elevator doors opened and a hotel clerk sent up to investigate the ruckus stood there with a collapsed umbrella as a weapon. He took one look at Dickey, who glared back, and didn't even step out of the elevator. Like a hilarious scene in a movie, he quickly tapped the close door button and disappeared, which was probably the single wisest decision that kid ever made.

Clean and sober Dickey is a sweet man, actually kind of quiet and gentle. But full of booze and blow he can be a storm best avoided. Skinny and wiry, he's got a fierce temper and isn't afraid of a fight — usually winning, much to the surprise of those who don't know him, particularly his unlucky opponents.

In the big picture of the times — The Who's Keith Moon, Led Zeppelin, and others — Dickey's antics hardly stand out, and he shouldn't be too harshly judged. I have enormous respect for Dickey, as a musician and as a man. He's written some wonderful songs and played some incredible guitar through the years. He's also been a solid friend to me, and I love him.

Credit © Chuck Leavell Archive

Rose Lane was on the road with me as often as she could be. After we'd been married for about a year and a half we decided we wanted children. The timing was perfect when Amy Leavell made her debut, as the ABB was off the road at the time and I was home with Rose Lane, living in a small house we'd bought in Macon. She had a fairly normal pregnancy with the usual discomforts and such, but was really healthy and all had gone well. When she went into labor early one morning, we

Starting our family … Rose Lane pregnant with Amy.

were prepared. We went to the hospital and checked her in, all excited. The doctor seemed to think all was well, and the whole procedure was going fine. But time went on, and no full dilation. Finally, they decided to induce the labor, and they gave her a shot to do so. More time, no baby. She wound up in labor for almost twenty-four hours, and we (her mother and I, and even our family doctor) were getting worried. They came out and said they needed to do a Caesarean. Her mother and I agreed, and they went in to get the baby. Everything went perfectly, and the doctor and nurses told Rose Lane's mother and me that I was the father of a healthy little baby girl. When we saw Amy, we cried such tears of joy! A couple of hours later Rose Lane was recovering nicely from her surgery, and we were allowed to go in and see her, shortly before a nurse brought Amy for mother and daughter to meet for the first time. More tears! To say this changed our lives is an understatement that only other parents can appreciate. A couple of rock 'n' roll twenty-something-year-olds now had a

Credit: © Chuck Leavell Archive

More keys, please! Me with my darling young daughter, Amy.

family. We embraced the joy of getting used to having a baby in the house but faced a harsh reality — I was the piano player for a rock band that was soon going to go back out on tour.

The band was in a precarious position and had been for more than a year. Gregg had quite truthfully fallen deeply in love with the singer and actress Cher, who reciprocally was deeply in love with Gregg. But their relationship, an on-and-off and on-again marriage, was so tempestuous that it became fodder for comics, talk show hosts, and newspaper cartoonists. Gregg appeared on a *People* magazine cover, which openly declared his heroin addiction. I remember when all this was going down, and people were so intrigued by Gregg and Cher. I also remember when I first met her. I was ready to not like her. I'm really not sure why, maybe because I saw her as a threat to the band somehow — that she might cause Gregg to lose focus in the band. But from the moment I met her, I liked Cher a lot. You can't not like her. She is direct, looks you in the eye and speaks clearly. She is funny and witty. I could tell that she was the type of person that wouldn't take any mess from anyone. I could also tell that she was not afraid to confront tough situations. She was very much into the band, and of course into Gregg. She cared about him deeply, and I believe she wanted to "tame" him. I never became what I would call close to Cher, but she certainly gained my respect, and after I got to know her, I have always had a strong appreciation for

her. I think she tried hard not
to be a burden on the band,
and when she would be there
at the gigs she'd try to be dis-
creet. But she was Cher, and
easily spotted. We'd see folks
in the audience pointing at her
when they would see her in
the wings, and together she
and Gregg got lots of stares and

Gregg with Cher on one of her first trips to Macon.

attention when they were moving about town, appearing in
restaurants, or wherever they went socially.

Dickey, too, was going through a rough personal time and
divorce from Blue Sky. He was also convinced that the Allman
Brothers Band was owed millions of dollars in royalties from
Capricorn, and the fact was we didn't have much money despite
huge record sales and a per-performance take of more than $100,000
a night, which was huge in 1975. Of course, we were blowing money
on private planes, limos, and posh hotel suites that we sometimes
never even made it into during binges. We'd never order one bottle
of expensive wine or champagne when five or six would do, even if
they went unopened. There were people hanging out who ended up
being on the payroll for no credible reason, and of course, there was
a lot of money spent on "recreational" substances. Dickey was the
first to launch inquiries into our financial situation. And the minute
you bring money into question, heat and a lot of hostility soon
follow.

The news just got worse. Jaimoe was in a bad car crash that seriously injured his back and from which he would suffer chronic pain
that haunts him to this day. Gregg was living, most of the time, in
California. The spontaneity of our music was waning, and that's
what had driven the band to begin with. The drugs and drink began
to assert themselves in earnest as our deepest enemies, and the band
members were scattered all over the place. People wouldn't show up
for scheduled recording sessions, or if they did, they were in no con-

dition to record. Sometimes, there would be just me, Lamar, Butch and Jaimoe sitting in the studio with Gregg and Dickey nowhere to be found. We weren't there to jam and have fun; we were there to record the band's next album, and the group's songwriters were not. Lamar, Jaimoe, and I wanted to move into a jazzier direction, while Dickey (when he was there) was moving a little more toward a country sound. Gregg and Butch were more for the status quo. But for months on end very little was accomplished. At one point, the local Macon newspaper reported that the band was in jeopardy after recording had ground to a halt and that Gregg refused to return to Macon to record his vocals. Eventually, producer Johnny Sandlin had to fly to Los Angeles with the master tapes to get Gregg's parts down. The whole thing had taken a year to do, which was ridiculous as far as I was concerned, though at least the timing of the difficulties was fortuitous for Rose Lane and me, as it gave us an extended period at home.

The album, *Win, Lose or Draw,* finally came out to much attention from critics and fans, much of it negative. The LP has its moments from all the members. I think I did some nice piano work on it, and I think it has a couple of Dickey's finest pieces of writing, such as *High Falls*, even if they weren't well represented by the combined performances. And some of Gregg's work — particularly on *Can't Lose What You Never Had* — is a highlight. But it was not a cohesive effort as our past LPs had been. The reviews were the worst of our career, and the album took a nosedive down the charts after starting out at number five. Trying to save face, Capricorn rushed out the release of *The Road Goes on Forever,* a two-LP compilation of already released tracks from the previous five albums. It barely cracked the Top 50.

There was no choice but try to salvage our reputation by doing what we always did best — hit the road and play intense two-, three-, and four-hour shows.

Rose Lane and I talked about it, and we decided that we would just take Amy with us. The band didn't mind. We had a private jet, so the travel was easy. So we would just load up the stroller, diaper

Just your average rock 'n' roll farm family. Rose Lane, me, and toddler Amy.

bag, backpack baby carrier, and other baby paraphernalia and hit the road. We loved it, and everyone else in the band seemed to enjoy having a baby around. Amy was a rock 'n' roll baby right from the start! I deeply felt the responsibility of being a father. It changed my attitude toward life considerably. For one thing, I decided that I wanted to be around for a long time, to see her and any other children we might have grow up, so I started paying more attention to my health and staying in shape. I started working out and jogging.

From that time to the present, staying in good physical condition has been a priority for me.

Amy was only away from me when I was on stage, but she was close at hand in Rose Lane's arms (with proper ear protection, of course!) We had such a blast and on days off we'd put Amy in a stroller or in a backpack and see whatever local sites were to be found — one of our favorites was the famous San Diego Zoo. I'm sure Amy doesn't remember much, if anything, because she was so young, but it was a wonderful time.

Sadly, it was also short-lived. There were moments on stage on that tour that suggested the old magic, but it was slipping away. We were all trying, but the spark dwindled rapidly. By the time we came off the road and returned to Macon, we faced our biggest challenge since the death of Berry. As it turned out, our final challenge.

We arrived back in Macon for Christmas, 1975, to discover that there had been a long ongoing federal drug investigation, which implicated a local pharmacy, band roadie Scooter Herring, and Gregg. The local Dixie Mafia was also involved. A truckload of charges and hundreds of years in jail sentences loomed — nothing, as I say, but a whole lotta ugly. Scooter feared for his life because of the mob and after a lot of legal wrangling and backroom discussions, decided to take the rap. Gregg was forced to testify to stay out of jail and was at one point put in protective custody on a nearby air force base out of fear the Dixie Mafia might whack him to keep him quiet.

You can imagine — if you weren't there to witness it — the headlines. In terms of the band dynamic it was a disaster, as some of the guys instantly hated Gregg for testifying — selling Scooter down the river, as they saw it. Especially when Scooter got a seventy-five-year sentence. (It was later, in a long legal debacle, reduced on appeal to a thirty-month term, which Scooter ended up serving several years later.)

In January Scooter's trial started and the Brothers briefly went back on the road for some lackluster gigs that sometimes bordered on miserable, at least from my point of view. Once in a while the magic would come through, but it was getting hard to find it and pull it out. A month later, we were told by Capricorn that we were broke. Well, not only broke — we owed the company a quarter of a million bucks.

Scooter's trial, which included Gregg's testimony, went on through June. At Capricorn, a cascade of lawsuits began spilling forth like an overturned jar of marbles, tripping up everyone.

By July, Gregg was persona non grata. I remember him calling around to each band member. I might have been the only one who would talk to him. He got me on the phone, and I told him the simple truth: Butch declared he'd never be on the same stage as him again. Jaimoe wrote a letter to the editor of the Macon paper saying that the band was finished, and that while he still loved Gregg and hoped he'd find peace with his demons, he could never play with him again. Dickey was next to go public, telling an interviewer that he'd never work with Gregg again.

I had mixed emotions. I didn't want to see the Brothers break up, and while I didn't know the truth concerning Gregg, Scooter, and the charges, I knew that the band was in deep trouble. Most everyone thought Gregg had sold out Scooter. But the truth is — as Gregg so correctly pointed out — none of us went to the trial. We didn't really know until years later what had gone down and what position Gregg had really been forced into by the feds, and I think generally the band members regret passing judgment on Gregg and came to believe that while certainly not an innocent party to the proceedings, he was given a raw deal by everybody and placed in the terrifying position of having his destiny at the mercy of others. He was really hurt by our rejection and had a right to be because we really didn't know the details. About a year later, the complexity of the case was revealed and even Dickey read the trial transcript and publicly declared that Gregg had been unfairly treated by everyone — the justice system and, more importantly, at least on a human level, the band. "It's about time he was let off the fucking hook," Dickey said. One by one, over time, we all fell into agreement and expressed our apologies to Gregg.

I may not remember all the dates or all the specific gigs, but there were so many moments of pure magic with the ABB, and it was that magic that made all the off-stage bull just disappear for me. I almost get chills thinking about it — Dickey sailing over the mountain, Butch and Jaimoe charging like a herd of wild horses, Lamar right there, pumping away with them, me and Dickey having dialogue, and Gregg's singing soaring high above everything. God, those times were great.

It didn't last that long, but for a while we truly, as Gregg once said, made "some music that would blow your hat into the creek."

Tragically, however, that drug trial changed everything and everyone.

The Allman Brothers Band was no more.

A jazz musician is a juggler
who uses harmonies instead of oranges.

Benny Green

Heading Out to Sea

The Allman Brothers flamed out in the drug scandal in Macon, but looking back I think Jaimoe, Lamar, and I had an unconscious feeling a fracture was coming, in part from the tumultuous year it took to record our last ABB album.

This is why I wasn't out of a job the minute the band shattered — the three of us had been jamming and working on material on the side long before the split with Gregg. We even, half-jokingly, called our little outfit "We Three" and made a few public appearances billed as such, and recorded some demos while cooling our heels in the Capricorn Studios waiting on Gregg and Dickey. (Recently, ABB tour "magician" and photographer/archivist Kirk West found the masters of our demos, and they're not bad. One tune called *Left Turn* has been released as a give-away in the *Hittin' The Note* magazine. And who knows, maybe more will see the light of day in years to come.)

In fact, as early as 1974, we'd played part of an ABB gig in Hartford, Connecticut, on our own when both Gregg and Dickey were more than an hour late for the show and the crowd started getting ugly. John "Gyro" Gilley, one of the stage technicians, came back to the dressing rooms and asked, "Listen man, is there anything you guys can do? They're starting to throw stuff on the stage — it's getting real bad."

So the three of us agreed to go on and play some tunes. John went out and introduced us, saying, "We've got our little band within the band, and they are going play for you right now."

We went out, and the crowd loved it. That night in Hartford — two years before the actual split of the ABB — was basically the birth of Sea Level, a pun based on my name C. Leavell, that Twiggs had come up with and painted on the side of one of my road cases. The case looked like a big safe, and he wrote on it "Sea Level Safe Co." But the band was a gradual thing that started long before the

Credit: Chuck Leavell Archive

Sea Level: Lamar Williams, me, Jaimoe, and Jimmy Nalls, with whom I'd played backing up Dr. John and Alex Taylor long before I'd landed the gig with the Allman Brothers Band.

ABB actually broke up. That's what made it so good. It was for pleasure and for the sake of the music rather than to make money. From then on, we'd jam whenever we got the chance.

At one of our impromptu sessions in Washington, D.C., my old pal Jimmy Nalls, from Alex Taylor's band and with whom I'd also toured with Dr. John, joined us on stage. Jimmy was a great addition, and we must have jammed for three hours. It was amazing, and we looked at each other knowing that there was some magic at work. Immediately, I told Jimmy that we needed to stay in touch — even though I wasn't about to leave the ABB.

Gregg and Dickey didn't care. I don't think they gave it much thought. They were so hung up on their own egos and were engaged in an ongoing battle for leadership of the band. Duane had been the undisputed leader of the Allman Brothers, but after his death there was never really a resolution as to who was the leader. (It was a constant struggle throughout the history of the band, which continued without me through a series of reunitings and further breakups and reunitings. The band's been on a roll for more

Jaimoe and I ham it up in front of the billboard on LA's Sunset Strip announcing the release of Sea Level's debut album.

than a decade now but fired Dickey in 2000, effectively putting an end to the struggle between him, Gregg, and the rest of the band.)

But for those years in the 1970s, Jaimoe, Lamar, and I just couldn't get our head around all the crap. We just wanted to play — and when that version of the ABB played, it was great. That's what pissed us off. When we were on and concentrating on the music, there was nothing like it. We were truly brothers.

I must give credit to Jaimoe for spurring the development of Sea Level. We'd be at a hotel somewhere, with a day off, and he'd call me. "Hey Junebug," (his nickname for me) he'd say, "What's you doin'?"

"Nothing really," I'd say, "Just watching TV."

"C'mon, man, let's go play. There's an empty ballroom downstairs. I'll have the roadies set up."

He'd do the same thing to Lamar. He'd pretty much call our hand on it, and we'd go play. We'd do it backstage; we'd go to the gig early just so the three of us could play. We started doing it all the time, and we'd play almost anywhere. I remember one time we were in Boulder, Colorado, and Jaimoe called me up and said, "Hey Junebug. You know that big empty field next to the hotel? I'm going to have Red Dog string our extension cords together and run them out to the middle of the field so we can play out there."

I thought he was kidding, but he was dead serious. Red Dog ran the extension cords, Jaimoe set up his kit, and Lamar and I dragged our rigs out there, and we played — right there in the middle of that field. People were walking by, wondering who the hell we were, but that's how it was for us. We'd play anywhere Jaimoe would put us.

"We just wanted to play," Jaimoe recalls. "We would always play. There was a setup at my place, so we'd play there. We'd play at schools, anywhere we could play. It gave us a chance to play other people's music, which we didn't do with the Brothers."

As Jaimoe recalls, the Brothers never did sound checks. The crew — most of whom were musicians themselves — would do the sound checks for us. They even went so far as to give themselves a name as a band — the Almost Brothers — and, Jaimoe recalls, did a few gigs around Macon, including Grant's Lounge.

"Red Dog played drums," Jaimoe recalled recently. "And Twiggs played guitar. They did a few gigs around town."

With the end of the ABB, I put in a call to Jimmy Nalls and Sea Level was born. I loved that band. That period is a very special memory to me. I'm very proud of what we did. We were a slamming group. Sadly, and despite our best efforts, things didn't last as long as I would have liked, to the degree of success I was hoping for.

Phil Walden and Capricorn were fully behind us and we recorded our self-titled debut album in 1977. Joining us in the studio were Rudolph Carter, Charles Fairley, Earl Ford, Leo LaBranche, and

The second generation of Sea Level, with the addition of Davis Causey, Jimmy Nalls, Joe English, me, Randall and Lamar.

Donald McClure on horns. For a producer, we thought of a lot of guys. But one stood out, Stewart Levine. Stewart had produced a lot of records for the Jazz Crusaders, who later dropped the Jazz from their name to become The Crusaders. We loved all of those records and loved the sound. We were able to get Stewart onboard, which was a great asset. We became great friends and still stay in contact. I even got to work with him again a few years ago on a fantastic show at Wembley Stadium in London, but more on that later.

We recruited former ABB tour manager Willie Perkins to be our manager. We knew and trusted Willie. He was our friend, and we liked his slow, even approach to things. He agreed to come on board and helped us structure the deal with Capricorn and to map out a strategy for where we wanted to go. He had some good contacts from our Allman Brothers days and was ready to move from tour manager to band manager.

For the first time in years, it was my time to step up with some serious vocals, which was a great challenge. The experience made me think of Paul Hornsby pushing me into singing all those years

Sea Level live.

earlier when we first got together, and I was again sure grateful for his influence. However, I didn't then and still don't think of myself much as a singer, taking on the role with some reluctance. Still, somebody had to do it, so it would be me. Much of the album is instrumental, and I wrote five of its eight tracks from material bouncing around my head for a while, a couple which came out of We Three jams. Of course, there's no way that we wouldn't in some way draw comparison to the ABB. While I thought this was not totally fair — after all, we were a four-piece band and had a totally different direction — I knew that we'd still have to deal with that. I tried hard to not worry about it, though. Just move on and do our thing. If the critics want to focus on that, there was no way we could stop them. We just wanted to play.

We went into the contract with Capricorn, actually, without much of a game plan. I've never been a prolific writer, so I was a little apprehensive at how quickly we were headed into the studio. But I came up with some of the band's now-classic tunes in a rather short time. *Rain in Spain* was something I came up with during the We Three jams. I finally sat down with the little riff I had and put my mind to finishing it. After a few days of fooling with it, it sort of finished itself. The title came after it was written — it just sounded sort of Spanish to me — and seemed to fit the mood of the piece. The second track on the first album, which has become a fan favorite, is something we threw in because we were certain it would spice the LP with a little fun. *Shake a Leg* was written by a New Orleans guy named Eddie Zip, and it was Capricorn Records' Dick Wooley who deserves the credit for bringing it to us. It's a delightful little track.

Tidal Wave is a song I came up with while fooling around on a Fender Rhodes. I'd been listening to a good bit of fusion music at the time: Chick Corea and the like. I thought we needed a sort of intense piece that moved along with some energy yet had some decisive changes to it. The title simply came from me thinking of Sea Level and the theme of water.

A new deal: Sea Level becomes an official Capricorn recording artist. From left, Alex Hodges, William Perkins, Jimmy Nalls, Phil Walden, Frenk Fenter, and (front) me, Lamar and Jaimoe.

One tune that we did that came directly from my ABB experience was the track *Country Fool*. Acknowledging the obvious Leon Russell influence, I was struck, at the time, with the reality of being on the road so much with the Allmans. I was living at the now-legendary Idlewild South but had been touring so much I was thinking of just getting back to the country. A silly little tune, in retrospect, but it was fun to play.

Perhaps the most serious of the songs on the Sea Level debut was *Nothing Matters But the Fever*, which also became one of the band's signature pieces. And its genesis is simple: Heroin. I had seen several of my friends dabble and had been witness to the destructive results. Some, like Gregg Allman, lived; some died. Simple as that. But the thing that they all had in common was addiction. I've seen guys when they needed a fix, and to them, nothing else mattered except that next hit.

The tune *Grand Larceny* was from a great keyboard player named Neil Larson, who had been hanging around Macon for some time. He and a guitar player named Buzzy Feiten would jam with us sometimes at Grant's Lounge or in the studio. Buzzy played guitar on some of the *Laid Back* record. Neil was a monster player and when he played me *Grand Larceny*, immediately I loved the tune and we began working on it in the studio, quickly knowing it belonged on the LP.

One of the stranger tracks on our debut was *Scarborough Fair*, which was entirely my idea. I'd first heard the Simon and Garfunkel tune in my sister's room when it came out and I'd always liked it. We Three started playing it for fun, and by the time we became Sea Level, I wound up drastically rearranging it and adding a lot of changes. We asked Paul Simon for a split songwriting credit, as the ABB had done with Donovan on *Mountain Jam* (if you didn't know, *Mountain Jam* was originally based on a Donovan folk tune), but he declined. We thought it was a bit unfair since there were so many parts of it that were unrelated to the song, but we liked it so much we decided to go with it anyway, giving sole credit to Simon

The last track on our debut was another We Three jam tune that we got into just about every time we got together back in the ABB days. It was a fun riff I'd come up with, though we got a little more serious about it when we got into the studio and made it a much more sophisticated tune than it had started out as and evolved into *Just a Good Feeling.*

We toured behind the record, playing across the country in the major clubs and theaters as a headliner and sometimes opening up

Credit: © 1974 Sidney Smith

for other groups like Jefferson Starship, Styx, The Outlaws, The Marshall Tucker band, and others. We were beginning to pull things together. One unique gig during that year was the honor of playing Jimmy Carter's presidential inauguration, with the interesting pairing for the night being the Buddy Rich Big Band.

Jaimoe recalls one funny story of us being up in Montreal on tour. He, Lamar and I were in a limo traveling to or from the hotel when Jaimoe asked the driver to

Jaimoe

stop at a local pharmacy to pick up some special skin lotion that he couldn't get in the United States.

"The guy behind the counter saw me get out of the limo," Jaimoe recalls. "He saw me come in and looks down at me over his glasses, sort of like Danny DeVito playing the Penguin. And he says, 'We have Robitussin by the case.' (In those days, it was pretty easy to score the cough syrup Robitussin AC — which packed a good punch of codeine and was a popular high.) I didn't know what to think. I thought maybe he was trying to get me busted or something. Anyway, I got my lotion and got ready to leave and got three bottles of the medicine. He said 'Is that all you want?' and I said yeah. I went out to the car, which was parked around the corner, and told Lamar that this cat was trying to sell me a case of syrup. He said 'Did you get it?' and I said I didn't. So Lamar went in and the guy wouldn't sell him anything. I figured it out — the guy had seen me get out of the limo, but after it pulled around the corner he didn't see Lamar get out of it."

We had a lot of fun on the road and played some great music but not too long into the official Sea Level band, Jaimoe's back really started giving him trouble. Part of it was the car crash he'd been in, part of it was an old football injury, and, he says, most of it was brought on by stress. The band was a blast and we were making great music, but not much money.

After we'd made some personnel changes, Jaimoe wasn't entirely happy with the musical direction in which the band was heading.

At the end of the touring, Jaimoe announced that he wanted to resign. He had already thought of a replacement, a drummer he knew from his R&B days named George Weaver. But he agreed to play on the record and help to break in George. He had hung in

Warming up for a college gig.

there like a trouper, touring with us under excruciating pain and trying every conceivable thing to help himself. He was on painkillers — always careful to never over-medicate himself so that he'd be sharp on stage — and tried everything under the sun to alleviate the pain. At one point I remember him even having a little pyramid tent in his hotel room. At the time there was a raging trend promising that any device or structure in the shape of a pyramid could do everything from sharpen razor blades to cure physical ailments. Besides, and I don't blame him, we were not making much money. It was a constant struggle.

"Chuck's a very respectful cat," Jaimoe said recently. "Always has been. He was always a good business guy, too. Musically we were doing a few things that others didn't have the opportunity to play. We were fortunate, man."

But staying in Sea Level just wasn't for Jaimoe.

"I don't want you to quit," he told us, "but I just can't go on tour." We accepted this, and with his commitment to do the *Cats on the Coast* record with George chiming in, we carried on.

I also wanted to expand the band, to make it "bigger and better." We began recording our second album, *Cats on the Coast,* and the arrangements were a little more intricate and advanced, and we truly began to grow away from our ABB roots. We brought in the famous Muscle Shoals horns to spike things up on a few tunes, and there were other bigger changes.

Singer/songwriter/multi-instrumentalist Randall Bramblett, whom I had known from the Cowboy and Gregg Allman Band days, came in to share front-man duties. I had also played on Randall's first two albums, *Light of the Night* and *That Other Mile*. With him came his long-time guitarist and co-writer Davis Causey. Davis and Jimmy worked well together, complimenting each other's guitar styles. Bramblett was, and still is, regarded among fellow musicians and critics-

Credit: © Chuck Leavell Archive

A little family fun with Rose Lane and Amy.

in-the-know as one of the great undiscovered talents in Southern music, and his and Causey's influence on the group was immediately apparent on the magnificent *That's Your Secret*, a smoking R&B tune with an unforgettable chorus and an outstanding dual-guitar solo. We honed our mix of rock, blues, and jazz through constant touring, particularly on the east coast, and ended up with a nicely charted hit single.

We played all over the country in all kinds of situations, but one of the most memorable of the year was when we enjoyed a terrific response playing the Montreux Jazz Festival in Switzerland, with Steve Morse's Dixie Dregs opening. I give large credit to Capricorn executive Frank Fenter for landing us that Montreux gig. He was a big supporter of Sea Level and I was heartbroken when he died of a heart attack a few years later.

Even though we missed our "guru" Jaimoe, we were rockin' right along and the Sea Level tours were fun and productive — constant tours, in fact, from the moment our first LP hit the stores and continuing to support our second effort.

I can't look back and believe I made the wrong decision, but the truth is that once Jaimoe left us things just never really gelled right with Sea Level. Don't get me wrong: we loved working with George. There was a wonderful feel to his playing, a wonderful R&B flavor with his own style and technique. The trouble was that the Sea Level material required heavy arrangements. There were just too many breaks and changes for such a straight-ahead player and he'd often have trouble with the arrangements. It hurt all of our feelings, but we all agreed that we should make a change. His departure was hastened by us hearing that there was some interest from Wings drummer Joe English. This surprised the hell out of us, frankly, since we didn't understand why he'd want to give up a great gig with McCartney to play with Sea Level. But the way he put it to me when I asked him was that he'd spent about two years with Wings, and he was tired "of playing silly love songs" and wanted a different kind of musical challenge. That I could understand — and certainly meaning no disrespect to McCartney, one of my heroes — but an

The beginning of the end ... the album *Long Walk on A Short Pier.*

accomplished drummer like Joe needed some challenges, and we were all grateful he came on board.

In the midst of our recording the next LP came a big surprise: The offer of putting the Allman Brothers Band back together. When the Brothers broke up in the spring of 1976, Phil Walden tried to find some financial relief in the mess a few months later by releasing a double live LP called *Wipe the Windows, Check the Oil, Dollar Gas,* culling songs from various shows we'd done from the time I'd joined the band until it broke up. Some were from the astounding Watkins Glen performance, others from the Warehouse in New Orleans, and still others from a great show we did at the Oakland Coliseum. The critics jumped on it and compared it unfavorably to the *Fillmore East* live LP. Time has been kind to it and it's now generally viewed as an accurate testament to the band's live shows at the height of its career, and I think *Ain't Wastin' Time, In Memory of Elizabeth Reed,* and especially *Come and Go Blues* are moments of true brilliance. It's not, as the critics so fondly put it, *Live at the Fillmore East.* But show me another live recording that is!

The first time any semblance of the Allman Brothers Band appeared on stage together after the nasty split was two years later. Dickey Betts had been recording and touring with his band Great Southern and was appearing in New York's Central Park. Phil Walden made the overture and Dickey agreed. Part way through the set the crowd went wild when Butch and Jaimoe walked out on stage followed by Gregg, who was very emotional about the uproarious reaction. Almost instantly, we were all in meetings to discuss a full-fledged reunion. Lamar and I had released two Sea Level LPs by this time and were in

Lamar Williams

the middle of recording our third and having a great time with Randall and Davis Causey and Joe, and we thought we had a serious chance of really breaking the mold of what people considered "Southern" rock. Lamar and I said we'd consider getting back with the ABB if its schedule could be worked around Sea Level's.

A further stumbling block was the contention that we thought the Brothers still owed us royalties from before the breakup. Needless to say there was no way Sea Level was going to take precedence over an ABB reunion, so Lamar and I were out. We hid this from the public when, a few days later, we all appeared on stage together at the annual Capricorn picnic in Macon, the first time we'd all played together since the breakup. It was a surprise for the crowd and went on to fuel huge hopes among fans but was uncomfortable for us — especially when Phil Walden announced the band was reuniting and headed for the studio — since privately we all knew Lamar and I wouldn't be participating.

But Gregg, Butch, and Dickey had made peace, as had Jaimoe. Besides, as Jaimoe says these days, "I owned too large a piece of that (ABB) history to give it up." They added guitarist Dan Toler and Rook Goldflies from Dickey's Great Southern band on bass, and the Brothers were reborn. Their first LP, *Enlightened Rogues*, went platinum. Despite this, Dickey began legal action against Phil Walden and Capricorn, which was on the verge of bankruptcy.

It can't have helped my chances of rejoining the group when, the following year, I filed suit against the band for what was first estimated to be over $50,000 in back royalties; my attorney later upped the suit to about $118,000. The band fired back with a lawsuit of its own, claiming it owned much of my equipment and got a court injunction preventing me from taking any of it out of Macon. Finally, the lawyers settled just as we had selected the jury and had begun the trial, and I was awarded roughly $40,000, much of which was consumed by my legal fees.

Meanwhile, Sea Level rolled on. Our third record, *On the Edge*, was something we were all very happy with. Again, it was a mix of instrumentals and more experimental, progressive stuff mixed in with more conventional vocal work; it did respectable business and was regarded well by the critics and, more importantly, by the fans, and we toured constantly.

As we began working on our fourth album, strains started to show up in the Capricorn office. While the catalog continued to sell well — it had the ABB, Marshall Tucker Band, Cowboy, Wet Willie, and others still selling albums — there were problems with the label. Phil signed a distribution deal with PolyGram, but it failed to turn the company around.

We were producing our disc *Long Walk on a Short Pier* — a rather unfortunately prophetic title, really, and thought it was our best effort to date. The only trouble was that I was convinced that Capricorn was soon going to be in such bad financial shape that there would be no way the label would have the resources to promote the work properly, and I believed it would have been a waste of all our efforts to put out an album that wouldn't be promoted or reach record stores; we asked Phil not to release it and to let us out of our contract so we could shop it to a more financially stable company. The label couldn't afford to even buy an ad in a magazine to promote it, but Phil wouldn't let us out of our contract. We were all downtrodden and so frustrated.

It wasn't a personal decision made with any sense of spite. Phil always had a deep, even blind, belief in Capricorn, and I know he did everything under the sun to keep it from foundering. And I'm sure he's always known it wasn't personal when Sea Level launched a lawsuit against Capricorn to get an injunction preventing the release of the album, since we didn't believe it could fulfill the terms of our contract. Our plan was to get the injunction, wait for Capricorn to go under, and then shop the album to other labels. The Marshall Tucker Band did exactly the same thing, as they were in the same predicament with their new album.

Well, we ended up winning the injunction, but Capricorn had snuck a few thousand copies out in Canada in an attempt to get the ball rolling and generate some sales; it effectively destroyed our ability to shop it to another label. Capricorn soon collapsed, despite Phil's best financial and business juggling. Years later Phil resurrected the company and did manage an American release of the CD in 1998, but it was widely ignored. A best-of CD has fared much better and is selling respectably as of this writing.

With the demise of Capricorn, our manager Willie Perkins and our attorney Joel Katz scored Sea Level a deal with Clive Davis and his Arista Records. We rallied and recorded an album called *Ball Room*, but Clive didn't like it, and it failed to garner much attention. Soon, some serious personality problems began developing within the band. Randall, who was handling horns, some keyboards, and vocals, and guitarist Davis both wanted Lamar out. This was a hard one for me and Jimmy, since we had such loyalty to Lamar. But Randall and Davis were right — Lamar was not pulling his weight. He was late for rehearsals and just didn't seem to be into the band, and when we played live he certainly didn't contribute what he always had in the past. It caused a lot of heartbreak, but we did it.

We fired Lamar. I understand his hurt and feelings of betrayal and wasn't surprised when he filed suit to prevent his dismissal. The whole thing was ugly for a while and there was lasting pain on all sides. Since we had an agreement in our original contract about individuals leaving the band, Lamar's lawsuit was baseless and he eventually dropped it. This was an incredibly rough situation, and for a long time we were at odds with each other over it. It remained an unresolved issue between us for years.

Amy and Rose Lane outside her store in Macon.

After Lamar left the band, Randall and Davis did a lot of scouting and found a local kid named Paul Broudour in a club in Atlanta. He was quite amazing. He was left handed but played right-handed bass. We hired him, did some dates and took six months to sit back and prepare for a second album with Arista. Clive Davis wanted us to turn into a sort of pop commercial band, which just wasn't us. This was a moment where I truly missed working with Phil Walden — Phil has always been a businessman who loved music but believed that the suits have no place in the studio and that artists should be left to do what they want to do. An executive's opinion on the music is nothing more than "meddling," he has always said. What magic that is to the ears of any musician!

Clive, however, was very kind and told me he'd let Sea Level out of our contract — which called for another LP — but I persisted. It was not a good decision. I should have accepted and moved on, but I had a deep belief in that band and what we had hopes of accomplishing with it musically. Plus I was weary after the Capricorn situation and didn't want to go shopping for another label at the time.

Another big problem that arose around this time was that some of the band wanted to change management. This, like the Lamar situation, was yet another toughie for Jimmy and me. We had loyalty to Willie and loved him. But we had to admit that we were having a tough time getting anywhere. It wasn't Willie's fault, though. He had helped us to get beyond the Capricorn problem and into a new record deal. But still, we were spinning wheels and so we reluctantly agreed to try something — anything — to see if we could get out of the mud. We checked around and found a guy named Bob Schwaid, had managed the band Orleans among others and would go on to even greater success. He lived in New

York and knew Clive Davis pretty well. We thought that might help our situation with Arista. He was OK and tried fairly hard to make it work, but in my opinion we would have probably been better off to hang with Willie Perkins. In any case, we made the change and moved on.

We planned on going up to Nashville to begin recording with a producer/guitar player named Steve Gibson that Clive had suggested. We checked out Steve and felt comfortable

Credit: Chuck Leavell Archive

Lamar and me on stage.

with him and began to make plans. Soon Clive freed up the budget for us to get started. I called all the guys to let them know the good news. When I called Paul, I got quite a surprise.

"Paul, fantastic news, man. We finally got Arista off the money, and we're ready to go."

"Well, that's great," he said. "But I've got one problem."

"What's that?" I asked.

"I've got to have some treatments."

"What kind of treatments?"

"Well, I've got a little case of cancer."

"*What*?" I asked. "Jeez, I'm sorry, man. How are you feeling How's it lookin'?"

"Well, it's come on me and I have to do these treatments. I don't know where this is going."

We began work on the album almost immediately, just as Paul began chemotherapy and radiation treatments, which turned out to be sensless tortures. His health declined at a shocking rate, and he just didn't have the energy, though we honored his wish to include him in the sessions. The whole vibe was so negative, however, that even Randall and I began having some personality conflicts. I have always had and continue to have the highest regard for him as a musician and consider him one of my best friends. We all knew it was over the first day we had to literally pick Paul up from his chair in the studio and carry him into the control room to listen to play-backs. We shut down the production with the hope that Paul might bounce back, but he died within a matter of weeks. What a horrible, unfair tragedy it was. The kid was so nice and so talented. It was a huge blow to us as friends, even though we hadn't known him that long. And it sucked up the last energy that Sea Level had. Paul managed to record only two songs on our last project. One of the best bass players I've ever played with and one of the best human beings I've ever known. It's cases like these that just make you wonder why — why him? But for whatever reasons, it was meant to be. It was a reality that none of us could run from. He died with grace and dignity. He told me when he was in the hospital that he didn't want to die, but that he had accepted it was inevitable. He told me that he was grateful to have lived his life and to have played with us. It was so sad, but I will always remember and admire the way he left us.

The album died with Paul. We carried on with Steve Gibson, who did an admirable job of trying to keep things running, but it was futile. Clive listened to the early tapes, hated the direction we were going, and pulled the plug on our financing. He fired poor Steve, and we were all out of sorts by then. It was nearing the end.

We did make one last feeble attempt at recording, however. Clive had come across this tune he thought was a hit. So with only myself and Davis Causey from the band, we went to Miami and recorded with some studio musicians to do some mediocre pop tune that Clive thought was a hit and wanted us to do. It was called *Make You Feel Love Again*. We did the track with a guy named Pete Solley producing. Now here's some cool trivia for you: Pete was the keyboardist in an English trio led by a great singer/guitarist named Terry Reid, along with drummer Keith Webb, that for a brief period looked like it was going to be the Next Big Thing. The trio was managed by Chesley Millikin, head of Epic Records London at the time and a life-long pal of the Stones, particularly Charlie Watts (and who would go on years later to discover and manage Stevie Ray Vaughan and become a friend of mine as well). Chesley had, in fact, hired Terry's trio to play Mick Jagger's wedding to Bianca at their lavish San Tropez ceremony.

At the same time, Jimmy Page was trying to hold together yet another version of the Yardbirds and asked Terry to be his new singer and rhythm guitarist. Terry declined because he'd already been hired to open across America for Cream (the only guy to ever open for Cream, as far as I know), and Terry had also landed the gig of opening for the Stones on the famous 1969–1970 tour of America. The only gig he didn't play on that tour was Altamont, which Terry says he just had a bad feeling about. Terry also turned down the lead-singer gig for Deep Purple because it looked like his trio with Pete Solley was going to be a hit.

When Terry turned down Jimmy Page, he did suggest a singer and drummer who might be suitable — a couple of guys who had been in a band that had opened for Terry, Keith, and Pete Solley the weekend before. Those two guys were John Bonham and Robert Plant! Terry still plays around the Los Angeles area and occasional overseas gigs. In fact, Keith Richards has joined Terry on stage twice recently at a Hollywood club with Waddy Wachtel and Rick "the Bass Player" Rosas from Neil Young and the Bluenotes and Phil Jones from Tom Petty's solo band on drums. But he will never be

Waddy Wachtel, Keith, Rick Rosas and Terry Reid play a Hollywood club in May, 2004.

able to escape the moniker of being the guy who turned down the gig as front man for Led Zeppelin — even if he is responsible for suggesting the singer and drummer who made Zep happen!

After the Terry Reid Trio broke up, Pete Solley was in Procol Harum for a while before turning to producing and session work for such diverse acts as Motorhead, Peter Frampton, Ted Nugent, Whitesnake, Eric Clapton, Mountain, and the Romantics — for whom he wrote and produced that famous song *Talking in Your Sleep*.

So it was great to have such an experienced and accomplished musician, arranger, and producer behind us, and I think Pete did a good job with what was essentially a hopeless situation. Through no fault of his own or the band's, nothing became of the single. The game was over. Sea Level never recorded again.

If things could be worse, we still owed money to some people, including our former manager Willie Perkins. Many people had been great supporters of the band and none of us wanted to stiff them.

Rose Lane and I were living in a house on a street called Twin Pines Drive at the time. Across the street from us lived our good friends Buck and Patti Williams. I had met Buck many years before with Alex Taylor. He had grown up in North Carolina with the Taylor clan and had eventually moved to Macon to work as a booking agent for the Paragon Agency, the agency that had booked the Allman Brothers as well as Sea Level over the years. We had become the best of friends, and would hang out together, cook meals, go to movies and such together. Our daughter Amy used to play with their son Hunter, and we were constant companions. Rose Lane and I became godparents to Hunter, and a few years later Buck would become my manager. He remains in that capacity for me today. Buck knew what I was going through with Sea Level. He had done his best to help us through this trying time, and I turned to him for help. He put together the best tour he could for us, and I was grateful. It wasn't easy, as by then we didn't have a lot of good options for gigs.

So we went on one last tour to pay off all the debts. We called it the Shopping Center Tour — six weeks in Florida on a shoestring budget. Before heading out we needed a road manager and I asked my pal John McCord, who owned The Cottage, a local Macon club we played and hung out at quite a bit. John had never done this kind of work before but graciously agreed to help us out. What a pal — and what a position we put him in! As John recalls, we towed a trailer with all our gear ... a trailer built to hold about five or six thousand pounds, not the ten thousand-plus pounds of stuff we were hauling.

Our first lightning strike came when somehow the gear came loose and the door on the back of the trailer swung open as we were flying down the interstate to Florida. We began dropping an assortment of monitors and other equipment — but, most importantly, Paul's bass amp, which crashed onto the freeway without our knowing it.

"I remember," John recalled recently, "that there were people driving up along side us and waving and gesturing and pointing back. It took a while but we clued in and pulled over. When we discovered what had happened we went back, but somebody had already picked up the amp and whatever else we'd dropped. That was our first day out. To this day I don't know how it happened."

In the summer of 2004, Rose Lane and I were at a party with John and when I mentioned I'd been working on my memoirs, he told me a story that he'd previously kept a secret: During that horrible "Shopping Center" or "Pay the Bills" tour, there was one evening during which he'd lost all our money. About $15,000 in cash. Lightning strike No. 2!

"Well," John says, "I was walking around with this briefcase full of cash. There was no safe or any place to put it. I was having a few beers and enjoying myself, like everyone else, and wanted to have a few more beers. But I knew I had to find a safe place to store the money. I went out to the trailer and hid it in a guitar case. Then I went back inside and forgot all about it until somebody from the band asked me for a $100 advance. That's when I realized I had no idea where the $15,000 was. I can't tell you what a feeling that was! I searched everywhere in a panic for two or three hours. Then, I guess I sobered up enough and it finally hit me … I went to the trailer and there it was. All these years, I've never admitted that one to Chuck!

"I think we were on the road for about 12 days. I came back and told my wife that if I ever agreed to do that again, to shoot me between the eyes."

Looking back, at least we gave poor John an adventure! The upside was that we paid everyone back, including what we owed Willie. The band ended not owing a dime to anybody. As tough as it was, I was proud that we lived up to our obligations. It was taking the high road — the only one I'm comfortable on. The break-up went largely unnoticed, and Sea Level, despite the brilliant musicianship, never got the acclaim it deserved. We had some great shows playing with lots of talented artists. I remember playing a few theaters with Jan Hammer as the opening act, who would then sit in with us. Jan was one of my heroes, and that was a great experience.

There were many other great times as well. Sea Level was a great band. We had a hard time with the record company and the retail stores because we were so difficult to tag. I could sympathize. We did instrumentals, but we also sometimes sang; we played rock 'n' roll, but we also played R&B, and we had tinges of jazz. I felt for the label and the stores because they couldn't figure out where to put us. Rock? Instrumental? Jazz? But we didn't really care. We just played and had fun. I guess the theaters were the most fun for me to play with that band. It just seemed to work better than clubs or big dates. I somehow think that Sea Level never really reached its potential, and that's a shame. But I don't like looking back over my shoulder, and really all I can say is that I'm grateful for the experience, and I think I'm a better musician for it.

Rose Lane and I ham it up in a photo shoot promoting her Cornucopia store.

Sea Level had many moments of brilliance on stage — a lot of experimentation — and we also had great moments in the studio, where we always embraced our second chances. But the touring was also a step back in some ways, traveling in a bus with a truck that kept breaking down, waking up in towns not knowing where the heck I was. Looking back at my diaries I found I spent considerable energy on worrying about money, being highly critical of my own personal performances, and to distract myself I guess, chronicling in fine detail the plots of the many movies I'd go to see to temporarily assuage my worries.

Here's one page from my diary: "Limbo Recording Artists Sea Level." In another entry, I scrawled: "On Plane: Good Morning, ladies and gentlemen, welcome aboard flight 102, jet service to LaGuardia with continuing service to BumFuck and points beyond." More than a little jaded!

It was with Sea Level that I recall having the most Spinal Tap moment. True, we never ended up as the support act at a puppet show, but there was one gig that I'll never forget. Again, from my diary: "Last night was one of the strangest gigs I've ever played. Way out in the middle of nowhere. I mean *nowhere*. These people just had a barn with one side opened completely up. That was the stage. There were about 1,500 or 2,000 people in the field in front of us. And there was no response from them whatsoever. If we played a song with more than three chords, they were just simply lost. I don't know what they were expecting but it was downright extraterrestrial. Paid good, though."

I can laugh about it now, but I was not in a good frame of mind at the time, clearly. I was getting bitter and fatigued and missing my family desperately. I was missing anniversaries, missing birthdays. I missed a lot of things that dads are supposed to be around for, no matter how small they might be. Like my daughter's first Christmas after learning that no, Virginia, there is no Santa Claus. I wrote in my diary that January that my little baby was growing into a little girl — without her father. I was surrounded by the band and fans yet I'd never been more alone.

But, of course, I wasn't going through this turmoil alone. On the other end was Rose Lane, raising Amy on her own while I was on the road, while also running her burgeoning business, a downtown Macon boutique called Cornucopia. She started it in 1977 from some funds from a timber sale that came from land she and her brother Alton inherited from their father. In the beginning she sold arts and crafts and antique clothing, as well as some current fashions. After a couple of years she gravitated toward newer fashions, dropping most of the arts and crafts, but adding some accessories. Later she had a second little shop called Dreamgirls that sold really cool clothing for young girls. Soon, she brought them together under one roof and eventually moved solely into adult fashions and accessories. She flourished and managed to purchase three buildings in the downtown core, which we've renovated in recent times, in some cases using lumber sawn from our own plantation.

This was great and I know educational and fulfilling for Rose Lane, but we were leading separate lives. After the Sea Level breakup, I began to play Mr. Mom while she went off to work at the store. While I loved being with Amy and spending more time with Rose Lane — and was actually became a pretty good cook in the process — I felt like I was beating my head against the wall.

After nineteen years, Rose Lane finally closed the business to concentrate on our efforts on the plantation, to spend more time at home embracing her own painting. "Besides," she jokes, "As I got older my customers got older and started going through divorces and menopause and constantly complaining about their kids. It was driving me crazy It was like I was their therapist!"

Sea Level fizzled out in 1980, and for the first time in my life, I was totally unemployed without any long-term prospects. I tried putting together a Macon-based trio and while it filled in some space, it wasn't going anywhere. I did have some fun, though. John McCord introduced me to a great local harmonica player named Buddy Green and we started a little jamming with percussionist Matt Greeley and Sea Level guitarist Jimmy Nalls, who came up with the name Fishmarket Five for the outfit. We kicked around and played John's club The Cottage a few times but it was more blowing off a little musical steam than anything serious. One of the good things to come out of this period was my reconciliation with Lamar, whom I'd always felt so bad about having to fire from Sea Level. In early 1981, Lamar came down to The Cottage and sat in with us, and we talked for a long time afterward. At first it was uncomfortable for both of us, but we finally loosened up and started to talk. We reminisced about the good times and talked about our families. We smiled and laughed together. We shared lots of personal feelings and got things out in the open. Finally, we shook hands and hugged. Much to the betterment of both of our minds and souls, we were friends again.

After his dismissal from Sea Level, Lamar had started doing sessions in Los Angeles but got really sick. Surgeons removed two ribs and most of a lung, but were unsure of his long-term prognosis. He'd contracted cancer from extreme exposure to Agent Orange when he was in Vietnam. The story I heard was that Lamar played in a Special Services band for a while, but eventually, was sent to Vietnam. Completely opposed to the war and the thought of killing someone, he went AWOL and spent months wandering the jungles and bases of South Vietnam. He would say that he had been separated from his unit and would stay with various outfits for a few weeks at a time before heading into the jungle again. That's how he got so much exposure to Agent Orange. He was finally given an honorable discharge in 1970, and he returned to his native Mississippi.

We had a long history and I'm grateful we were able to repair our fractured friendship. I'm pleased and proud to say that we were able to look each other in the eye and say that we loved one another. I'm happy we had that chance to visit because his doctors were right in their discouraging diagnosis. His condition steadily worsened and Lamar died on Jan. 21, 1983. He was thirty-four years old.

I miss Lamar and remember him first and foremost as a family man. I remember going over to his house in Macon, and he'd be there with Marian and the kids. He'd have his bass around his neck and a baby in each arm, and he was just so happy. He really loved family life. On a personal level, I truly enjoyed discussing race relations with Lamar. The beautiful thing about music is there is no room in it for racism or prejudice. By playing rock music in a white band, he — and Jaimoe — helped break the color barrier that existed in the Deep South in the early 1970s, and that was important. I thought it was great that a white man from Alabama and a black man from Mississippi could sit down and openly discuss our upbringings. We were never uncomfortable talking about our backgrounds — as a matter of fact, we both rather enjoyed talking about that. I appreciate our relationship and will always admire the goodness that Lamar had in him.

The trio Lamar had seen me with didn't work out, which turned out to be of little concern. Soon after, my life changed forever when Rose Lane's grandmother passed away. No one on the planet could have guessed what I'd do next.

Music is spiritual. The music business is not.

———————————————————

Van Morrison

From Keys to Trees

So what does a keyboard player do after having made rock history with one of the best bands to ever come out of America only to find himself unemployed without a prospect on the horizon and with very little energy or enthusiasm for taking on the music business as a solo artist?

Grow Christmas trees.

OK, that's a bit of a leap. But that's ultimately where I found myself in 1981 after my previous musical efforts had exhausted themselves — and me and my young family. This was no arbitrary decision, however; it was fate slipping a few extra-strength Duracells into my soul. Not that it was an easy time, mind you.

Rose Lane's dear grandmother, Miss Julia, passed away and left her about 1,200 acres of land and a homestead — the "Home Place." We were living in Macon and at first didn't know what to do with the property. Selling it was not an option we even considered — Rose Lane's family has been living in the area since the 1700s. And if you want to talk history and fate — the family's land is just four miles away from where Civil War Union General William Tecumseh Sherman swept through in November and December of 1864 on his so-called March to the Sea. He and his 62,000 troops slashed and burned a wide swath of destruction through Georgia after having destroyed parts of Atlanta with the fall of Confederate forces there and continued on to Savannah. Sherman and his men burned every plantation, homestead, and town in their path. It's truly a miracle that Rosie's family escaped the destruction, but I've come to believe there's a magic in this bit of land, so I guess I shouldn't be all that surprised.

Credit: Chuck Leavell Archive

General Sherman: His March to the Sea destroyed a wide path through Georgia … and missed our plantation by just four miles.

The specific parcel Rose Lane inherited was land purchased by her grandfather, Alton V. White Sr., back in 1932. Mr. White was a forester, and he and his business partner would buy and sell tracts of land and timber. This particular tract caught Mr. White's eye, as it was only a few miles from where he and his wife, Miss Julia, lived. Eventually, he bought it. We think he paid a little more than a dollar an acre for it, probably a tidy sum back then.

For many years Miss Julia would hitch up a horse and wagon at daylight with her then-infant son Alton, Jr. and head to the farm, where she spent long hours overseeing the operations. She would either take little Al with her or leave him in the care of some of the workers while she supervised the activities of the farm throughout the day, heading back home at dark. The family moved to the farm in 1944. They dubbed it Whiteway Farms and raised cotton, corn, soybeans, some cows, and had hay fields for the cows in addition to forestland.

With the Depression and then World War II, life was tough and they worked hard for what they had, but they were making it. It was a rural existence. It's rural now, out in the middle of nowhere, so you know it was really rural then. Dirt roads, no highways, and making a phone call meant a trip to the little community store, which was a couple of miles away. The Whites became pillars of the community, active in the local Baptist church, with many friends and relatives nearby. Cars were still relatively scarce there at the time, and farming methods were very old fashioned. I've heard many tales of the farming back then, of mule wagons laden with hand-picked cotton that were so heavy the mules strained to pull the enormous load, so all the hands would get behind the wagon and help push it up the hills.

For fun and recreation there were horseback rides and foxhunts. Mr. White had about sixty fox dogs in a big pen out back. I can just imagine the scene when they turned those dogs loose at the cross-roads and Miss Julia and Mr. Al, or Chief as many called him (although Miss Julia like to call him "White"), rode through the woods on a beautiful afternoon, the sun filtering through the trees and the horses dancing over fields and ditches and other obstacles as the dogs howled. What a spectacle it must have been!

In 1953, tragedy struck. Chief had a heart attack and died on the way back from a trip to look at some foxhounds. It was a terrible blow to Miss Julia, who was quite a few years younger than Mr. White. She vowed not to remarry and to keep the home place going by herself — a tough decision for a woman on her own in the 1950s. But she did it and did an admirable job of it.

She had her own two children to help, Alton, Jr. and Mary; of course by then they had lives and children of their own. All went fairly well, and they were making ends meet with their crops and

timber. But in 1974, when her son Alton, Rose Lane's father, contracted cancer and passed on, it proved too much for her. Although I
never met Mr. White, I was privileged to know Miss Julia, quite an
incredible woman, sweet, but tough at the same time. She had to be
to survive. She was headstrong and determined with an iron will.
She loved to socialize and it was usually at her house that the big
events were held — Christmas dinner, Thanksgiving. Miss Julia
loved to throw a party, a trait she passed on to my wife. But she also
had a soft side and was, I think, vulnerable at times and certainly
lonely for the companionship of her beloved "White."

In 1981 When Miss Julia passed on and left the land to Rose
Lane, we really didn't know quite what to do. While I was at a loss
musically, Rose Lane had her store, which she'd opened in 1977, and
was very busy with it and events surrounding it, such as fashion
shows. Our daughter Amy was just past a toddler at six, and we had
another child on the way. Of course, the first thing was that we had
lost a loved one, the matriarch of the family, Miss Julia. We went
through that period of grief and recovery when families come
together. But when we began to come out the other side of that, we
started to realize there were many challenges that faced us. Estate
tax laws were much different in the early 1980s than they are now,
and the good ol' IRS was, naturally, banging on our door. After realizing what our situation was, it seemed like we didn't really inherit
the land at all; the federal government did, and now we had the
opportunity to buy it back from them. And in the end, that's exactly
what we did, over a very long period of time. The next thing we
faced was more of a personal decision. We were comfortable in
Macon and didn't really want to change our lives. Miss Julia had left
the old house, the home place, to Rose Lane, but now that she was
gone there was no one to stay there and look after it. Her brother
Alton had his own family and farm, as did Aunt Mary. Alton was
also helping to run the farm where their mother Rosaline lived. So
the family asked us to consider staying in the house for a while to
prevent vandalism and look after things until we decided what we
wanted to do. We agreed and began staying out in the country.

But the cutthroats at the IRS were all over us, and we, heartbreakingly, had to sell a tract of land that Rose Lane and Alton had inherited from their father a few years earlier to raise the money to make the first payment on the inheritance tax. It was a tough decision, to give up land that had been in the White family for more than a hundred years, but there was really no choice. I've always carried a pretty bitter feeling about the injustice of this; it was really no different than the government sweeping in and stealing the heirloom wedding ring off a deceased ancestor's finger. That's what this land was and what it meant to Rose Lane's family. It was an heirloom, and we were never able to buy it back. The IRS wanted its money. Another hurdle was interest rates at the time. They were very high, in the upper teens. This made us shy away from borrowing a large sum to deal with the problem. It also added significantly to the remaining amount we owed after the initial payment. In all, it would take us a long fifteen years to pay the federal government for the land that Rose Lane's family had owned for generations. It took a great deal of the income I made as a musician and money Rose Lane made from Cornucopia to do it, and there were many times when we wanted other things but had to pass on them to make the IRS payments. But we did it. We survived the challenge and after digging out from under the IRS, ultimately added nearly 1,000 acres to the estate. If only we'd been able to buy back the original tract we were forced to sell to make that first payment.

I had no idea I would fall in love with the place or that Rose Lane would fall back in love with the lifestyle. But we became hooked. Miss Julia had been ill the last ten years or so of her life and the place needed a lot of attention. Much of the timber had been cut for income and the few remaining cows were left to Rose Lane's brother, Alton. The house was badly in need of repair. What could we do with this land? We began to investigate the possibilities. We knew we couldn't grow crops or raise cattle. Though my musical career was in shambles in the wake of the demise of Sea Level, playing music was all I knew and being on the road for extended periods was a large part of that, so the prospect of crops or cattle was simply unworkable.

We considered peach trees, nursery stock, and pecan trees. These are things that do relatively well in Georgia. But those things also require a lot of attention, almost daily attention. Then one day Rose Lane's brother Alton said to me, "Look, there's that fifty-acre field over there that we used to plant corn on. If you're not going to have any row crops, you might think about planting trees." The idea clicked. Trees take a long time to grow meaning they don't require day-to-day attention, allowing me to resume touring without having to be so concerned with what might go wrong. Also, it seemed like an environmentally sound thing to do. I liked the idea of planting trees.

At that point I began to ask questions about forestry. I sought advice from the Georgia Forestry Commission and started reading about forest management. I went to the library and checked out books on forestry and land management. I also called upon some industry programs like the Landowners Assistance Programs offered by timber companies such as Georgia Pacific, Weyerhaeuser, and others. I went to meetings held by landowners groups and tried to learn. I sought out others that were involved in family forestry and pried them for information. I tried to soak it all up and get a feel for this new challenge in my life.

Credit: © Chuck Leavell Archive

Seems there's pyro everywhere I go. On stage or out in the bush, here working with my forestry team on a controlled burn.

On my career front, I began guesting on every album and tour that seemed reasonable, all the while trying to learn as much as I could about forestry. On tour with Dickey Betts' solo band once, I insisted we stop by the Audubon Society in Washington, D.C., to search for a specific book on quail management called *The Bobwhite Quail: It's Life and Management* by Walter Rosene, that was very hard to find. They had it, I bought it and read it, and I still refer to it when I need to these days.

Eventually, I found out about a correspondence course on forest management offered by the Forest Landowner's Association in conjunction with the Georgia Extension Service. I enrolled while touring with The Fabulous Thunderbirds. We'd be riding down the road in the tour bus and I'd be in the back, doing my homework. Or I might do some of it backstage, or in the rare times we afforded ourselves hotel rooms. The course culminated in writing a long-term management plan, which I did with some help from a consulting forester. Then came the hard part: implementing the plan. We began to manage our family forest. We identified all the different tracts for what was growing on them and began to mange them individually. We did some thinning here and there; we planted lots of open fields in loblolly, longleaf and slash pines. I learned how to operate tractors and other farm machinery. We began to manage our wildlife, planting feed plots for our white tail deer, quail, wild turkey, ducks, and other species. We managed to do the same for songbirds and non-game species. I got my hands dirty in the process, working on cold winter days and sweating in the hot Georgia summers, and I loved it. Slowly, surely, we began to see progress. The trees grew healthier and the wildlife became more abundant as we did our work and the years passed. It took a long time to

Goin' hard at my day job on Charlane.

see the results of practicing sound stewardship of the land, but that has been a great lesson in itself. It has taught me patience.

All of this led me on a journey. A wonderful, fascinating journey that has taught me a lot about many things. And it seems the more I learn, the more I realize there is to learn. I've learned a bit about biodiversity, our ecosystem, forest management, and wildlife. I have learned a lot about myself just by taking long walks in the woods and having what my dearly departed, talented friend Eddie Hinton once wrote in a song: "a commune with nature."

Probably the most important thing I have come to understand is that there is a wonderful and fragile balance in our world, and it's up to us — you and me — to help maintain it. Rose Lane and I have been fortunate. We've been able to not only keep our family farm but also to add to it. We believe strongly in the heritage it brought to us, and we want to pass that to our children and to our grandchildren and great-grandchildren. We want them to know the values we have learned from the wonderful and awesome responsibility of this family heritage. As the old saying goes, they aren't making any more land, and we are so very grateful to have this to live on and to work.

We did run a Christmas tree operation for about twelve years but ultimately decided that it wasn't as economical as we'd hoped — for various simple reasons. There was little profit if we used middleman retailers and the plantation is too far from the cities to do a large-scale "choose and cut" operation. But it was fun for those years that we tried it, and there was always a special joy when folks left smiling and laughing in the Christmas spirit with one of the trees we had grown. It was a great learning experience and our first step into the world of forestry.

Through the years, we used our own vision to steer Charlane into a new era. We've turned the forestland around, and in addition to improving the existing stands, we've planted many more. Recently, we had a milestone event: thinning the first area Rose Lane and I planted ourselves back in 1982. I can remember those trees going into the ground as little seedlings no more than twelve inches in size. I even have an old video of the planting. Now they are more than fifty feet tall and growing strong, especially after we "weeded the garden" by taking out the lesser trees, leaving the best ones to grow.

Through all this process of learning and living as foresters, Rose Lane and I discovered how much misinformation there is in the general public about the forestry industry, so I took another

unexpected step for a piano player from
Alabama: I wrote a book to try to boost
the profile of what we're doing and what
so many other family forest landowners
across America are doing. With the help
of writer Mary Welch, I published *Forever
Green: The History and Hope of the
American Forest*, which is now in its
second edition. It has also been translated
into German and published in Europe.

I believe in sound forestry management. I believe that man is part of this
equation. And I believe that we are here
to be good stewards of the land. The
keyword in all of this is "balance." If we enjoy using products that
come from the forest, we need to face the fact that harvesting has to
be done. On the other hand, do you want to preserve for aesthetic,
wildlife, and the future? Of course you do.

We face lots of challenges in our country and beyond concerning
our forests and our environment. But I believe we can meet these
challenges with sound solutions and in some cases good ol' common
sense. One of the major things we face here in the United States is
our own growth and development. What's not a function of nature
is urban sprawl. We can't have forests if we don't have room for
them. Let's talk about building a strip mall and putting in an operation for fifteen years, shutting it down, and moving up the street and
building another one: That's deforestation. It's real hard to get a tree
to grow in concrete. I'm not anti-growth, but I certainly am for *smart*
growth. We have to be careful and think of the consequences before
we act.

As I said, I have learned that there is a delicate balance in our
world, and it's up to us to understand that balance. People tend to
take a lot of things in life for granted, and certainly in my mind,
natural resources are one of those things. Naturally, some people
give it a lot more thought than others, but sometimes people say,

"Well, look at that tree. What a nice tree," and then go on by and continue on until something else strikes them. What I'm trying to do is make them stop and look at that tree and ask, "How old is that tree? What kind of tree is that? What does that tree offer us? Is it a fruit tree? Is that one over there a pecan tree? Are there other nut trees around here? Is that one a red oak? What things do oak trees go for? Flooring? Fine furniture? Is that a tree that means something for an animal? Are there nests up there?"

I want people to think about the trees that we harvest and saw up into lumber in order to build houses, a church, or a school. I want them to think about the wood fiber that we use to make books, magazines, and newspapers. I want them to know about some of the medicines and vitamins that come from trees. Then you begin to realize, "Wow! Isn't that a lot of things to give?" My piano is made out of maple and of spruce — most soundboards are spruce, and maple is quite often used to make the casing of the piano. Many other musical instruments come from wood: violins, cellos, violas, guitars, drums, and so many others. I've always loved Keith Richards' quote when he said, "Just think ... all this vast amount of money is generated by sitting down with this little wooden instrument."

Wood is a part of all of our lives. And it is an organic material. It grows back. It grows even better if you manage it right. Of course, we want to use wood, but we want to do it wisely and carefully and in a sustainable manor. And we also want to have protected areas for public and recreational use. Again, it's about balance, and I believe we can find that balance.

My hope with *Forever Green* is that it might give some people this pause to think about this wonderful resource of wood. We have 6 billion people on our planet and population growth is accelerating at an alarming rate. All you have to do is look at a city like Atlanta: the growth is staggering. I remember as a boy growing up in Alabama and going to the big city, a city then of 1 million people. Now it has over 4.5 million people. That's rapid growth. What will the population be ten years from now? Twenty years? We need to think about these things now, as we are going to be handing these challenges to our children and grandchildren. I hope we can hand them some solutions and not just problems. Wood is one of our most valuable resources, and to truly appreciate what it gives us, we have to look at how we're going to best use it. Gone are the days of slash and burn; we do things much better now. We've learned that we have to pay attention to what we have. We have to manage it — that's the keyword. Another keyword is stewardship; we have to be good stewards of the land. We are in a new millennium, and I think it's appropriate to make people aware, to give them something to think about, to start debate. That is why I wrote *Forever Green*.

Since Rose Lane and I took over the plantation I've learned so much about so many things — forest and land management, wildlife management, the ecosystem, and the importance of biodiversity. This ol' piano man has even learned how to fix a tractor that's broken down in the field!

It's been a joyous journey and continues to be as I work in my woods more, do more public speaking on the subject, and work with others who are involved in forestry and help educate the public. There is good news in our country concerning our forests. Our forests are not disappearing, as some might suggest. For the most part they are healthy, vibrant, and growing. This doesn't mean we aren't facing challenges, however. Trees are susceptible to fire, insects, and disease. They are susceptible to weather events like storms, floods, and droughts. People that grow trees on family forests like ours are challenged by things like these as well as things like taxes and regulations. Urban development is a problem. We need to think of growing up, not out, in some places. Many of our cities can't continue to grow ever outward. We have to slow that down, and make it smart. We need to go back into the cities and spent money on existing infrastructure and make it better, make it livable, and clean up a lot of the dilapidated buildings. Let's spend time on that, and allow these other lands to be used for recreation, national parks, agriculture, or timber resource. The more we cut into that timber resource and recreational land, the more we see our future slipping away. You can't grow a tree in the middle of the asphalt.

To know that the woods I'm a steward of are better now than they were before I had them and the satisfaction that comes with walking and looking at the deer jump out, seeing a covey of quail, a bobcat or bear, that is the big reward. This land is Rose Lane's heritage — her family's heritage, and now it's also my heritage and our children's heritage. It's in our blood and our roots run deep here. We love our land and will always do right by it. We will always work hard to keep it healthy. And when we have the time, we love to enjoy it, like when we go horseback riding, hunting, or just walking in our woods. That's a great day.

Like I said, it's been a wonderful journey, and the journey continues. If I had to put my feelings about forestry and conservation into a couple of sentences, it would be this: Man has been connected to the forests since the beginning of time. And if we take care of our forests, they will take care of us.

Without music, life would be an error.

Friedrich Nietzsche

Rolling with the Stones

The Rolling Stones called. Christ. The last bad joke this Southern boy needed. I was sitting on a swing in the front yard of the main house on our Charlane plantation in 1981, bemoaning the demise of Sea Level and all the frustrations of a career that had yielded so many highlights, so many good times and moments of great music, but yet had collapsed once again, leaving me scared for my family's financial future.

What was I doing? I had a huge property that needed a great deal of attention and care — and money — I had a wife and a daughter and soon another child on the way. I'd exhausted myself spiritually and creatively with Sea Level, given it my all only to be crushed by Goliath, the insurmountable collapse of Capricorn Records and a rash of physically, emotionally, and financially draining lawsuits. To paraphrase David Byrne — "This was not my beautiful career."

Where had the magic gone? The magic I remembered coming off those ivory keys thirty years earlier under the tender touch of my beloved mother and the soul-steeling charge I got out of seeing Ray Charles and Billy Preston for the first time live in concert. The magic with Dr. John, the Allman Brothers, Sea Level, and all those great recording sessions of the past. Where was I going? I briefly tried fumbling about with a local trio, but it was a dead end.

Even the unlikely prospect of rejoining the Allman Brothers wasn't in the cards; their reunion, which began in 1978, had already flamed out and the band broke up a second time.

I told Rose Lane I was giving up music. I was going to sell my piano and all my gear and hunker down to be a Georgia farmer, beholden to the weather and the seasons perhaps, but no managers or attorneys or drug-addled musicians or corrupt promoters. I was going to support my family. I made this announcement to her in earnest, thinking it truly might be the answer.

Rose Lane laughed at me. The love of my life — the mother of my precious little Amy, and soon my delightful little Ashley —

Credit: Chuck Leavell Archive

Original Rolling Stones keyboardist, Ian "Stu" Stewart and me in 1981.

laughed. The Rolling Stones were trying to get in touch with me, she said. She had taken a message from Alex Hodges, a friend of ours we'd known for years who was in the music business and living in California. He had talked to Bill Graham, who had told him they were looking for me. Maybe I should look into it and stop sulking. It was one of those guy moments of really enjoying a good depression and the chance to blame it all on someone else only to have it ruined by your wife, who is, let's face it, smarter than you and who more often sees the big picture. But I had no connection to the Stones, so I simply had no reason to believe it. Nevertheless, I agreed it was worth a shot to at least see if it was for real. I got a phone number from Alex and made a call, getting a secretary on the phone.

"I'm Chuck Leavell," I said, expecting an immediate brush off. "I'm calling because I understand the Rolling Stones may be trying to find me, and if they are, here's my number." I hung up feeling somewhat foolish, but I'd made the call. No regrets. Nothing lost.

A few hours later, Stones keyboard player Ian (Stu) Stewart called me back.

"Yeah," he said. "We've been looking for you."

I was briefly speechless. Bill Graham, who I had met in the Allman Brothers days and become good friends with and who was producing the Stones tour, threw my name into the hat without me knowing it. Stones bassist Bill Wyman was the first to voice support for me, I've been told, since he was somewhat of a fan of my playing from the ABB days.

The Stones were rehearsing in Massachusetts at a place called Long View Farm, which is a sprawling studio complex with accommodations and a rehearsal hall. This was a Thursday night, and I had, for lack of anything better to do, booked a club gig in Macon for that weekend.

"Well, sure … great. I've got a gig this weekend, can I come up on Sunday or Monday?" I asked.

"We'd really like to have you here tomorrow," Stu said.

"Hmm … can I make a call and get back to you?" I said without trying to plead, hoping for the right answer.

"Sure, here's the number."

I called the club manager and explained the situation. Luckily, he was totally sympathetic. "An audition with the Stones? Go, man! Don't worry about us, we'll be OK. I know someone else we can get for a couple of nights."

One is unlikely to forget few details about this kind of life event — and I assure you I haven't! I remember arriving at the small airport near Long View. I arrived about noon. Stu was there to pick me up, and it was our first in-person meeting. He was very cordial and welcomed me, helping with my bags and into the car.

Bill Wyman and me on my first Stones tour.

Long View Farm Studios

The drive to Long View was about forty minutes, so we had time to talk a bit. We made a bit of that small talk that goes down when you're just getting to know someone. But then we got into music. He loved the South, loved Southern music and musicians. He asked me about a small town in Georgia called Waycross. He had heard the name in an old blues tune and loved it. He asked me about the Allman Brothers and Sea Level. He didn't know much about Sea Level, but had liked the Allman's records. I asked him how it was going, if there had been others in for an audition. David Sancious and a couple of other guys had been in, so I knew I had competition. Finally, we arrived at the place. I saw Mick a hundred or so yards in the distance in a jogging outfit running with three or four other guys who looked like security guards. Stu took me in, and the first person I met was Bill Wyman. He was sitting in the catering area, just hanging and having a bite. Quick introductions were made. I was shown my room and settled in for just a few minutes, soaking it all in. Then I went back to the catering area, where most folks were hanging, and met Charlie. Actually, it was our second meeting. Many years before we had met at a party in London. The Allmans had gone to Europe to do two shows, one in Amsterdam and one at the famed Knebworth festival. Also on that bill were The Doobie Brothers, Van Morrison, Mahavishnu Orchestra, and some others. It was a huge gig and very successful. There had been a big party afterward in a swank London club and Charlie was there. Someone asked me if I wanted to be introduced, and of course I said yes. We met, and I asked him how it was going. He replied, "Well, do you mean for me, or do you mean for Mick and the rest?" I said, "Well, both, I guess." He said something like, "Well, not so well for me, but it's going quite well for the others." He seemed so quirky, yet very friendly and honest. We chatted a little more, but that was about it. That day at Long View I reminded him of it, and he remembered straightaway with his sly smile; it made me feel a little more at ease that he remembered me, and we talked for a bit.

There were lots of crew guys around, and I met some of them. I was introduced to Allan Rogan, Keith's guitar tech at the time and a fellow with whom I was to become great friends; the wonderful and legendary Chuch McGee, who was Ronnie's guitar tech and Charlie's tech. He was a really nice guy, and both of them tried to make me feel comfortable, asking what I needed in terms of the keyboard rig and so forth. I got the grand tour of Long View, which had been converted from a working farm into a massive recording complex. A very interesting and cool set-up, I thought. There was a recording room, a stage just for rehearsing, lots of nice rooms for us to stay in, and a great place for the meals and for hanging out — all on this beautiful farm in the hills of almost the geographical center of Massachusetts. I also met a group of people who worked for the band, including Alan Dunn, who served as a logistician for the Stones (still does), and several folks that worked at Long View. I thought, man, this is a big organization. Everyone was nice and made me feel at home.

Finally, Mick came around after his jog and I met him. Very nice and charming, I thought after introductions and quick talk about the new record, what time we might start up, and so on. It wasn't until much later that I met Keith and Ronnie. The music wouldn't start until around 7 or 8 p.m., so I had some time to hang. After a while I was curious about where the guitar section was and asked about them. I was told they were in a room playing pool. So I made it a point to go introduce myself. There they were, smoking, laughing, drinking, and playing a game of eight-ball. I felt a little out of place, but I wanted to get to know them a bit and so I joined in on a couple of drinks and played a bit of cutthroat with them. They were fun to be with, making silly puns and cutting one-liner funny jokes. After about an hour, it was time to play.

It was supposed to be a one-day audition with the band, but they kept me there for about four days, jamming and hanging out. On the first night, we started with a few Chuck Berry tunes and some blues, which put me right in my element. I was having a great time, feeling relaxed and at home. I was amazed how much fun the band was to play with, and how natural it felt. Charlie was swinging so hard on everything we played, just driving the band like a freight train. Keith was playing those fantastic riffs, Ronnie floating around on his guitar, Bill holding steady and solid, and Mick singing so soulfully and every now and then playing some mean harp. Eventually, we got to a few Stones tunes off the *Tattoo You* record, which had just come out, such as *Start Me Up*, *Hang Fire*, *Slave*, and *Waiting on a Friend*. It was nice and loose, and a great vibe. We jammed and got to know one another. I was quite impressed with their knowledge of the blues and early rock 'n' roll. It seemed that Mick knew every word to every blues song and every Chuck Berry song there was. Keith knew all the changes. In between playing we'd talk about a particular tune, and I became aware of how much they knew about this roots music. They knew who wrote a particular tune, who the musicians were on the record, and when it was recorded. They were like walking encyclopedias of blues and early rock. Later, I would learn how true that is, and for the moment it made me realize how much I didn't know about these records!

I got along wonderfully with everyone, especially Stu. We hit it off immediately. Like the rest of the Stones, he was British (a Scot, actually — a very important distinction!) and was fascinated by the American South and the cradle of the blues and R&B. He was like an instant big brother to me and we got along famously. After perhaps the most exciting four days of my life, I left Long View and was told that a final decision on who would accompany the band would be made soon. I was certain I'd landed the gig and went home beaming.

I was crushed to learn a few weeks later that I'd been passed over in favor of former

Bill Wyman and Charlie with Brian Setzer and the Stray Cats.

Faces keyboardist Ian MacLagan. I found out years later from Charlie that Stu wanted me there and told them, "I quite like that boy from Georgia!" I've never been told the whole story, but I believe some of the band wanted me and others wanted Mac, who had played with the Stones on a previous tour and who, of course, had been a buddy of Ronnie's since the mid-1960s. Since it wasn't long before they were to hit the road, it probably seemed safer going with Mac. It made sense, I rationalized, but I was truly heartbroken. It was like being one number off in the lottery.

A few days before the tour hit Atlanta, Stu called the house again and invited me to come up and sit in with the band as a guest. It was Oct. 26, 1981 and the very first show I played with the Stones, to a sold-out audience at the Fox Theater. The Stray Cats were the opening band. They were really hot at the time with their hit single *Rock This Town*. They had a good set, and I remember Stu introducing me to Brian Setzer. Little did I know that years later I'd be playing with him, too!

The Stones took the stage to a frenzied audience. The whole room was buzzing with excitement, people screaming their heads off. The band was playing great — Mick strutting around the small stage, Keith banging his guitar furiously, and all the guys tuned in and swinging. I watched the show from the side of the stage behind a curtain, waiting. When it came time for me to sit in, Stu waved me over and just left the stage and let me take his place. Man, it was great. Sure boosted my spirits to learn that even if I didn't get the job for the tour, the guys respected me and had invited me to do this show. Mick quickly introduced me, which was cool. This was the first time I had met Mac. Of course, I was disappointed I didn't land the gig myself, but I certainly had no ill feelings toward him — good for him, I thought. He's a sweet guy, a gentleman and one hell of a keyboard player. We were introduced to each other briefly before the show, but didn't get to talk much. When Stu called me to the stage, Mac was playing organ and I was on piano. As the keyboards were set up right next to each other at a right angle, we were in close quarters. Halfway through a song Mac leaned over to me and joked, "Oh, you've done this before, have you?" It was a nice compliment and really helped me feel at ease. We hit it off and became fast friends and remain pals today. He's a great player and has contributed so much to rock 'n' roll history and continues to, working with Woody on projects and fronting his own Austin, Texas-based Bump Band.

The tour went on and the North American leg finally wrapped up a few months later. I didn't give it much more thought until Mick Jagger phoned me. Mac was unable to do the European portion of the tour, for whatever reason, and the gig was mine if I wanted it. I wanted it! Talk about fate pitching a curve ball, however: Rosie was pregnant. It wasn't an easy decision to make, but for our long-term security and certainly my career, going with the Stones was the only choice to make. We knew that I would be out of the country when the baby was born, and therefore she would have to deal with the final stages of pregnancy and the birth without a partner there to help. But she took it all in stride, telling me to go and do this gig; she could handle it. It was a tough situation for both of us, but it was her carrying the child and she had the harder road ahead.

I flew to London in early summer for the rehearsals. Stu picked me up and it was so great to see him again. The rehearsals were to begin straightaway, and even though I was pretty weary from the flight, I was energized to be playing with the boys again. We had a good rehearsal, and I had taken time back home to learn a lot more Stones songs and felt prepared. It all went well, and as they had already had a few days of playing before I got there, they were going to take a day or two off after this one, which was fine with me, as I could use a day off to shake the jet lag. At the end of the rehearsal, Stu was taking me back to the hotel. I was a burnt-out puppy, tired from the flight and from the rehearsal, just wanting to go to bed. Behind us was Keith in his famous orange Bentley. He had Allan Rogan in the car with him along with two other guys that worked for him: Gary Shultz (whom we called "Shultzie") and a fellow named Svi. Of course, I had met Allan at Long View Farm and we had become friends. It was good to get to see him again. Svi was a kind of personal assistant, and Shultzie helped out with odd jobs and whatever might be needed. All great guys who had been very welcoming to me.

As we were pulling up to the front of the hotel, Keith leaned out his window and cried, "Hey, Chuck, we're going to my place Redlands. We'll come back in a couple of days for the next rehearsal. C'mon, man!" Oh, jeez, what a situation. I was dying to get some rest, just crash for a while. But this was a great chance to hang with Keith and get to know him a bit. I wavered for a second, but then I realized there was only one choice. "Sure, give me a sec and I'll be right back." So I got in what was a pretty crowded back seat for the two-and-a-half hour ride. A ride I shall never forget. It was late at night, and I was already fried. But Keith and all the guys were pumped up, ready to ride and party. Keith was driving … and driving very fast. Very, very fast. Really very, very fast! We flew through the outskirts of London and into some open roads. We flew through small little communities with barely one lane available in

My first full Stones gig … a surprise show at the 100 Club in London, 1982 … we were billed as Diz & the Doormen … and played to about 350 people.

them. We missed parked cars by inches. I figured I was going to die that night. It was all over. This was the way I was meant to go out, I told myself. Just sit back and accept it; it will all be over soon. I tried to be cool and not say anything — what was I going to do? Tell Keith Richards to slow down? I don't think so. So I prayed hard and closed my eyes, hoping that maybe there would be an outside chance that I'd get to open them again. I did. We made it, thank God!

Redlands is a neat place. An old sort of manor house with a moat around it. I understand that's where Mick wrote about "my best friend he shoots water rats … and feeds them to the geese" in the song *Live with Me*. It had some beautiful grounds around it and was placed in an Old English setting. We got out of the car, and after a silent prayer of thanks, we went in. It was already morning, and we were all getting hungry. Keith sent Shultzie to the local butcher to get some sausage and some other meats with another stop to the grocers for eggs and such and to the bakery for bread. He got back and we cooked a huge breakfast. I was barely able to keep my eyes open by then and eventually fell asleep on a sofa. Later I woke up to loud music being played. Keith was listening to some reggae, and

Keith only listens to music one way: loud. As loud as he drives fast. But I had gotten at least a little sleep and felt almost human by then. He greeted me and we talked for a while. The other guys were in various states of up and down, but eventually everyone got up and joined the "party." Later, we played some. Keith had an old piano there. It was out of tune, but it didn't matter. We played the blues and some boogie, soul tunes, and ballads. Great fun. We basically just hung out and played music for the whole day, taking some short breaks here and there. I enjoyed walking around his estate and getting some fresh air during the breaks. We finally crashed. Then the next day it was back into the Bentley for another wild ride. But at least this time I knew what I was in for! Amazingly, we arrived back at the rehearsals all in one piece. I was again very grateful to have survived.

Rehearsals went by quickly, and couple of weeks later the 1982 European Tour began. I was feeling good about things, trying to figure out how I was supposed to look with these guys on stage, so I went out and bought some new threads, trying my best to fit in with the vibe. I had fun shopping and was happy with what I had bought. I thought, "Well, at least I should fit in with the look."

The first show came and we were all dressed up in our "rock regalia" out there in front of 80,000 people — except for Stu. He wandered out in his old Levis and the same white golf shirt he wore almost every day, carrying his camera, and half a sandwich. He put the camera and the sandwich on top of the piano and just played his heart out. His head would bob and weave while he was playing, and he had that "Stu grin" going. Between songs he might take a bite of the sandwich, and if he saw a good picture, he'd stop and take a couple of shots of whatever looked interesting to him. I'd never seen anything like it in my life! Fantastic. He was just so casual and comfortable, and I think all of the flare and fluff of the Rolling Stones meant absolutely nothing to him. It was all about just playing what he wanted and having a good time.

I don't take a half sandwich out on stage with me, but later I did pick up Stu's habit of having a camera somewhere amongst my gear up there, and over the years I've been able to get some great, intimate photos of my band mates and the fans as well. I've included a few in these pages. Describing what it's like to be on stage with the Rolling Stones is next to impossible, but at least I can show you what it looks like from my piano seat.

Stu was so funny to be with on stage. So casual. Sometimes after playing a song that was really rockin' he'd say something in his soft Scottish accent, which was rather higher pitched than one would expect from a man of his stature, like, "Well, that was lovely" or "That was quite nice." He was just so understated, and it was wonderful. Of course, if he didn't like the way we played a tune, it would be "rubbish," or "corr, blimey, that was useless!"

He always spoke his mind. I remember being at one of the highly produced Stones tour parties in London one night, Stu and me sitting in the back. We just did not fit in with all the glitz of the "rock star" social crowd of the time, all the groupies and hangers-on, and the people on the fringe of the band. There was loud dance music being played in the crowded room. After a while Stu looked around with a slightly bewildered look on his face and told me that he thought disco had "significant shortcomings." God, I laughed!

Man, was it an education hanging with Stu. He taught me some of his tricks on the piano. Like the way he approached the song *Honkey Tonk Women*. He had this great way of giving it a swinging three-against-four feel and sprinkling some cool rolling licks on the top. He showed me his secret, and I've done it every night on stage with the Stones for two decades now. He used to have these little comments about his approach to playing piano in the band that he would tell me in his lilting Scottish brogue, "Make 'em sound like diamond tiaras, Chook … diamond tiaras."

As the tour rolled on, the birth of our next child got closer. This was the only time that was really hard on me during that first tour with the Stones. I couldn't be with Rose Lane when our second daughter, Ashley, came into this world. We knew when the baby would be born, as Rose Lane had had a Cesarean section with Amy, our first child, and would have another this time. Amy was seven

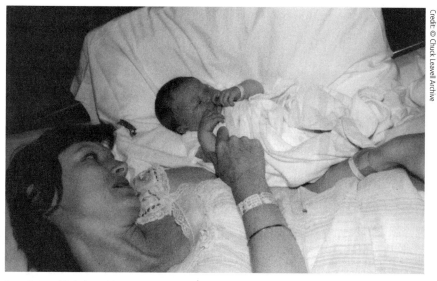

Credit: © Chuck Leavell Archive

Rose Lane with baby Ashley in the hospital.

years old and was also very excited about the birth. At the time we didn't know what the baby would be — boy or girl — and of course were ready to accept whatever came. The band was in Madrid when Rose Lane went into the hospital, and it was simply impossible for me to be back in Macon for the birth. It was hard on Rose Lane, I know, for her husband and the father of her children not to be there. It beat me up pretty badly not to be able to participate in the birth. If there's anything that can take the shine off joining the Rolling Stones on stage it's becoming a father — whether it's the first, second, or tenth time. In all the years I've enjoyed playing music, being in front of a crowd, and hearing the roar of audiences, I've never lost sight of the fact that it's all a big show, a circus that goes on for a couple of hours a night. Real life is family, and I felt terrible that I couldn't be there for Rosie, for Amy, and for the new little Ashley. And, yes, selfishly, I felt bad I couldn't be there for me. The call came on Jul. 8, 1982. The baby had been born. Rose Lane called me, and the first thing was to know that she was OK, which she was. Then, "Soooo, what is it?" I was dying to know.

"I'll let Amy tell you," she said, handing the phone to her.

"Hey, darlin', how are you" I said to my firstborn.

"I'm fine, Daddy. I miss you."

"Oh, baby, I miss you, too … so much. Is Mommy OK?"

"Yeah, she's fine."

"So tell me darlin', do you have a little brother or a little sister?"

"Guess!" she teased me. I was about to fall apart by then with anticipation, and she wanted to play a guessing game!

"OK," I said. "It's a girl."

"You're right, daddy!" Finally, I knew. I had the feeling all along, as my life has been so filled with the influence of strong women. Now I had another one! I was over the moon.

The Madrid gig was a very special one. A good friend of mine and Rose Lane's, Scott Baker, had taken photos of Ashley right after she was born. Then he had the photos overnighted to me in Madrid, just before the show. You can imagine how emotional it was for me to see pictures of my little baby right before the show. I taped a few of them to the fallboard of the piano where I could see her the whole night. I remember Ronnie floating over to have a look every now and then giving me a big smile. That night it rained, really rained hard. We had delayed the start of the show for quite a while, waiting for it to subside, but it just wouldn't. Finally, we had to go on rain or no rain. On that tour, on the opening song, *Under My Thumb*, there was a release of thousands of helium-filled balloons on both the left and right sides of the huge stage. The balloons were hidden from the audience by the face of the set of the stage and released right when a curtain was lifted and the band revealed. Thousands of these beautiful and colorful balloons would float gracefully up into the sky while the band started playing, a nice and fun intro. But this night, because of the heavy rain, when the balloons were released they were knocked back down on us on the stage. The band was totally obscured by a mountain of multi-colored balloons. Ronnie, always the joker, began popping as many as he could with his lit cigarette. Mick and Keith were kicking at them, trying to get them out of the way. It was quite a scene, unexpected but fun.

It was a fantastic gig, one of the best ones of the tour. Of course, I'm prejudiced, but I have to think it was because of Ashley. Ronnie even commented about it after the show, saying, "Man, that was really a great gig, and it had to be because of your daughter!"

The next night the band threw a big bash to celebrate Ashley's arrival, which I sincerely appreciated. Didn't I tell you this was one big family? Mick, Keith, Ronnie, and Charlie did a handmade card of congratulations — covered in Woody's great illustrations — which they mailed to Rose Lane. It was a very sweet gesture. At one point in the evening Keith got up and gave a toast: "To Ashley Rose and her first pose!" Then he, Ronnie and a couple of the guys from the J. Giles Band, who were opening up for us, got up and sang a really great acapella version of *Sea of Love*. We stayed up until the early hours of the morning, celebrating, singing, playing, and laughing. It was an exceptional night, indeed.

The thirty-five-or-so European dates were fantastic. It was the first time in six years that the Stones had played there and tickets were at an all-time demand. We played to more than a 1.5 million people. I'd hadn't played to such crowds since my days with the

Keith and me on my first Stones tour in 1982.

Allman Brothers. Except for not being able to see my family, I was having the time of my life playing with such a well-organized, not to mention huge and well-funded, band. I had met so many new people on the tour and had renewed my friendship with others that I'd worked with in the past, like Bill Graham. Bill was a big part of that tour. He worked closely with Mick and Keith and was instrumental in helping things run smoothly and successfully. He was a man in charge, on the case at all times. I remember once we were going into Sweden, and he had received word that there had been a new politician put in place as head of the country. He was apparently a hard-nosed anti-drug type and had instructed the customs authorities to search the band thoroughly as we came into the country, even to the point of strip searching us. Bill found out about it and gave us ample warning that it would happen. Indeed, upon arrival we were all really run through the drill. They looked in every bag we had, one by one. When it was my turn and I went into the room, they asked me, "Do you know why you are here?"

"Well, I think I do. I've been told you wanted to search all of us."

"Yes, that's right." They went through every piece of clothing and everything I had in every bag I was carrying. They told me to

The pre-show routine I've done since joining the Stones on tour ... a little warm-up jam in Keith's dressing room. Charlie doesn't often join in but it's always great when he does.

take off my jacket, my shirt, my undershirt, shoes, socks, pants. I was about to take off my skivvies, but they stopped there, telling me to get dressed and move on. They actually did go further with some of the folks. Bill was incensed and didn't hold back on them. He ranted and raved at them, asking why they would put us through such an ordeal. He told them: "We come into your country to bring some great music, some joy and happiness, and you greet us with indignity. Why? Why do you do this? It's stupid. It's wrong." He was really in their face, giving them all hell about it. He never let up the whole time, telling them how ridiculous the extreme search was. Of course, they didn't find anything, and we entered Sweden with no further problems. One thing that struck all of us was that all the customs agents were older, like retirement age. We found out later that all the younger agents had called in sick in protest to doing such a search, and they had to recruit some of the retired guys. I thought that was very cool.

That's the kind of guy Bill Graham was. When he was on your team, he was going to go to bat for you all the way. Bill was an amazing man and did so much for rock 'n' roll. He was a joy to work with, and I admired him greatly, as so many others that worked with him did. He would work as hard or harder than anyone. I can remember moments like seeing him sweep water off the stage when it would rain at a show or helping the stage crew with the load in or load out. He ran a tight ship, but he did it in a way that made everyone feel part of the whole, the big picture. He was smart, funny, dedicated, and loyal to his team. And he loved the music. When he died in a helicopter crash in California many years later, it marked the end of an era in rock 'n' roll.

One thing about my gig with the band did intrigue me: Why, when the Stones had the incredible Ian Stewart, the master of boogie woogie, behind the piano, did they need a second keyboard player? And they always had one — Nicky Hopkins, Billy Preston, Ian MacLagan, and me. So I asked Stu. Simple. He loved playing on the rockin' tunes, some of the country things, and the soul sort of songs. But, he said, "Chook, I don't like slow songs. They're boring. And I don't like minor chords. They're useless and they sound Chinese." I once heard or read somewhere that Stu was such a blues purist that he refused to play piano on the recording of *Wild Horses* because he hated minor chords so much. "Stu would just lift his hands off the keyboard in protest when we went to minor chords," I recall someone saying. All Stu wanted to do was to play the boogie and blues stuff. He was wonderfully eccentric. And so kind to me. One of the truest human beings I've ever met.

During the 1982 tour, when we got to London, he said, "You're not staying in a hotel. You come stay with me." He had two grand pianos at his place. And it was almost like he had a system worked out every time I'd visit. He'd turn me on to some great piano music, like Albert Ammons, whom I'd never heard before, and we'd listen to some Mead Lux Lewis, Pete Johnson, James P. Johnson, and others, all fantastic boogie-woogie players. We'd go have a bash on the pianos. What a great time. That's when I really was awakened to where he was coming from and started to get into that style of piano playing myself. I'm still so grateful to him for what he taught me. He loved to play, loved boogie-woogie, and I can still see that look on his face, that grin and his head bobbing when he played. I can remember the way he held his shoulders, at a slight angle and with just a bit of a hunch. He'd be so into it, and you could tell he was in seventh heaven. He was modest about it, but he was really a very talented and special player, and he loved it. He taught me a lot about the left hand and boogie-woogie patterns that I had never really bothered to figure out before. He made me go and listen to those records and then really pay attention to what the guys were playing on the left hand. That style of piano playing is sometimes very hard; it requires two levels of thinking, left and right hand. Those left-

Bill with Stu ... and Stu in his ever present golf shirt!

hand patterns can be very difficult, and you have to lock in and make it bounce, make it rock and swing. Your right hand goes off on a whole different thing. That's what Stu was referring to when he talked about "diamond tiaras," the bright "sprinkles" in the upper register. You can sort of fake the left hand and that's what I had been doing before I knew Stu. At the start, I'd play it straight, but Stu would say, "No, you're missing out," and he'd show me how to fill out the left hand, how to put the swing in the groove. There's a lot more room for swing in the Rolling Stones than people realize. Charlie Watts is a huge part of that. Here's a guy playing in the world's greatest rock band, and really, all he wants to be is a jazz drummer. He can tell you who played what on almost everything Charlie Parker, Miles Davis, or Count Basie ever recorded. The point is, he brings that swing factor into the band. That's one of the things that make the Stones unique. And I totally lock into that.

I got off that first tour in 1982, and I went down to my studio and worked on my left hand. Stu taught me that I needed to pick out any given pattern — and there's so many of them in boogie-woogie — and just play the left hand. Just put your right hand down and forget about it. He said, "Do it over and over until you're sick of it and your hand gets tired and you're aching. Then do it some more."

And he was right because once you're comfortable and steady with it, then you can really swing and float around the groove. Stu could really swing. It was a beautiful thing to watch and hear him play. He was a wonderful influence, and to a large extent, I believe he's the reason I ended up with the gig with the Stones. He was my best friend in the band. We spent so much time together just listening to music and having fun.

One special time that occurred during that tour was when we played in Turin, Italy. During the course of the tour, the World Cup of soccer was going on. The guys in the band were all "football" (what they call soccer) fans and had watched the whole competition unfold. Their favorites (England, of course) had been knocked out of the rounds earlier, but they kept up with what was going on almost daily. After a couple of months, it came down to the finals. It was

Italy against Germany. We were in Italy at the time, and the day of the big game we had a show in Turin. Even though the finals were held in Madrid, all of Italy was watching it on television. The game was played in the evening, I think around 7 or 8 p.m. Knowing that we would have heavy competition for that event, we moved our show earlier in the day, playing at something like 3 p.m., finishing at 5 p.m., and giving the Stones fans time to see us and still catch the game later on TV. The show was great, a real rocker. Mick always takes the time before a show in a foreign country to learn a few phrases in the native tongue and spoke to them in Italian, congratulating them on being in the final and wishing them well. Of course, they loved that, and the show was a huge hit with the fans. Never having experienced a World Cup final and not knowing much about how big an event it is, I didn't really pay much attention to the situation. I got back to the hotel in the late evening and was hungry. I went to the hotel restaurant and ordered a big plate of spaghetti. It was so good (I found out it's almost impossible to get a bad meal anywhere in Italy!) and being so hungry I ate more than I should have. Anyway, afterward with a full tummy and a few glasses of wine in me, I went to my room and dozed off for a couple of hours. I was awakened to the sound of horns honking, yelling, chanting, all sorts of loud commotion going on outside. Italy had won, and the whole town was celebrating. I've never seen anything quite like it in my life. The streets were full of mad Italians, all going completely nuts. They were parading all around the town, waving their flag, jumping up and down, screaming shouting, laughing. It was just a huge bash. I ventured out to get some firsthand flavor of the celebration, but just for a little bit, as it was getting pretty dangerous. The raving went on all night and into the morning. It was impossible to get any sleep, so some of us got together to hang out and watch the town going bananas. We watched into the wee hours of the morning from the balconies of our hotel rooms, enjoying such a wild and joyful celebration. It was an amazing experience, and I now have a much better appreciation of the World Cup!

After the tour we had a few months off before starting to record the *Undercover* album in Paris. The routine was that Stu, Alan Dunn, co-producer Chris Kimsey, myself, Bill Wyman and Charlie Watts would leave the hotel around eight at night and go to the EMI Studio. The rest of the band would show up anywhere from about 10 p.m. to midnight, and we'd work until nine in the morning or so. Sometimes it would go even later, and some nights not everyone would show. In any case, there was a lot of waiting around. Sometimes Stu and I would jam some boogie while we waited ... sometimes Charlie and Bill would play as well. It might be a blues jam, or a Chuck Berry song or just about anything. We had lots of fun doing that, and it helped to keep us from being so bored waiting for the rest of the guys.

As the sessions progressed, Chris and I became good friends. We were staying at a hotel right off the Champs on Rue de Berry called Le Warwick. After the session would end and we got back to the hotel in the morning hours, Chris and I would usually hang out for a while before going to sleep. We'd talk about the music, about our families (he and his wife Kris have two children, a daughter Cloe and son Joe), about some of the other artists we'd respectively worked with and life in general. It was comforting to have someone like that to talk to, and our friendship grew over the course of those sessions and beyond. Chris had a great energy, wonderful sense of humor and is truly an extremely talented engineer/producer. He had worked on several Stones records prior to these sessions and had the respect of the band. He did a great job on *Undercover*, helping to keep things moving along, getting great sounds and pushing all of us to perform our best. Chris and I spent quite a lot of time together during those days, and I'll always be grateful for his friendship and encouragement. We would work together many times after that, as you'll read later.

Stu and I also spent a lot of time together when we weren't recording. He had a turntable and a small stereo system in his hotel room. He didn't like cassette tapes and always carried his LPs with him. I'd go visit him and he'd have a glass of fine malt Scotch and be boppin' to Count Basie, Duke Ellington, or a boogie record. Stu didn't drink very much, but he did enjoy a glass of proper Scotch or a lager every now and then. He never did drugs.

Other times we might go out. I remember on the Champs Elysée there was some little bistro where he liked to get ice cream. He loved ice cream, tarts, that kind of thing. Often he'd ring me up in my room and get me to go with him. Whether it was the ice cream or a dinner, Stu would never let me pick up the check. He always had a wad of money with him, in his back pocket in a big old wallet. He also kept notes with phone numbers, receipts and other stuff in that wallet ... it was like his "briefcase" with his phone book, his accounting records, two or three different currencies of cash, everything. I don't know how he could sit on that thing, it was so thick. Anyway, I would try and sneak ahead of him and get the bill, but he would always have it sorted out somehow, and it just drove me nuts. I would get upset with him and he would just smile and say, "Oh, no worries Chook, it's only little bits of paper."

In early 1985, we gathered again at the studio in Paris to begin work on the album that would become *Dirty Work*. This time the band had recruited a young producer named Steve Lillywhite. Steve had several successful records to his credit including the early U2 recordings, records by The Psychedelic Furs, Peter Gabriel's third solo record, Simple Mind's *Sparkle in the Rain* and many others. He brought a different approach to the proceedings. I found him to be sort of a quiet man, a bit reserved. While I missed my pal Chris Kimsey, Lillywhite did an admirable job for the times, keeping things rolling along in his own unique way.

Sessions continued through June before moving to New York in July and finally finishing in October. There were some other tracks we started that were pretty cool but didn't make the final album. There's one recording, in fact, of a track called *Deep Love* that I've always liked — in part because I played drums on it! It was one of those late-night jams of Keith's, with Ronnie on bass. Charlie wasn't around so I jumped on the kit for fun. Like some other Stones tracks, it has leaked out of the vault and when we were in Japan during the Voodoo Lounge tour I discovered a bootleg CD version of *Dirty Work* with *Deep Love* on it. *Goin' To Memphis* and *Invitation* are another couple of tracks that were never released from the *Dirty Work* sessions that have leaked out and are quite popular among collectors.

One track that did make it to the album, however, was a tune that I'd come up with called *Back to Zero*. Basically, I'd been sitting in the studio alone, tinkering on a new keyboard and came up with a little groove that I was amusing myself with. Mick came in and started jamming on it, singing gibberish to the melody as he does before he comes up with lyrics to a tune.

The next day I went to Mick. The Stones have always been very protective of their songs and their songwriting credits. So it was with some trepidation — I was the newest kid on the block, after all — that I went to Mick and told him that if the tune we were working on progressed any further, I wanted the credit I deserved. "No problem," Mick said, with such ease that my concerns evaporated. We brought in a few percussionists, Keith added his input, and the song was done. It may not be a classic, but I was honored to have my name alongside the Glimmer Twins.

One funny story about that keyboard was that I came into the studio one night and caught Stu playing it with headphones on. Stu really hated synths of any kind, and it was a surprise to see him playing it. He didn't see me at first, and I watched him for a while. He would play it a bit, frown, play some more. He punched buttons, twisted knobs, played, and frowned. It looked like he was trying to give it a chance, hoping to come up with something that would inspire him, turn him on. This went on for about ten minutes or so, and I was enjoying watching him experiment. Finally, I couldn't take it any longer and walked up to him. He was sort of embarrassed; he didn't want to be caught playing a "machine." I asked him what he thought about it. "Did you find any interesting sounds, Stu?" He looked at me calmly, took the headphones off, smiled, and said, "Chook, I can say without reservation whatsoever that the best thing you could possibly do with this is to throw it in the ocean!"

Our sessions could sometimes be brutally long and sometimes didn't start until very late. The standard procedure was that Charlie, Stu, Bill, myself, and the crew and staff would go down around 9 or 10 at night. Most nights we'd have to wait a while before Mick, Keith, and Ronnie would show. Sometimes Mick or Keith might take a night off and we'd just plough through with whoever was there. But as the aforementioned constituted the rhythm section, we had to be there every night. I remember one night when we arrived and waited. We jammed for a while, then waited some more. Jammed, waited. Took naps, waited. No Mick, no Keith, no Ronnie. The sun came up. We waited some more. Finally, about 9 or 10 in the morning, we figured it was a bust. We were dead tired, sort of pissed off, and confused, and were ready to get some rest. So we gathered our coats and scarves and whatever else we had brought and were just about out the door when Keith and Ronnie showed up, raving. "Get your arses back in there. Where do you think you're going!" snarled Keith. Oh, man. We had no choice but to go along. He wanted to play, and he was not going to hear about us going back to the hotel. He kept us there all that day and on into the next night's session. A couple of times during breaks, I would sneak up under the piano to catch a nap, but it wouldn't be long before Keith would want to do another take of a song, and I'd climb up on the piano stool bleary-eyed but trying to do my best. I'm not sure if this was the way he came up with the song, but I remember him looking at me at some point saying, "Yeah, you'd better get some sleep tonight, Chuck!" Indeed, we began to play that song that night, and while at the time it was just a sketch, it eventually made it on the record as *Sleep Tonight*.

We worked in Paris through June and then moved the sessions to New York, finally finishing the album in October. After a lot of hard work, all the people in the Stones camp scattered to their respective home lives and settled in for the holiday season and the wonder of what great things the following year might bring.

Stu himself did what he loved to do — play. On Dec. 11, 1985, he sat in with some friends in a band called Rocket 88 at the Old Vic, a club in Nottingham in England. The next day, he wasn't feeling well and went to his doctor for some tests. After some sort of heart scan, Stu sat down in the waiting room and died. Just like that, forty-seven years old. We were all devastated, totally crushed. Many in the Stones camp had known Stu since the early 1960s. He'd been with the band from the start.

It was simply unbelievable that he was gone. I flew to London for the service. We were all just dumbfounded, numb. It was hard to even talk about it. It was so surreal, so impossible. We all grieved. We were all at a loss. We sort of wandered for a couple of days and then had to go to the funeral. It was tough on all of us. At the funeral, I remember a moment when Charlie leaned over to Keith and said simply, "Who's gonna tell us off now?"

After the funeral there was a wake at the club where Stu played golf. All of us were there, the whole band, lots of other musicians and friends. Stu loved golf just about as much as he loved music. There's a story that Bobby Keys tells about the band finding themselves in these weird far-away hotels on one of the early American tours. At that time, Stu was in charge of overseeing all the travel arrangements for the band. Bobby says they would wake up in the middle of nowhere in a hotel, way away from the town they were playing in. Finally, somebody said something to Stu about it, and of course he replied that there was "quite a nice golf course nearby." He had booked the whole tour around these golf courses he wanted to play! So we all went to Stu's club after the funeral, sat, and talked about Stu — how much we loved him, how great a character he was. Lots of stories floated around the room. At one point Keith said, "He's got to be in the room with us now, and I can hear him saying 'Well, if this is the only way to get the band to come to the club!' "

We played a tribute show at London's 100 Club for friends and family a month or so later. Jeff Beck, Pete Townshend, Jack Bruce, Eric Clapton, and others joined us on stage. It was a great and, as one might imagine, emotional evening. We hadn't had a rehearsal or anything. It was totally wide open and impromptu as far as the music went. I remember Mick picking some songs out of the air and telling the folks in attendance, "I'm trying to remember the ones Stu liked." Jack Bruce gave a particularly moving tribute to Stu with a few words, saying how much he loved him, how much we all would miss him, and how much he had all influenced us. Others gave short remarks, and all spoke highly of the love they had for Stu.

It was the last time the Stones played together for several years; Keith wanted to tour immediately but Mick didn't. *Dirty Work* was released a few months after Stu's death, but there was no tour. It would be years before we'd get back together as the Rolling Stones and marked the beginning of their individual solo efforts. No one — I'm not certain even Mick or Keith — knew whether the Stones had come to an end or not.

Good music is very close to primitive language.

Unknown

Gathering No Moss

I ensconced myself in the plantation and a long series of sessions, having a great time but wondering if the Stones would ever get together again. It was almost five years later when, finally, I got a call — the big machine was going to start rolling again.

First, we went into the studio to work on the first album without Stu, *Steel Wheels*. This was a critical time for the band. There had been a long gap with no record since *Dirty Work* and no tour since 1982. There had been solo projects by all the guys, but the fans wanted to hear the real deal. The sessions began in Montserrat at George Martin's Air Studios. Chris Kimsey was in the co-producer's seat again, and there was another change: the addition of another keyboard player named Matt Clifford. Mick was looking for someone that was good with synthesizers and programming, and Matt fit the bill. Kimsey had known about him, worked with him a bit, and suggested his name. The basic tracks were recorded with the core

Paradise. At home with my young daughters and beautiful wife on a brief break from the road.

Matt Clifford (right) and us on Steel Wheels.

band and Matt in Montserrat over a month or two, and then the band went into the overdub process. That's when I got the call. I went to London for my overdubs, glad to be back in the saddle again with the boys and curious about this new guy. Matt and I quickly became pals and there was certainly no rivalry between us. He is a technical genius and a master when it comes to programming. I'm neither. I remember later when we went on tour, we were playing RFK Stadium in Washington, D.C. Lee Attwater, a "spin doctor" in the political world who worked for George H. W. Bush came to the show. He was a fan of the band and had become a pal of Woody's. Lee was a really nice guy with a quick wit and a true Stones fan, having further appreciation since he played guitar. He watched the show and afterward came backstage and complimented Matt and me. He said, "Man, that was great the way you guys handled the keyboards. It was like high-tech and red-neck." I love that! It was a good description of how Matt and I worked together.

So I got to London and heard the tracks for the first time. Songs like *Mixed Emotions*, *Sad, Sad, Sad*, and *Rock and a Hard Place* stood

out to me, as well as Keith's numbers *Can't Be Seen* and the wonderful classic *Slipping Away*. I got to do my bits and was happy to be
back with the band, especially with such a good record in the works.
The sessions wrapped up, and we began to make plans for a tour.

The rehearsals took place in Washington, Connecticut. It was a
beautiful sleepy little town, and we had found a great place to stay —
like an old summer camp. Most of us stayed there, but a couple of
the guys had rented houses in the area. The actual rehearsals were to
take place at an abandoned girls' school that the scouts for the band
had found. They had to do some extra wiring and bit of fixing up,
but it was spacious and perfect situation for us. The school wasn't
far from the accommodations, and since the town was a good bit
away from the public eye, it was a perfect setup for us to get down to
business. We hit it hard over
the next two months. This was
a very critical time for the
band, and we all knew that we
had to put on a spectacular
show and have the music tight
and swingin'. I believe it was a
turning point for the band. We
had to step up to the plate and
hit the ball out of the park.

My view of Charlie on the B-stage.

The best of the best were
called in on the tour. Patrick
Woodroff, who had done the
1982 tour, was to design the
lights. His talents are considerable, and he has great
innovative vision for not only
the lighting design but other
creative aspects of the show.
Veterans Mark Fischer and
Jonathan Park were brought in
for the set design. Their credits

My view of Ronnie and Keith.

had included Pink Floyd and many others. Michael Cohl had won the bid to produce the entire tour and was breaking new ground with his approach to promotion. All the crew and staff were the cream of the crop. Musically, we recruited the Uptown Horns, a great horn section from New York for the tour. This was also the first time that Bernard Fowler and Lisa Fischer came on board as vocalists, as well as Cindy Mizelle, another talented backing vocalist. Bernard and Lisa had worked with Mick on his solo tour, but this was the first time for them working with the Stones. The rehearsals went well, and the pieces of the puzzle fell into place. But it was also tough without Stu there. It was so different.

Finally, after two hard months of planning, rehearsing, meetings, filming videos, and other preparation, we were ready to go. It was hard work musically. We went through lots of songs from the past as well as putting in a lot of the new tunes from *Steel Wheels*, and we felt good about the tour, confident and rarin' to get it in front of people. We did the usual small-club gig before moving to Philadelphia for the big opening show. This time we picked Toad's Place, a small club in New Haven that I had played before with Sea Level, The Fabulous Thunderbirds, and a couple of other bands. The

Credit: Chuck Leavell Archive

A great homecoming: Mick and me in Birmingham, Alabama.

gig rocked, and we left Connecticut in good spirits. The tour, which was called Steel Wheels in America but with a name change to Urban Jungle when we went to Europe, was dedicated to Stu's memory. This was the first time the Stones were on stage without Stu, and I think it was on the road that it really struck everybody that he was gone. It seemed like no time at all had passed since his death, and it was a very open wound with all the band and crew who knew him. I remember clearly back in the dressing rooms before the first show in Philadelphia we discussed that this would be the first time we'd take the stage without first hearing Stu's voice. Stu was the one who would tell the band when it was time to go on stage. We never went until Stu said it was time. He had these wonderful little phrases he'd use to come get us, like "All right, my little three-chord wonders, you're on!" Or "All right, my little shower of shit, it's time to earn your wages!" It was like a huge empty hole was there, but the band carried on and of course that's what Stu would have wanted.

No one could ever truly replace him, but I guess it was a natural thing for me to slide into a role that sort of makes sure his presence is still felt. I'm just so fortunate to have spent all that time with him,

Credit: © Chuck Leavell Archive

Soundcheck with the best ... Lisa Fischer and Bernard Fowler.

watching him, studying his playing, and learning from him. But I'll never be able to play like he did. He just had a special thing all his own, and his contribution was so strong.

There's a Stones B-side called *Fancy Man Blues*, which in a way was my tip of the hat to Stu, in terms of the piano playing. I think about Stu probably as much as I think about my father, who died when I was seventeen. Sometimes I'll laugh out loud at a memory of him, catch myself playing something that I learned from him, or look at a picture of him and this flood of emotion will come pouring out. Stu had a profound and everlasting effect on many people. He certainly did on me. During rehearsals, I found myself playing all the parts Stu was known for and on the tour there wasn't a night that we played a show that he wasn't there with us in spirit.

The band looked to me to slide a little bit into those shoes. They're very heavy shoes, and I could never fill them, but they looked to me as someone who understood Stu, understood the way he played, and could cover that territory. So I went into a slightly different role with the band. And then as time went on, the role

Credit: © 2003 Jane Rose

The Rolling Stones band doing its Forty Licks in 2003.

evolved further, into being sort of the "gatekeeper," someone who keeps track of the arrangements, will work extra rehearsals with the horns and with the vocals, and do whatever it takes to make it easier for the main guys to feel comfortable, allowing them to do their thing with minimal pressure. I began to feel more a part of the big picture. So in that respect, I'm given a lot of reign and freedom.

Steel Wheels and Urban Jungle were indeed turning points for the band. They were fabulous tours, both as shows and musically. The set was something that no one had seen the likes of before with its huge *Mad Max* stage, big blow up dolls for *Honky Tonk Women*, and other features. It captured fans and held them in awe. The band played better than it ever had, and more consistently. One of the highlights was going to Japan for the first time. The band sold out ten shows at the famous "Big Egg" in Tokyo. The fans were ready for us, and we were ready for them. No one had done that many shows there, making it another record breaker. Our stay there was incredible, and Rose Lane and I made many new friends in that wonderful country. I made a guest appearance at a music school there, the ESP Music School. ESP is best known for their guitars, but they also had this music educational facility that was very impressive. After touring the school, one of the professors asked me if I'd be willing to do a clinic for one of the classes. We put it together, and it worked out great. We had many other memorable experiences during the stay in Japan: going to museums, special sites, temples, some cool parties, restaurants, and just generally soaking up the culture. The ten shows all rocked, even if the audience was more reserved than we were used to. Tokyo was abuzz with Stones news, Stone sightings, and reports of the shows. The Stones were still breaking new ground.

We did something like 114 shows all over the world on the Steel Wheels/Urban Jungle tours, from August 1989 to August 1990. The reviews were strong, the band worked hard and reached new heights of success. The greatest rock 'n' roll band in the world was back with a vengeance. It was just what it needed to re-establish itself.

After that there were a couple of years off for the band. Everyone scattered and did solo projects — back to more domestic lives. I was busy with Charlane for a while, but it wasn't long before I got a call for some pretty cool session work. More on that later.

In 1994 the band wanted to crank up again. The big deal this time was that Bill Wyman had announced he wouldn't be on board. Mick and Keith tried to talk him out of it, but he had made his decision and was going to stick by it. It was a tough situation. He was a well-known founding member of the band and had been a big part of it from the beginning. But his mind was made up, and the band had to move on. There was nothing personal. No scandals, conflicts, anger, or tension of any kind. Bill just simply had had enough. He'd toured for as long as he cared to do it, and he wanted a change of lifestyle. I understand that completely — I have a different lifestyle when I come home. Also, he had developed a fear of flying. He didn't care to fly anymore, and obviously that wasn't going to work. He'd tried to do it once or twice before, to convince them that they could do it without him, and they kept negotiating a way around it. But this last time, his mind was made up. I respected his decision and I know he's never regretted it. In the years since, I think there are mostly just fond memories for everyone in the band, and Bill showed up to say hello to everyone backstage at the last English show on the Forty Licks tour.

Darryl Jones, Charlie and I discuss an arrangement during rehearsals.

Auditions were held to try and find a replacement, mostly being held in New York. After going through scores of players, the decision basically came down to Charlie. Keith told him that he had the last say on it, and he should make a choice. He suggested Darryl Jones out of all that had auditioned, some thirty or so, I believe. It was a great choice. Darryl added a new punchy sound to the band and brought in some new blood, which kicked everybody up a notch. Plans were made to go to Dublin, Ireland for the sessions.

The first album without Bill was *Voodoo Lounge*, and we gathered at Ronnie Wood's place in Ireland to begin writing and recording in early 1994. Released the same year, it ended up winning the 1995 Best Rock Album Grammy award. How's that for a band that had been together, essentially, for more than thirty years at the time!

With Don Was producing, the core band with Darryl and myself began recording what was to be *Voodoo Lounge*. There were strong songs written by Mick and Keith, and with a renewed energy we were all inspired to carry on beyond *Steel Wheels*. Darryl's presence proved to add in a freshness, and Don's even-handed guidance kept us all on track. With the record complete, songs that stood out to me were: *Love Is Strong, You Got Me Rocking, Brand New Car* and Keith's wonderful tune *The Worst*. I also liked the ballad *Out of Tears*, as it gave me an opportunity to do some more melodic playing. When I went into the studio to record the piano part, I distinctly had my mind on Nicky Hopkins. He was such an inventive player, a real motif-meister who always came up with those great melodic parts of songs that make them so memorable. Like on *Angie*, his piano part is more than just fills, it's full of beautiful melodies, just gorgeous, and his parts helped make the songs what they are. I wanted to do the same with *Out of Tears* and thought of Nicky's playing when I sat down to record it. It was one of the pieces I'm particularly proud of — one of those songs that I left my mark on, while honoring the memory of Nicky. Every piano player has done it in his own way with the band. Stu's contributions were immeasurable. And think of what Billy Preston did on organ for *Slave* and *Melody* or *I Got the Blues*. And when he toured with the band, Ian MacLagan added his incredible playing as well.

Of course, the tour was coming. Michael Cohl started to put it together and after rehearsing for a couple of months in Toronto, we were off to do it again. Matt Clifford was out of the equation this time. He and Keith were friendly enough but never really seemed to gel on stage, so it was inevitable that a change would occur. Mick had several other keyboard players on hold for auditions but I went to him and told him that I didn't think we needed another keyboard player. I wasn't trying to protect my own position; to me, it just didn't make sense. As I told Mick, we only really needed two keyboard players on a select few songs a night.

"Do you really want to carry another guy around the world, pay his salary and expenses for a year for a few songs a night?"

Mick looked at me rather astonished because he'd never considered the practicality of this.

"Why don't we get a horn section with a guy who can play keyboards?" I suggested. "Somebody who can pop over and play when we need him, but the rest of the time can play horns."

Mick agreed.

Two different horn sections were auditioned and the band quickly chose the New West Horns, with Kent Smith, Michael Davis, and Andy Snitzer, who could play keyboards quite adeptly. The New York-based trio played and recorded with everyone from

Credit © 2003 Jane Rose

Kicking it up with Ronnie and Ketih.

Aretha Franklin and Frank Sinatra to Al Green, Bob Dylan, Paul Simon, and dozens of others. More recently Tim Ries replaced Andy on the road with the Stones because Andy didn't like being away from his family and home for such extended periods. Of course, Bernard Fowler and Lisa Fischer were called in again. The new team was in place and ready to go.

And again, it was a record-breaking outing. One of the highlights for me (and I'm sure for all of us) was going to South America for the first time in the band's career. There was a lot of anticipation about it since it was a first. The shows sold well — incredibly well. We wound up playing five sold-out shows in Buenos Aires' River Plate Stadium to nearly 55,000 people each night. We also played big shows in Sao Paulo and in Rio de Janeiro. It was amazing. We had a long trip to get there, as we had played Japan just before. After a

One of the highlights during the Voodoo Lounge tour ... Keith and I salute Jerry Lee Lewis during my *Honkey Tonk Women* piano solo.

flight that seemed to last an eternity, we arrived in Buenos Aires in the wee hours of the morning. Waiting on us were about 500 or so fans, all excited, all screaming and yelling. We were pretty surprised to see that many people at that hour of the day waiting, but there they were. We loaded in the vans to go to the hotel, and this amazing chase ensued. The fans wanted to catch a glimpse of the band and were chasing us hard. Our drivers were trying to avoid them, but the faster they went the faster the fans followed us. It got to be pretty dangerous. There was so much commotion, hollering, waving, and close misses with the vehicles going on. Lisa was in the car with me, along with a couple of members of the horn section. She was getting a bit freaked at the whole scene, and we were all a little uncomfortable about it, but it was intensely exciting as well. It was probably close to what the old days were like in the 1960s with Stonesmania and Beatlemania. We finally got to the hotel, and there were even more fans waiting there. They all began to crowd around the cars as we made our way in, and all of a sudden our car was covered in Latin bodies, all screaming and beating on the car, shaking it as well. At this point Lisa started to cry and scream. We somehow managed to push through past the secure area and were safe. Man, what a wild scene. Then the fans broke out into their soccer chant ... "Ole, ole ole-oleeeee! Rollings, Rollings!" Their short name for the band was "Los Rollings." Our stay there was just incredible. Anytime Keith, Ronnie, Charlie, or Mick could be seen from the balconies or anywhere, the crowd would burst into the chant again. Rose Lane and I — and of course most all members of the band and crew — made it out into the cities and explored. We all loved it. Most of us had never been to Buenos Aires or to South America. It was a fantastic trip, and the shows were wild and electric there. Watching all those beautiful dark-skinned and dark-haired people jump and sway to the music was a sight to see, so passionate and caught up in the spirit. It energized and inspired us to play better, I believe.

There was an interesting recording situation during *Voodoo* as well. The record company had seen the rise in popularity of the *Unplugged* series done by MTV. While Mick refused (for whatever reason, I don't know) to do an *Unplugged*, he did agree to do a record that would strip the band down a bit. Thus the name, *Stripped*. We went into several studios during the tour in various different cities. The band rerecorded some tunes that had been done long ago, like *Spider and the Fly*, *I'm Free*, *Wild Horses*, and others. We also did some live gigs in small theaters to round things out, which included

Keith, Lisa, Bernard, Mick and me during a theater gig.

a smokin' version of Bob Dylan's classic *Like A Rolling Stone*. That was picked as a single and showed that the Stones were still great at doing a cover tune. In my opinion, *Stripped* is probably the most overlooked Stones CD. Re-doing some of those old tunes showed how great they were in the first place, and how much better the band played them at this point. *Not Fade Away* pumps with passion, and *Shine a Light* brought a somewhat obscure but great song back to the surface, giving me a chance to play some gospel piano in the process. *Dead Flowers* and *Sweet Virginia* lets the band remind the world that the Stones can still do country with the best of them, and *Little Baby* puts the band back into the blues where it began. Mick sings so cool, and Keith and Ronnie play some mean and beautiful guitar work. I get to throw in my "diamond tiaras."

The Voodoo Lounge tour was a great experience for all of us. There were five club gigs and 130 other shows before 6.6 million people who forked over $350 million for the opportunity to be a part of the experience.

One day we were in South America, and Stones' road manager Alan Dunn said to me that he'd been thinking Stu would have really gotten a kick out of what had become of the Rolling Stones. Stu had been with the band from the start, when they were driving from English gig to English gig in a van — the band and all its equipment. There we were, in the middle of more than a year of solid, sold-out international gigs and we needed fully loaded 747s to get around. And getting around to places that most of us have never been before and might never be again. I remember being in Africa on the Voodoo tour and getting a chance to head out on a specially arranged safari: I saw elephants in the wild and a leopard climbing a tree with a freshly killed kudu. It was unbelievable. And what did I dream about that night? Training the bird dogs and being back on Charlane! I laughed to myself the next morning when I woke up.

One really great and fun person that works for the band is our ticket co-ordinator, Shelley Lazar. Shelley is a legend in the business and does the guest tickets for not only the Stones but for many big acts such as Bruce Springsteen, Paul McCartney, and many more. She is a wonderful person and can be a real hoot. Sometimes she does fun things during the course of the tour to spice things up. Like when we check into a hotel she'll greet us dressed up in some wild garb that has something to do with the city we're in. When we arrived in Boston once she was dressed as one of the Founding Fathers with the powdered wig and fancy coat tails. In Australia she had a kangaroo with her in the lobby. In New York she dressed up as a street person and was laying in the middle of the floor of the fancy hotel. In Sweden she dressed up as "Helga" with the blonde pig-tails and costume. But she is also our "Jewish Mother" on the tour, doing some wonderful things like arranging a Hanukkah ceremony once when the holidays were near and we were staying in Miami. It's so great to have folks like that on board, and it keeps things fun and interesting — and goes a long way to maintain that family spirit of the Stones.

Shelley also started a tradition of the "best and worst" of the tour. She printed up a questionnaire and distributed it to everyone,

Credit: © Chuck Leavell Archive

Soundcheck with Mick.

asking to list the best and worst hotel, best and worst city for shopping, best and worst opening band, best and worst restaurant, and so forth. One category was best and worst police escort. Through the years, we've had hundreds of police escorts all over the world. The one that took the cake was in Albuquerque, New Mexico. Apparently, the whole police force there was made up of Stones fans. There were at

Credit: © 2003 Jane Rose

Another day, another soundcheck.

least twenty motorcycle cops, all with the Stones' red tongue logo on the back of their helmets. In addition, there were six police cars and a helicopter! Now that's an escort!

There was one shattering moment for me during the tour, however. We were just starting the outdoor portions of our European tour when Rose Lane called to tell me that our good friend Matt Greeley, percussionist and singer, who joined Sea Level in about 1978 and hung in there through all the tough times with Capricorn Records and then our trouble with Clive Davis at Arista, had died. He'd called me just before I went on tour and told me he had cancer and that he was refusing all those ugly, invasive treatments, preferring to die with dignity. He did.

After the Voodoo Lounge tour wrapped there was, quite understandably, a bit of a break, and I didn't hear from anybody for a while. I was too busy on Charlane to make many overtures myself. The Stones would pick up next with the *Bridges to Babylon* record. I had heard that the band was going into the studio, but this time the call didn't come. I found out through a friend that they had begun the recording and had thought the phone would ring, but it didn't. I waited and waited, but no call. It was frustrating and I was very disappointed. I wondered if I'd done something wrong. But in the end I came to grips with it. There were other keyboard players that made it on the record, like Benmont Tench and Billy Preston. Great players that did a good job. But I know in my heart that it should have been me. I would have done better.

The CD struck me as a bit unusual — not to say it didn't have highlights. One of the songs that would be a staple on the tour that followed, *Saint of Me*, was a tune Mick wrote. Session veteran Waddy Wachtel played guitar on it, rather than Keith. Maybe Keith didn't want to be on it. I don't know. Pretty strange, though. Another tune I liked like was *Out of Control*. That also became an important song for the tour. Keith's soulful *How Can I Stop*, a beautiful track, and his reggae *You Don't Have to Mean It*, also caught my ear. But for me, it sounded like there were too many cooks in the kitchen for the *Babylon* record. There were lots of producers listed: Don Was, The Dust Brothers, Rob Fraboni, Danny Saber, and more. All talented producers, but the end result was pretty scattered in my opinion. Still, I give credit to the band for being able to work through what must have been some tough sessions to put the CD together. That's one thing about the Stones: they see things through and will get done what needs to get done.

The phone did ring soon, however, before the record came out. Time to crank up that big machine again! So we embarked on the Bridges to Babylon tour. This time the team was the same,

Darryl, Lisa, Bernard and Blondie Chaplin ... what a team.

but with the addition of Blondie Chaplin. Blondie is from South Africa and is a veteran singer/songwriter who worked a lot with the Beach Boys in the mid-1970s. Keith had met him when he was recording his *Wingless Angels* project in Jamaica. Blondie had been brought in to the *Angels* project by co-producer Rob Fraboni to help with vocal arrangements. Keith liked the results and invited Blondie to work on the *Babylon* record and to join the tour. Having another male voice in the equation added a nice touch, and he began playing a little guitar and percussion here and there as well as some keyboards if needed, making the band more versatile.

The Bridges to Babylon tour was simply incredible. The "bridge" that would telescope out over the crowd to the B-stage in the middle of each venue cost about $1 million alone and was so complex that it wasn't even ready for the first few shows of the tour. That gives you

an idea of how elaborate the effort was. For me, our show at the newly built Georgia Dome in Atlanta was a sheer highlight. I don't know whether it's just being close to home or what it is, but for me Atlanta Stones shows always seem to be among the best.

The tour was fun musically, as well, since there were a number of

Lovebirds Ronnie and Jo Wood.

new tunes from the *Bridges* CD that were in the set, including *Saint of Me* and Keith's wicked take on the electric chair, *Flip the Switch*. We cruised through the world yet again, doing 108 shows. The tour was extended because of a weird situation: the tax laws in the UK. There were some changes to the laws early in the Blair administration that severely affected the British subjects who were working with the band and staff. The changes resulted in a lot of folks taking home a lot less from the tour than was initially anticipated. There was another problem with the new laws that affected the UK portion of the tour. The bottom line on that was the band had to postpone the scheduled shows for about a year. So Michael Cohl and his team went to work, coming up with the idea of following the release of *No Security*, the live record from the Babylon tour with another tour. The plan was to come back to the United States and do select dates in arenas instead of stadiums. It had been decades since the band

In the studio in Paris with Don Was, June 2003.

had done an arena tour, and this raised interest from the public — he prospect of seeing the Rolling Stones in a smaller setting. With this in place, and the UK shows rescheduled, the band continued to work. Of course, it all went even better than expected, breaking more records and earning more multi-millions. The concept of doing the arenas was a big hit, and the band started to see the value in mixing up the venues. This idea laid the framework for the next tour.

Having extended the Bablyon tour into the No Security tour, the band had been on the road for a long time: two years. We had started Babylon in September 1997 and then worked No Security up to late April 1999 in the United States, ending in San Jose. But we still had to make up those shows. There was a break of a couple of months, and then we went back to do the UK shows in the summer of 1999. Finally, we were done. A break was much needed, and an exhausted band, crew, and staff were happy to get a rest.

Then in April 2002 the phone rang again. The Stones were to celebrate forty years of rock history by releasing forty songs on a comprehensive retrospective with four new tunes added in the mix. It was to be called *Forty Licks*. We flew to Paris for the recording, taking a month to record some twenty or so songs. Most were just rough ideas that we put down for reference, but some were complete. Out of these, four were chosen for the *Forty Licks* CD. *Don't Stop* is a catchy single; *Keys to Your Love* is a nice floating R&B mid-tempo tune; *Still in My Heart* is a harder song; and the cool, almost jazzy ballad that Keith sang was called *Losing My Touch*. On this last one I got some nice space to play some more sophisticated chord voicings and some nice melodic phrases. All in all, the sessions went well, and we looked forward to the tour that would take the celebration on the road and to the people. There was a unique idea that surfaced about playing three different kinds of venues: stadiums, arenas, and theaters. We'd pretty much gravitated toward doing this at the end of Babylon/No Security, but this was a chance to design it so that in some cities we could do all three in one time period. Cohl — as always — arranged the tour nicely, and this was also a chance for us to try to lay out three fairly different shows. So when we arrived in Toronto to begin rehearsals, we knew we had to explore the catalogue deeply. We dove way back, trying tons of songs, around 140. Not all of these made it to the final tally, but we did wind up with something like eighty different songs to choose from for the tour. Mick and I worked hard on picking the songs that would work well in the stadiums, the ones for the arenas, and the ones for the theaters. It was a fun challenge, and after we all chipped in on ideas we had an impressive list. We honed it down, and after about six weeks of rehearsing we found ourselves doing the traditional warm-up show at the Palais Royal club on Aug. 16, 2002. From there we went to Boston for the official opening show at the Fleet Center on Sept. 3. We did the Fleet, then the Gillette Stadium in Foxboro on Sept. 5, and the theater show was held at the Orpheum on Sept. 8. The result was a huge buzz, and all were totally successful, setting the stage for the rest of the tour. We took this concept through the United States first, and then went on to many other countries around the world with the same results. It was a total success, proving yet again that no one rocked harder than the Stones and that with forty years of experience the band was better than ever. It's hard for me to believe that it's been that long. Hard for me to believe I've been there for over half of those forty years. Not many bands can make the claim of having a creative career for as long as that and to have stayed on top of the heap the whole time. Even though I'm in the middle of it, it still blows my mind. And how far can it go? It's like Keith says, "We don't know. We're making this up as we go along!"

Since joining the band I've tried to get them to play some of the more obscure material from their massive catalogue. And through the tours in the 1990s and more lately with the Forty Licks tour, I've been increasingly successful. Of course, it's not all my idea, but I try hard to encourage them to dive into that fabulous body of work. In the process and just by virtue of the fact that I've been there so long now, I've have become a lot closer, both personally and profession-ally, with Mick, Keith, Ronnie, Charlie, and all the people behind the scenes without whom the organization simply wouldn't exist.

I love them all dearly. I came onto the Stones scene after the real bad-boy period that's legend to the band, so thankfully I don't have any secrets to hide about anyone — including myself! The primal element is still there, but the secret for survival seems to be to leave the animal on the stage, and that's generally what the Rolling Stones are about these days. It's a gig that everyone takes very seriously. It's interesting: they are all serious about the music, the recordings, and the performances, but they don't take themselves too seriously. They know it's only rock 'n' roll. On the private plane and between gigs, it's not a constant party, but, believe me, we do have a great time! And there are certainly some unbelievable and fantastic parties that we all go to. There were a number of incredible parties just on this past tour. There was a wild party thrown in Los Angeles that was a "Rolling Stones Fashion Show." The band had released an expanded line of clothing designed by Chrome Hearts that included lots of flashy clothing, including women's underwear. Lots of beautiful girls modeled those goods, much to the delight of all the guys in attendance. Ronnie and Jo had a huge party at their house in London. It was held on their beautiful grounds, with lots of specially decorated tents all around. There was reggae music pumped everywhere and a couple of dance floors. One of the main features of their party was a light show that was constantly going on, being projected on the trees and shrubs of their grounds, making everything look alive and moving. They also had several special food areas throughout, as well as a health-drink bar along with the regular bars.

Mick had a big sixtieth birthday bash in Prague at a place called the Duplex during Forty Licks. This was a big deal, as you might imagine. Lots of his friends and family flew in from all over the world. Even his dad, Joe, was there, enjoying the scene. All the band and crew came, and of course there were hundreds of fans outside the place just trying to catch a glimpse of some of the band and other celebrities going inside. Lots of famous people were there. There was a big bar and lots of food everywhere. Very loud

An invitation to just one of the great parties on the Licks tour.

dance music was playing all the time, and lots of folks (including Mick) danced the whole night and into the morning. During our stay in Paris, Rupert and his daughter Dora threw a biggie at a club called La Suite. This was held one night after a show and was right across from our hotel. Dora had these people dressed up in white butterfly costumes on stilts with wands in their hands outside the club. That made it hard to miss! Inside we were treated to open bars, fantastic food, and cool dance music. Of course, there were lots of

French celebrities and chic in-crowd types there along with all of us. There was a bash in London given by the band and Virgin Records. That one was quite a rave. When we walked in, we were frisked by "police" (hired actors in costume), and then we were told to go see the "doctors" in the next room. When we got in that room, there were more actors dressed as doctors and nurses. They did a quick "exam," with stethoscopes and such, prescribing that we needed drinks and fun. The next room had a group of black guys that were in body paint, naked except for some loincloths, sort of grabbing and groping people as they went by. From there we all walked down a set of stairs and into a corridor of "tongues." This was a hallway with curtains on either side about forty feet long, and behind the curtains were people you couldn't see except for their arms, which were covered with big red patent leather Stones tongues. Everyone was "licked" as they walked through the corridor. Then we walked into the first main party room, and as we walked in we realized that everything we'd gone through was being projected on a big screen in the room. Everyone that came in went through all of this, and it was all on camera, so everybody was sort of announced. And there were quite a few celebrities and friends of the band there that night, too, and I simply ran out of time to speak with everyone, including Jeff Beck, who spent most of the night there chatting, which was a little unusual since he's a fairly shy guy. There was a great band playing in the main room, and several bars set up throughout the huge club. It was quite a party! During the course of the tour there was a Super Bowl party, a World Cup party, a Final Four party, a World Series party, parties thrown by friends, parties for some of the children's birthdays, parties for birthdays of folks in the band, and several great parties thrown to celebrate Ronnie's terrific artwork. There was one art show in Hong Kong during the last time we were all together that was wonderful. Of course, we had parties for no apparent reason at all, so don't think that the reputation is entirely undeserved! But it's not the 1970s anymore, and it's certainly not the kind of decadence of the past.

We're also generally paired off with our families during the course of the tour. Tour director Cohl is often on the phone doing business, as is Mick. Keith is often reading. Besides music, his other great passion is reading, which is why the guy knows so much about just about any topic you'd care to mention — from history to geography and beyond. The riff meister is a human library. I swear!

I'm usually with Rose Lane just relaxing and talking. If Rosie's not with me, I catch up on my reading or perhaps do some writing, computer work, or think about future set lists. All of us, Bobby Keys, the other guys in the horn section — Mike Davis, Tim Ries, and Kent Smith — Darryl, Lisa, Bernard, Blondie, all the staff and crew, as well as the Rolling Stones certainly hang with each other and each other's families throughout the whole tour. We often eat together, travel together, talk on the plane and the busses, at the rehearsals and backstage. On off days we go shopping together, go sightseeing

On stage or off, we like to hang together.

Keith and I catch some rays in the Med.

I love it when Rose Lane can join me on the road and enjoy some of the romantic and exotic locales.

Credit: © Patti Hansen

together, go to concerts to hear other artists sometimes, or go to a
theater or to another type of event. We have a committee called the
TAC (Tour Activity Committee) that helps to put together fun
outings from time to time. We share our thoughts, our secrets, our
feelings. It certainly is a big family, and we all care for each other.
But the odd thing is that when the tour or the recording comes to the
end, then it's over and everyone scatters. Sure, we stay in touch a bit,
but we all have our own situations and our own families. And we all
look forward to seeing each other the next time the big machine
cranks up. And it isn't a bad gig. It's everything you can imagine it
would be and more. I won't say it's a job; I have had a duty with and
a loyalty to the band for more than two decades.

I don't discount that it's a legendary band and that this means a
lot to millions of fans — something that adds to my already substantial work ethic of wanting to
give my all to whatever I'm
doing. But it isn't the early
1970s any more, either. I think
everyone is more tuned into
the gig these days. We go to a
sound check at four o'clock
and then stay at the gig waiting
for show time — four or five
hours later. We pass the time
chatting, doing some work, and
preparing for the show. Keith
and Ronnie play snooker or
pool, and Mick and Darryl like to play video games as a way of
relaxing before the gig. I catch up on my emails, practice a little, meet
with some friends, or just kick back and hang. We all have a bite to
eat. The last hour before show time, we're all getting pretty antsy to
get up there and play. In a sense, it adds to the anticipation and the
excitement for us. Finally, when the moment arrives, the lights go
down, the crowd goes wild and the music starts. Just another day at
the office!

Credit: © Chuck Leavell Archive

Mick working with Lisa and Bernard.

Of course, many fans and reporters I encounter still think it's the bad old days and are looking for dirt that isn't there. They ask me, "What's Mick Jagger really like?" or "What's Keith Richards, Ronnie, or Charlie really like?"

Mick and I – well everyone – had to bundle up for an outdoor October concert in the way-north Canadian city of Edmonton.

Most of the time, I answer with a quip: "I'm not telling."

But, since you've gone to all the trouble to buy and read this book, I'll tell you. Just keep it between us, though, OK? The truth is: they're people, just like you and me. They happen to be extremely talented at what they do and they've become inordinately famous and wealthy because of that. I wouldn't mind their bank balance, but I don't think I'd like their fame; I believe a lot of the time it's a burden for them. I mean, it's nice to be appreciated, but when you can't go to the store or a restaurant without causing a scene, being stared at, photographed, and hounded for autographs — sometimes by people who are asking not because they're fans but because they figure they can make a few bucks on eBay from a few strokes of your pen on a picture — success and that kind of high achievement begin to exact a toll that I don't think I'd care to pay.

As people, they're still hurt by lies, insults, and betrayals; they're no more immune than you or I to the tragedies of life like the death of a loved one. They're friends and, like many in the Stones organization, family. And we are a family. We play on each other's solo works — Bobby Keys

The great Bobby Keys ... one of the Rolling Stones' secret weapons!

and Lisa on mine; Bernard on Woody's and Mick's solo work. And I've been on Mick's, Keith's, and Ronnie's solo projects. As individuals they're all kind and have their own individual levels of personal generosity about them. I was blown away once when the band gave me a vintage National Steel guitar worth thousands. I'd seen it when guitar tech Pierre de Beauport was looking at some other guitars for the band and had a bunch of instruments lined up backstage. Pierre saw how much I like it and told Keith. He had the band buy it for me. I was speechless.

Naturally, like all families there are sometimes tensions that only intimacy can create. It's no secret that part of what makes the band tick is the rivalry and uncommon brotherhood of Mick and Keith. They are very different people whose history will link them forever, whether they're on the same stage together or not.

But a lot has changed over the years. It's like a combination of Barnum & Bailey and Microsoft these days. It's big business, high risk, and there is a lot of money at stake with every tour, every album, and every theatrical release. The two hours or so on stage have lost none of its allure. In fact, I believe the band has gotten consistently better over the years. The greatest rock 'n' roll band in the world? Some nights, yes. Other nights … well … there are "moments." During the Forty Licks tour, film director Marty Callner, who was shooting the *Four Flicks* DVD set, told me about a conversation he had with the cameraman who shadows Keith (for the image projected on the big screen behind the band at stadium gigs). Marty asked him, "So, what happens when Keith makes one of those blatant mistakes on an intro or some other part of a song … what do you see him do?"

"Well, when that happens," the camerman told Marty, "Keith sort of looks up towards the sky with a twinkle in his eye and a bit of a scowl on his face, as if to say to the music gods, 'Fuck you!'"

God, I loved that! This is exactly the attitude and response that makes the Stones the Stones — the unpredictably of musicians, equipment, weather, technicians, and even audiences is what gives any live performance its edge. And the tripping over ourselves —

With Keith before a Licks show.

songs beginning in wrong keys or switching mysteriously part way through — is just part of the magic. In fact, I sort of half-seriously think the Stones should put out a CD of these "precious moments!" It would probably be a huge seller! Hey, if you've checked out the *Four Licks* DVD set, in the backstage footage just before we go on stage Keith quips something like, "Well, I'm going to go and screw up. Who wants to join in?"

Because it's about the feeling, the groove, not trying to render chart-perfect renditions of the studio recordings. Feeling? Groove? That means Keith Richards. Keith is the musical director of the Rolling Stones, as far as I'm concerned. He's the bandmaster. But they do look to me for certain duties, like setting some tempos, counting the band in to some songs, giving cues when certain parts of songs come in, and also occasionally helping with arrangements.

Another day at the office.

I've got the theory of the big picture. Throwing solos at me doesn't make sense for the Rolling Stones. After all, as Keith reminds all of us quite often, The Rolling Stones is a *guitar* band! What does make sense is to blend in and sprinkle the fairy dust in there ... Stu's "diamond tiaras." And that's those sparkly bits on the

Charlie, Keith and Mick during rehearsals.

high end of the piano that pop up occasionally in those boogie-woogie songs. And that's part of what this gig is all about from my end.

Musical navigator is the only way I can really think to describe my role. I keep track of all these hundreds of songs. We'll be in a rehearsal, and Mick or Keith will say, "What's the bridge? I can't remember the bridge." I keep charts and info so that it makes it easy for them to be reminded of what the bridge is or what some of the other changes might be. I work with the horns, with Darryl, Bernard, Lisa and Blondie ... whatever it takes to make the big picture. In that respect I'm given a lot of reign and freedom. Since joining the band I've tried to get them to play some of the more obscure material from their massive catalogue. And, tour by tour, it seems to be working. I remember going all the way back to the 1982 European tour — Bill Wyman's last — he signed my tour program, adding, "Thanks for all the cues!"

My role is to be a catalyst between the guitars and the rhythm section. The way I do that depends on the song, of course, but in general, that holds fairly true. To me, Keith is like the Count Basie of rock 'n' roll. Thankfully, he's not some flash guitar slinger, but he certainly throws in some powerful solos when it's needed, and he's the guy who holds the band together and directs it. Mick does that too on some tunes, but as he's out there working the crowd, it's usually Keith that is pushing the band.

The incredible Bernard Fowler and me during a soundcheck.

It's not chaos up there on stage, but there are times when someone is unsure of what's coming up and will lose track of how many bars have gone by and get a bit panicked. Hey, let's face it, there are literally hundreds of songs in the Stones catalogue and on every tour I've done we've rehearsed more and more so that we might be ready to toss them into the mix. It isn't easy to keep 160 or so tunes straight in your head — whether or not you wrote them!

So I do my best to look around all the time, giving little nods of yes or no about a section of a song coming up. I know the arrangements very well and don't mind helping. I have two huge books, full of notes and charts on all the songs. A lot of this I keep in my head, but if we haven't done a song in a long time I too need to review it so I can be on top of the situation.

As Bobby Keys described in an interview, "With the band being the size that it is, and with so many arrangements to remember, somebody has to be in charge, and Chuck has performed a real service to the band in that regard. He is the person that you look to for the count-offs, and during rehearsals, he'll point out the adjustments and changes from song to song. He fulfills his role very well, and it's something that no one had done before him. When I joined the band, Nicky Hopkins was the piano player, and there was no musical leader as such. Keith and Mick were always the guys you looked to, and when they quit playing, you quit playing! Back then, the arrangements of the songs and the presentation of the shows were a lot different, so now, someone has to be in charge, and Chuck serves a real necessary musical purpose for the Rolling Stones."

Darryl, too, has spoken very flatteringly about me in the press: "I think that traffic administrator is a really good term for what Chuck does when we're playing. He is also the keeper of forms, and everybody will kind of go to him and ask, 'What do we do after that? Where do we go from here?' Chuck always has the answer, and with his personality, he is the perfect guy for the job."

Sometimes Mick is so engaged with working the crowd that he forgets where he is in a tune, so he might look at me for help. Charlie may not feel confident about where a break is to occur. Just think about the size of those stadium stages. If Mick, Ronnie, or Keith, go running off to stir up the crowd, Charlie can almost go a whole song without seeing anyone but me or Darryl, so I'll give him a nod or help with a hand movement.

The Stones is a guitar band, loose and open. I think that the guitar playing actually reflects the whole attitude of the Rolling Stones. They are not afraid to have fun and have a laugh. Some bands like to put on that look: "Oh, we're going to be really serious and just play the music." The Stones work hard to get things right, but they also like to throw it up in the air, have a good time, and not be afraid to make a mistake and laugh about it if they do. With a lot of bands, if you get to a spot in a song and it falls apart, everybody looks at each other real seriously, like it is a real terrible thing. When the Stones do it, they look at each other and laugh, like somebody farted. That is a real part of the attitude of this band: they have fun with the music. After all, it's only rock 'n' roll!

Ronnie recently told a reporter that he's glad he's sober — a better player — and joked about some of the mistakes that kept happening on the Forty Licks tour. "Sometimes on stage," Woody says of Keith, "He'll start the wrong song. It's usually any song with 'rock' in it — it could be *If You Can't Rock Me*, *It's Only Rock 'n' Roll*, or *Rocks Off* or any one of a number of others. He still plays great even if he's out of it."

One moment that stands out for me from that tour was a massive blunder that was absolutely hilarious. Keith was supposed to start playing *Brown Sugar* and was wearing the guitar for that song. If you've ever wondered why the guys change guitars all the time, it's because they're in different tunings for different songs and are for different sounds and tones. Anyway, Keith started to play *Jumping Jack Flash* instead in the wrong key, G, two steps down from where it should have been. Pierre (Keith's guitar tech) ran out with the right guitar for *Jumping Jack Flash*, but by this time Ronnie had joined in and took it to the key of C. By the time Keith was back in action we wound up playing *Jumping Jack Sugar* in three different keys. I think that was a landmark and should go down in Stones history! The philosophy isn't about getting it perfect — it's about having fun and picking yourself up if you fall down having that fun. What a great outlook.

One thing that has really helped me along the way was getting to know some of the guys that had the seat before me personally, like Nicky Hopkins. Back in 1982, during my first tour with the band, Nicky came to the show at Wembley Stadium, and Ronnie came up to me and said, "You've got to meet Nicky." I went, "Oh my God! I'm a nervous wreck. I can't meet Nicky Hopkins." Ronnie told me, "Naw, come on. It's cool," so I went and met Nicky, did that "I am not worthy" thing, and he was just the nicest guy. He asked me, "Would you like to have lunch over the next couple of days?" I told him sure, so we got together at this little sandwich shop, and we had this fantastic

Credit: Chuck Leavell Archive

Mick and me during band introductions.

afternoon. He told me some stories from his time with the band and asked me how things were going for me. We talked music for hours and had a marvelous time together. We remained friends after that, writing several letters and occasionally exchanging phone calls until his unfortunate passing in 1994. It helped me so much to get to know the man a little bit and not just listen to his stuff on the records, something I tried to express in a tribute letter I wrote for his wake. Bobby Keys so kindly read it for me since I couldn't attend myself.

Getting to meet Billy Preston really helped, too. I mean, I had seen Billy with the Stones in the 1970s in Auburn, Alabama, when Mick Taylor was still in the band, and I got to see Billy play with Ray Charles when I was a kid, so meeting him was a big thrill for me. Getting to know the guys has been a help for me in trying to translate what they did and to do it with respect.

Through the years I've been faced with my share of frustrations and disappointments with the band. I'm often disappointed with where the keyboards end up in the mix in some of the recordings and performances. I remember Keith inviting me to his room one night to listen to the mix for what would become the *No Security* live CD. When *Waiting on a Friend* came on and I heard how much I'd been taken out of the mix it kind of knocked the wind out of my sails. Don't get me wrong — it's an honor to work with these guys and most of the time it's a hell of a lot of fun. And I know that I'm not going to get out front with a lot of solos with the Stones. That's not my place, and that's OK with me. I get plenty of licks in. Some tunes, such as *Loving Cup*, *Monkey Man*, and *Can't Always Get What You Want* have great piano parts. And songs like *All Down the Line*, *Rip this Joint*, and *Brown Sugar* have piano raging all the way through. I get to sing a lot of harmony too, and that's fun.

It's just disappointing to hear the contribution I'm making when I'm on that stage or in the studio being brought down a few notches when the end mixes are done. That having been said, there are also times when for whatever reason the keys do make it up there in the mix. I was very pleased with the mix of the *Stripped* record, and somewhat surprised to hear myself so clearly. And there have been other tracks through the years that I thought put me in a nice space in terms of the mixes. Certainly, I understand that mixing is a subjective thing, and someone has to have the last say about it. It can be difficult to sit on the sidelines after the tracks are cut and have to accept what comes. But all in all, I'm a happy member of the Stones family, and the only reason I care to disagree about things with the family sometimes is because I want the music to be right, and I have to speak my mind about it because I love the music and love them so much.

There was a sense on the Forty Licks tour that it might have been the last of its size for the Stones. What else can they do? That tour was another ground-breaking effort — playing stadiums, arenas, and theaters all in the same major cities. No one had done that before. Who knows? Every tour I've been on has supposedly been the last one for sundry reasons. But in Zurich, I remember Keith telling me that he envisions a future in which the Stones take a more toned-down approach, playing a few months and then taking a few months off. Yeah, right. By the time this book's in your hands I'll bet another 100-plus-date tour has been planned and a new CD of future classic Rolling Stones tunes is in the works. There's tons of stuff in the famous Stones vault, dozens of songs that I'm on and no guessing how many more that I'm not, dating back to the band's beginnings. I know Keith wanted to dive right back in after the Forty Licks tour, explaining to one reporter that he and Mick don't get along only when the Stones aren't active.

"Now that we're working together, everything's fine."

But during our Paris, 2002 sessions, everyone was really friendly and Ronnie was looking and playing great after his stint in rehab. There were a lot of numbers that were for the most part finished, and some that were sketches. One we did with Keith was a little boogie number called *Smooth 180*. I hope it gets polished and released, since it's a fun track. Keith told me he'd written it because he was angry about a few things in his life and was going to send out some blistering letters but, at the last moment, "pulled a smooth 180" and decided to play it cool. It was this notion of changing his mind that gave him the idea for the song, he says. I always think it's a blast to hear about where Keith finds his inspiration.

The analogy has been made so many times about a "marriage" between Mick and Keith, but I think it's true. With marriages, some of them work, and some of them don't, but all marriages have challenges, and certainly the partnership between Mick and Keith has had them. The big testimony is that after forty years, they are still working together, and that is an amazing thing, and such a rarity. Is there tension there? You bet there is. There are times when you can cut the tension with a knife. Somehow, though, at the end of it all, that tension breaks into laughter. There will be a tense moment going down, and then one of them will look around and grin or giggle, and that's it, it's over. In the end, they always find a way to diffuse things.

You know, the Rolling Stones are a family that you can always come back to. No matter what you do, and whether the other family members like it or don't like it, they are always there for you to come home to. In other words, Keith may not like the fact that Mick goes out and does these solo projects, and it may not be what he wishes Mick would do, but in the end, as long as the family still gets back together, it's OK. It's not just that they realize that they can make more money as the Rolling Stones than they can as solo artists, they just realize that this band is bigger than each of them.

Let's face it: the songwriting relationship, like many songwriting relationships, has changed. You saw it with Lennon-McCartney at a certain point. They began to write more and more separately and would then bring those songs into the band to have them worked up, and that is the case with Jagger-Richards. Maybe there is a lot less collaborative songwriting these days, but there were a couple of tunes that we just did in Paris where they were kind of forced to sit down together and put both their thoughts into one song. That was a beautiful thing to see. So collaboration still goes on, but it's a little bit more separate these days than it used to be in the beginning.

It is amazing to me to watch how they react to each other's material, and their willingness to listen to one another. One may not particularly feel that a tune from the other is fantastic, but they are both willing to listen to each other. They allow it to evolve, and they work together in that manner. They are always willing to listen to a song and to give it a fair shot. Whether the song belongs to Mick or Keith, it has a chance to become something.

On stage, if ever there's a war going on, it's between Mick and Keith over tempos. Mick likes them up while Keith prefers them more laid back, so I often get glares from one or the other, depending on what speed the song goes. If they're both glaring, then I know I'm right because I've hit it right in the middle! Not that this is always good. I remember one show in Rio when Keith ran up to me after *Ruby Tuesday* with a glare and said, "If you ever count that song in that fast again I'll slit your fucking throat." Of course, I counted it in as I always do, even using a metronome to make sure I had it right, but Keith still wanted it slower, and that night he let me know it in his own peculiar — and, despite how it sounds if taken literally, funny — way.

The late, great, Chuch McGee, who passed away during Toronto rehearsals for the Forty Licks tour.

Like past tours, the Stones decided that Toronto was the place to rehearse for Forty Licks. We set up shop in a building in the downtown area, which was a comfortable place to work and we just getting settled in. We were just a few days into it when tragedy struck — another death in the family. Chuch Magee, who had been Ronnie's guitar tech for more than thirty years and who had been the band's backline crew chief for nearly as long — one of the guys the fans never saw who nevertheless made the show happen — died tragically before our very eyes. From my diary:

> It seems as if an entire lifetime has gone by the last 10 days. The last thing in the world that any of us expected was to lose one of our own here. Our dear friend Chuch Magee had a heart attack July 18. We had rehearsed up to dinner time. Chuch had complained of heartburn and sore left arm (I didn't know this until after). Classic signs of a heart attack. He got

sick after he ate, and decided to lay down for a nap on one of the road cases filled with guitars. Then someone noticed he was convulsing. They ran to get Torje Eike, the band's physical trainer. Torje performed CPR while the paramedics were called, and they arrived very quickly. They continued to work on him ... finally using electric shock to try and bring him back. But Chuch was long gone. All of us watched this happen. So surreal. I had come down after dinner and was practising on the piano, doing some boogie-woogie while all of this transpired; so it's likely that the last music he heard was that. Guess I serenaded him home. An incredible shock to all of us, Ronnie was standing near Chuch calling out to him when the paramedics were working on him. Others called out, too, me included. It was Ronnie that phoned Clare (Chuch's wife) to tell her. Jo Wood (Ronnie's wife) and Keith spoke to her as well. We were all crying, in shock. Of course, the next few days were tough on all of us. We've all been grieving.

We had to start back rehearsals on Monday, which was a difficult thing for all of us. We all flew to Marquette, MI on Wednesday for his memorial service. It was held at the Lutheran church that he and Clare were members of. It was a very fitting service for Chuch. Lots of people there to say goodbye. A wonderful tribute shrine was set up in the church lobby with lots of photos of him through the years. It was said that he had two families, his with Clare at home, and his family with us. Clare said she was so glad that Chuch was with one of his families when he passed. Ronnie, Keith, Darryl, Mick and I played *Amazing Grace*. Don't know why Charlie didn't play ... I guess he just thought it best to sit out. Beautiful words were spoken about him and then it was time to let go. We flew back, arriving in Toronto around 10 p.m. It's been an emotionally draining time for all of us. We know we have to carry on ... Chuch would want nothing less, but we'll all have a scar on our own hearts from this.

Chuch was such a sweet guy and we had so much in common. He, too, preferred to live close to the land. He and Clare, an artist and seamstress, were married for about eighteen years and lived on the upper peninsula of Michigan. When he wasn't on the road with the Stones or with Ronnie's solo shows, he loved fishing, snowmobiling, and hiking in the woods with his dogs. He also volunteered time and effort to local community youth groups, helping found the Cedar Tree Institute, which works with troubled kids and has so far planted more than 1,000 trees in Northern Michigan. A lot of people — in the world of rock 'n' roll and the real world — are going to miss him forever.

Chuch and me in Paris.

The Stones didn't want to go back to the building where Chuch had died, so we moved to a different facility in Toronto and carried on with rehearsals. No matter what, we need a big room. Mick likes to move around a lot, and we all

Darryl, Pierre de Beauport, Chuch and me in Paris.

need a bit of space. The crew needs room to work because there is obviously a tremendous amount of stuff for them to do.

It can't have been easy for him, but the crucial role that Chuch played was taken over by his good friend Johnny Starbuck. In Toronto, I remember, he went through all of the guitars that Ronnie, Keith, and Mick play. The total count: seventy-seven. That's seventy-seven guitars that need to be maintained, tuned, cleaned, and cased. That's a lot of work, and it requires a lot of space. The monitors need to be set up and tweaked so that everyone is happy with the sound. When we're on tour, there are about 100 monitors spread around that stage, so space is very important in rehearsal. Every day, the band is in there, concentrating on what we're doing. We discuss the songs. The crew is busy. It's a very active time. Keith's tech, Pierre de Beauport; Dave Rouze, who does Mick's guitars; Mike Cormier, Charlie's tech; Johnny Starbuck; Russell Schlagbaum, who does the B-Stage guitars; and the tech that has worked with me for the last couple of tours, Peter Wiltz, all have their hands full during the rehearsals and during the tour, and they do an amazing job. All the other guys like Robbie McGrath, our house engineer; Christopher Wade Evans, our monitor mixer; Jake Berry, the head of the production personnel; and all the hundreds of other hard-working folks on the tour are much appreciated by all of us in the band. The Stones crew is the best there is, and that's what you'd expect!

If rehearsal is going to delayed by a business meeting or something, I'll take the time to get together with Bobby Keys and the horn players to go over a few things, so there is always something going on.

Just a couple of Ronnie's cool song lists from the Toronto rehearsals.

Ronnie does these cool boards chronicling the songs we're working on. The guy's a great artist and isn't satisfied just jotting down some notes, so he's always got grease-pen boards mounted on easels. We'll start listing songs, and he'll list the key the song is in and draw something fun with each song. For *Dead Flowers*, he'll put wilted roses next to the title; for the last single, *Don't Stop,* he put a stop sign up there. By the end of rehearsals in Toronto we ended up with more than 20 of these boards lined up in the room, with more than 100 songs on them, and they were all very colorful because Ronnie constantly changes pens. He creates an on-going document in front of everybody, and we all can start to get a feel for what is going to make it into the set, and what is going to be dropped.

Credit: © Chuck Leavell Archive

The boys at the Toronto rehearsals.

The Forty Licks tour was the best yet. In part it was because the band was playing so well. The Roseland Ballroom show was a real standout as I recall, but as the *Four Flicks* DVD attests, the band played well in each venue, and we did some songs that the band either had never done live before or had only done rarely. We played tunes like *She Smiled Sweetly, Can't Turn Loose, That's How Strong My Love Is* …. We rocked around the world again, playing in some places that the band had never been before, like India. We were diverted from doing gigs in Hong Kong, Singapore, and Beijing because of the SARS outbreak, but we did finally make it to Hong Kong in November of 2003. A few days of rehearsals and then two shows at an open harbor festival. At the second show, I was quite surprised to see former President Bill Clinton sitting just a few arm-lengths away from me in the wings. He was in China at the time working on his AIDS awareness campaign and stayed an extra day to catch the show. It was nice to see him again. The president had introduced us as at a special show we'd done in Los Angeles earlier in the tour. That show was a benefit held at the Staples Center and was sponsored by the National Resource Defense Council. The idea was to raise awareness about global warming and other challenges we face in our environment. Clinton made an engaging short speech, then introduced the band. I was able to slip him a copy of my book *Forever Green* before it was all over.

Maybe it was the last time I'll share a stage with the Stones on a year-or-longer, world-wide tour. Maybe not. But it's been an experience I'll never forget. Sitting at my keyboard watching Mick perform. There's no one I've ever worked with who can hold an audience's attention like Mick. There is a passion that goes into every chord Keith plays. I love looking over there and seeing Charlie smile and hearing that wonderful back-beat that no one else could play. You hear fans say that the golden era was when Brian

Credit: © 2003 Jane Rose

As always, putting more than a little feeling into it!

Jones was in the band or when Mick Taylor was in the band. Well, I don't know. Ronnie Wood came in and kicked ass, and it's been a golden era since then, too. It's all golden to me. Every tour I've done with the Stones was supposedly "the last time," according to everyone but the Stones themselves. I think they'll go on for years in one manner or another.

The point is that this is a band with an extraordinary work ethic. All you have to do is look at the body of material; it's insane how broad, deep, and great it is. There are so many incredible songs to enjoy. And they're poised for more. One reason is the passion. They love writing songs, recording them, and performing them. And because of this they've just become better and better at their craft.

Keith, as usual, is a little more blunt. He says criticism of the band continuing is "pure physical envy. We shouldn't hear, 'How dare they defy logic?' People want to pull the rug out from under you because they're bald and fat and can't move for shit. We keep touring for the same reason dogs lick their balls. If I didn't think it would work, I would be the first to say, 'Forget it.' We play rock 'n' roll because it's what turned us on. Muddy Waters and Howlin' Wolf — the idea of retiring was ludicrous to them. You keep going. And why not?"

It's a trip, man, really. To think: I was a kid playing the YMCA in Tuscaloosa when the Rolling Stones were appearing on *Ed Sullivan* for the first time.

Music is the vernacular of the human soul.

Geoffrey Latham

A Little on the Side

One of the many great things about playing with the Rolling Stones is that, generally, their productions are so huge and take so much money and effort that there's often a pretty decent break between projects.

Traditionally we're on the road for twelve to eighteen months, and everybody needs a long break after that. More practically, when you're on the road that long it takes a huge toll on not only your family life, but attracts the very unwelcome attention of the tax man. When you've played the world countless times and are nearing what many would consider retirement age, that kind of hassle is just not worth it, in my opinion.

But over the two decades I played with the Stones, these long hiatus periods have given me the chance to really stretch out as a session player — and a couple of times have offered teasing possibilities of rejoining the Brothers.

In fact, it was just as I was being considered for my first touring gig with the Stones, back in 1982, that I was approached once again by the Allman Brothers management with an offer of putting the band back on the road.

Tentatively, I agreed, since I didn't land the gig playing with the Stones on the North American leg of the tour. But the band was with Arista at the time, having landed there, like Sea Level, in the wake of the demise of Capricorn, and there was a lot of tension with label honcho Clive Davis. He didn't want to pay the band to come up with new material and go into the studio. But we worked together anyway, and came up with some stuff that I thought was pretty good. Some of it appeared on later ABB and Gregg solo projects.

Rose Lane and I were expecting the birth of our second daughter, Ashley, as well, and I was eager to stick close to home. Then I got the call from Mick Jagger about the European leg of the Stones tour, and I told the boys in the ABB that it was time to get things going or call it off. I had to record a new album with them or bail because there was no way I was going to turn down the Stones gig. But Davis wasn't going for the bait, and the entire reunion project fizzled as I headed to Europe.

The Allmans scattered. Gregg went off to play with the Toler Brothers while Dickey and Butch went out opening for the Charlie Daniel's band. Along the way, Dickey got intrigued by some of the acts he saw on the road and started to develop a plan for a maverick band that included fiddle, sax, guitar, organ, and other instruments. He went through a long series of players to hand pick the band he wanted, and by the end of the summer, I was free from my Stones commitments to join them. I didn't know what the result would be when I got back. I didn't know if Dickey and Butch would be interested in pursuing it any further, so I was very pleased when they told me they still wanted us to do something together.

It was a chance to re-establish something with the guys. During the time that I had spent with Dickey in the Allman Brothers, he had reached out to me on several occasions. He had invited Rose Lane and me to go to the Indian reservations with him, and that allowed us to become close for the first time back in that era. That was something I always cherished about Dickey, so when both he and Butch personally called and told me that they wanted me involved with this project, it meant a great deal to me. I saw a rekindling of some good relationships, and I wanted to pursue it. Circumstances dictated that rather than it turning into the Allman Brothers again, it turned into Betts, Hall, Leavell, and Trucks.

By the time we debuted in Fort Worth, Texas, on Dec. 2, 1982, we had Dickey on guitar and vocals, Jimmy Hall on sax and vocals, me on keyboards, Butch Trucks on drums, David "Rook" Goldflies on bass, and Danny Parks on violin. For lack of a better name, we came up with BHLT. Amongst ourselves, we called it the "Sandwich Band," simply because of how the name sounded. But make no mistake, this was no musical fast food. We played a brilliantly unique blend of music, I think. Rock, country, swing, Southern boogie, and R&B. We played some of Dickey's solo songs like *Nothing You Can Do*. I sang lead vocal on his song *Rain*. We also tossed in some of the ABB classics like *Jessica*, *Southbound*, *Ramblin' Man*, and Jimmy Halls' *Cadillac Tracks*.

We had a strong band, and it cooked. In fact, I've always said in the years since that BHLT was the best band you've never heard of. Aside from a few bootleg board tapes from performances in New York, there is no audio recording of the band. We did some demos of a series of original tunes, including *Stop Knockin' on My Door*, *Pick a Little Boogie*, *Love Needs a Hero*, *Memories*, *Need Somebody Bad Tonight*, *Lorraine*, *Keep on Rockin*, *Run Away*, *One-Track Mind*, *Rock*

Credit: Chuck Leavell Archive

The best band you never heard: Jimmy Hall, Dickey Betts, David Goldflies, Butch Trucks, me and Danny Parks ... BHLT.

and Roll Town, Still in Love, and a great rocker called *No One to Run With,* which would eventually, about fifteen years later, found its way onto the Allman Brothers album *Where It All Begins.*

Most of the material came from Dickey, and I think he had a very good vision in terms of the music he was writing. BHLT kind of came along during Dickey's "Nashville period," and so he was writing songs with a country tinge to them. With Danny in the band, it made it interesting in that it was more like the Vassar Clements' *Highway Call* kind of thing. Jimmy of course added the R&B influence, and that made it just strange enough to get my attention. One thing I have always regretted is the fact that I didn't bring more to the table in terms of material. I really wanted to, but Dickey already had a good bit of material, and Jimmy had recorded the *Cadillac Tracks* album. I know in his mind he wanted to use BHLT as somewhat of a vehicle to promote it, and that was fair enough.

One of the unrealized potentials of BHLT was collaboration, and I think that if we would have had time to rehearse more, to explore song-writing options, the band would have gone to even more interesting heights. I was grateful that Dickey had all that material already lined up because we needed something new, and he had it. It would have been great to have written some songs collectively and to have explored those possibilites. We never made it happen, and that's too bad. I think it would have been quite intriguing, and that was the unrealized potential of BHLT.

One tune I got to step out on was *Rain.* I'd drastically rearranged it from the version Dickey wrote and we recorded on his *Highway Call* album. But I'd always loved the tune and one day I sat down alone and wondered how I'd play it by myself. It's such a beautiful piece of music that Dickey

Credit: Chuck Leavell Archive

We never did an album, but a couple of BHLT shows, like this one in the Blue Mountains, were filmed.

created. By the time I'd done my own rearrangement on it, most people didn't even realize it was Dickey's song. I ran it by him, and we included my version, and my vocal, into the set. He liked what I did with it, and he respected it. That's the kind of thing I was talking about. If we had more collaborative efforts, I think we could have come up with some really interesting things.

We didn't know what to do with the band — we shopped it around to record companies but came up dry. So we'd just head out on two-week runs to play clubs and colleges for people who wanted to hear us.

Credit: Chuck Leavell Archive

For trivia buffs, I remember that at one gig in Nashville, we had a young twenty-two-year-old guitarist get up and jam with us on *Ramblin' Man*. His name was Warren Haynes. I'd heard of Warren before, though an old buddy named Doc Fields, his manager at the time, and he kept me regularly informed on Warren's progress. Then, many years later, he called me to say that he'd landed a record deal for Warren and asked if I wanted to produce. Doc sent me a tape of demos and I was quite impressed with what I heard.

Warren Haynes and me (center) with Mark Richardson and Rick Meyer (front) in the studio recording Warren's first solo CD.

The only trouble was that I was just barely between Stones tours and didn't have much time, so I told them that if we did the record in Atlanta, I'd produce. Otherwise I'd have to decline, since I didn't have the time to travel to Nashville, where Doc and Warren were living.

We went through all of Warren's demos, discussed which ones should make the final cut and then put together a good team of musicians, rehearsed the material, and started the process of recording. It went so smoothly. I was pleased and so were Warren and Doc. The album was good, but it was on the Megaforce label, which is far better known for hardcore stuff. Warren came up with the title:

Tales of Ordinary Madness. Megaforce did at least give it some support, but in my mind it wasn't the right home for Warren and the CD. In any case, it didn't sell very well, although it did garner quite a lot of critical acclaim.

Warren, of course, ended up playing with the ABB before launching his own very influential, and terrific, spin-off Gov't Mule. He then kept the Mule kicking when he returned to the Brothers when Dickey was fired from the ABB in 2000.

I'll always be grateful to Warren for getting me in on a cool little jam one night that ended up turning into an important recording gig a little later on. I'd never heard of this cat named John Popper before and I was a little taken aback when I walked into the room and saw him in a wheel-chair. He'd been in a motorcycle crash and was recovering. I was also a little surprised to see Noel Redding, from the Jimi Hendrix Experience, playing bass. But it was one hell of a jam! I was downright freaked out when I heard Popper pull out a harp and start blowing.

A BHLT guest spot with the Marshall Tucker Band.

A short time later his band Blues Traveler invited me in on the sessions for their *Four* CD and I played on several tracks. The single, *Run-around* became a big hit, and it was cool to hear my B3 work on the radio. It had been a while since I had been on a hit single, and it sure felt good. A fine experience I am proud to have been involved with.

Looking back on BHLT, however, I agree with the critics who said we were playing the right music at the wrong time. It was the height of new wave, electronic music and what we were doing was just not what radio wanted at the time. I myself remember very well traveling in the vans and doing some great shows at the Bottom Line in New York City, The Pier in North Carolina, and many other clubs. At the Bottom Line, we'd do two shows a night, and they would be sold-out. We really kicked up some dust there. We were a tight group. It lasted just seven months and in the end pretty much fizzled out. There are a few bootlegs out there and at least portions of two shows were videotaped, a gig at a rural East Coast club called the Coffee Pot and one of Charlie Daniels' Volunteer Jams at Bailey Stadium in Clinton, South Carolina. But we all had bills to pay, and BHLT wasn't producing the paychecks.

In a recent interview, Dickey himself said that, "We had a sound that I think would get attention on today's country radio. We had a unique blend of music, and Danny Parks had so much to do with that. He was a tremendous fiddle player, and that gave what we were doing such a flavor. You combine that with Jimmy Hall's vocals and sax, Chuck's piano playing, and Butch's drumming — I'll tell you what, we were some heavy hitters, man. I think we made tremendous music, but that was a rough time for what we were playing."

I have some great personal memories as well. Dickey had long been a bow hunter, and, on one of the tours, he took me out at my request to give me an introduction to the sport. When I got off the tour, Rose Lane bought me a bow for Christmas. I got a target, and I would go out there and shoot the bow, and I enjoyed it. I learned that from Dickey, and I really appreciate it. I remember Dickey getting me out on the golf course, and although I'm not a golfer, it was his way of reaching out to me and trying to find some social common ground. I enjoyed that, and it meant a lot to me. Butch was the same way. He was taking up golf at the same time, and he got me out there too. It never became a passion for me the way it did for them, but I went along with it, because I was trying to reach out, too. The reason for that was because we had such a great, strong, successful history together.

My era with the Allman Brothers Band was absolutely golden. It worked for the band as well, because *Brothers and Sisters* was the biggest record they've ever had. So what does that mean? It means we connected back then. We had a musical connection, we had a personal connection, and with BHLT, I saw the potential of having that again. But I guess it was just never meant to be.

In 1986 — a full decade after the band first split — tempers had cooled, and the Allman Brothers Band all got on stage again, this time in Nashville at Charlie Daniels' annual Volunteer Jam. A few months later we regrouped at New York's Madison Square Garden for an anti-drug benefit promoted by Bill Graham. From there, Gregg and Dickey did a weird tour with their respective solo bands, each night joining together to jam at the end. When that tour hit Macon, Butch, Jaimoe and I joined in. But there was no follow-up reunion.

About three years after that, Epic Records made the first move to put the (as near as possible) original band back together, and I got a call. Gregg and I had a long talk and soothed whatever lingering sourness there had been over my lawsuit against the Brothers. We got together in Florida and did a little bit of jamming, which I enjoyed. But things weren't spinning fast enough for me, and there was no formal agreement on the horizon when the Stones called me to rejoin them for their next album and tour. Again, I bowed out of the reunion.

Many years went by without much communication. Perhaps a call from Jaimoe or Butch, but not much contact otherwise. Still, the vibe between us was good, and I have to say that the Allman

The short tour I joined with Gov't Mule after the death of bassist Allen Woody.

Brothers have really had my admiration for the way they kept things together and carried on. Even though I got a couple of invites from Jaimoe and Butch to sit in, scheduling and timing seemed to keep it from happening. In March 2001 I got a call from Butch. He invited me to be a special guest at four of their shows during one of their acclaimed annual runs at the Beacon Theater in New York. It meant a lot to me and was a really special thing. It had been more than twenty years since I had played in public with the ABB, and it was a joyous reunion. The music rocked, and we renewed our friendships. It's a joy to know that even though we don't see each other for years at a time, that wonderful musical dialogue between all of us is still there.

"I was as happy as a lark when Chuck joined us at the Beacon," Butch said recently. "He's so level-headed, sensible ... the most stable guy I know. It feels so good to play with him. And, well, sorry to beat a dead horse, but ... *Jessica* ... hearing Chuck on that again ... the song just isn't the song without Chuck."

Gregg was just as sweet when asked about my guest spot with the Brothers. "I have always loved and respected Chuck and his wife Rose Lane," Gregg said. "The Beacon shows — it was great. It really was; it really was. Absolutely. We had some good jams at the Beacon."

It's always been a blast to sit in with Warren and Gov't Mule, as I've done on a few occasions. I was able to become a more integral part of the band when Warren and Matt Abts got me to commit to a tour after the tragic death of bass player Allen Woody in August 2000. I had already had the pleasure of playing with them on several tunes at a wonderful New Year's Eve show at the Ritz theater in Atlanta before Woody's death, which resulted

Credit: © Tamara Guo

Kicking with the Mule: On stage with Warren Haynes.

in the special packaged *Live with A Little Help From Our Friends* CD that was recorded that night. We stayed in touch, as we always had. Then came Woody's passing. Along with many other musicians and friends of the Mule, I called to offer my condolences about Woody and to encourage them to keep the Mule going. Ultimately, Warren and Matt decided to pay tribute to Woody by carrying on and taking a rather unique approach to the situation. They recruited not only one bass player, but many, to do a tribute CD to their departed bandmate. The result of this was two CDs called *The Deep End,* volume 1 and volume 2. I made cameos on both CDs, and there was quite a cast of bass players involved. From Jack Bruce to Bootsie Collins to John Entwistle and many, many more. Even though I played on a couple of tracks on the CDs, it was an honor to be involved. Warren and Matt asked me to go out on tour with them, and, with Dave Schools of Widespread Panic on bass, we hit the road. Since Dave had commitments with Widespread here and there, Otiel Burbridge of the ABB stepped in on some gigs. On a couple of special shows, one in New York and in San Francisco, we were able to get some of the other great bass players that had contributed to *Deep End* to play with the band, such as Tony Levin, Jack Casady, Les Claypool, Alphonso Johnson, and others. The Mule rocked across the country, playing lots of clubs and theaters over several months. It was a gas for me, and I've always loved both Warren and Matt and really admired the way they carried on after Woody's death. It was nice to be able to chip in for a while, and man, did we have some smokin' gigs.

Speaking of Dave Schools and Widespread Panic, I've been privileged to be a small part of their family through the years. We became friends a long time ago when they were doing their first recordings for Capricorn Records and Johnny Sandlin was producing. We stayed in touch, and I have been invited several times through the years to sit in with the guys. John Bell, Dave Schools, Sony Ortiz, JoJo Herman, Todd Nance, and Michael Houser are all great people and musicians, and every time we get together it's a groove. It was a truly sad day when Houser died of pancreatic cancer, but the band has carried on with George McConnell, who has done a great service since coming in. With Widespread, I wound up on a few recordings, including the *Live in The Classic City* record and a really swingin' pre-New Year's Eve show held on Dec. 30, 2003. We stay in touch, and I'm sure we'll have more fun together in the future.

My latter-day appearances with the Allman Brothers Band, Gov't Mule, and with Widespread Panic have been nothing but pure musical joy. Actually, I've had a lot of that on the extended Rolling Stones hiatus periods. Many will always stand out in my mind, but two of the most unusual were Legends shows, which took place in Rome, Italy, and Seville, Spain. Both of the shows — like a lot of my most successful session work — were under the tutelage of my old pal Dave Edmunds. Dave has been, in some ways, a real guardian angel.

Credit: Chuck Leavell Archive

Dream come true: Meeting Ray Charles in Rome.

The Italian show was called Legends of Rock and was really a masterstroke, shot in 1989. The idea was to duplicate the all-star lineup as it might have been on a Saturday night at Harlem's Apollo Theater in the 1950s. It was a smash. All the guys were in terrific form. Little Richard, B. B. King, Bo Diddley, Fats Domino, James Brown, Jerry Lee Lewis (OK, he probably wouldn't have been on the Apollo bill!), and Ray Charles. James Brown and Fats insisted on bringing their own bands, but I got the huge honor of backing up all the other artists, which was a dream come true. After all, it was seeing Ray Charles for the first time that led me down this path in the first place. We had a great time, both on and off the stage. What a gentleman.

We belted out fifteen songs in a one-hour set, followed by an all-star jam. Chuck Berry, it was said at the time by critics, was conspicuously missing, but I can't say I was surprised. He's not the easiest cat on the planet to get along with, and I'm sure there isn't an agent or attorney alive who could come up with a contract that he would have been happy with, though I know they tried to get him on the bill. Looking back at it now, he wasn't really missed. Everybody else was in such top form that it was a pleasure to be in the backup band.

Me with B. B. King at the Guitar Legends show in Spain.

I was thrilled to see that the show has been preserved on DVD for a whole new generation to check out these true legends. Dave did an amazing job as musical director and played most of the guitar for the show, though he somehow managed to stay in the background and let our musical idols bask deservedly in the spotlight. Interestingly, joining us in the backup band was the Uptown Horns, who'd I'd played with on the road with the Stones. We kicked off with James Brown, who did *Papa's Got a Brand New Bag* and *I Feel Good (I Got You)*, and continued with Bo Diddley and his signature song and *I'm A Man*.

Ray Charles then came out and did *Mess Around* and *I'm A Fool for You*. Playing with my hero was such a rush, I just can't tell you. When we rehearsed the day before, I was able to take a picture with him and to tell him how that concert I went to in Tuscaloosa, Alabama, so many years before had changed my life. I treasure that picture and that moment being with him. Of course, when we did the show he just ruled the night. He was so good, so soulful, and I was truly in heaven!

Little Richard then came out to do *Great Gosh A Mighty*, but before he sat at his piano he walked the stage, waving to the crowd and came up to me as the backup band was playing the intro. Apparently, before the show, Richard's musical director, Travis

Womack, had mentioned to him that I was living in Macon — Richards' birthplace. Before heading back to his own piano and getting into his tune, he walked right up to me and said "I didn't know you was from Macon Georgia, honey!" It was like we were supposed to stop and have a conversation … very funny. It was a great show.

Jerry Lee came out next and tore the place up with *The Wild One*, *Great Balls of Fire*, and *Whole Lotta Shakin' Goin' On*. He just set his own pace and went with it, and the band kept right there with him. We were all going for it, pushing the artists and loving every second of the music! It was great.

The very sweet Fats Domino came out next to a wonderfully warm cheer from the Italian crowd and played *I'm Ready* and then a splendid version of his big hit *Blueberry Hill*. Finally, B. B. King came

out and, well, was B. B., which is to say flawless. We played *Let the Good Times Roll* and others before everyone else joined us on stage for the ending jam. It was a dream come true to play with these guys … and all in one night!

Credit: Chuck Leavell Archive

Blur of blues … really letting go in Spain with Keith Richards, Steve Cropper and others.

Not long after, again on a break from the Stones, Dave was on the other end of the phone again. This time, we were headed for Seville to honor some of the world's great guitarists during a five-night Legends of Guitar festival that the Spanish government was funding in the fall of 1991 to help spark tourism for Expo 1992.

Some nights were dedicated to classical players such as Paco de Lucia and John McLaughlin, while there was a night of heavy metal guitar stars such as Joe Satriani and another with players as diverse as Joni Mitchell and Les Paul. Dave was the musical director behind the blues segment and asked me to join in on keyboards.

I agreed in a flash — what a thrill to back up Albert Collins, Robert Cray, Steve Cropper, Bo Diddley, B. B. King, and others. We rehearsed for a few days in London and then flew down to Spain for the shows. Ours was on Oct. 19, but I was quite surprised to see Keith Richards would be playing there a few days earlier. He had no idea I was coming to the gig either, and he invited me to sit in with him and Dylan on the night of the Oct. 17. The whole experience was great. We all hung out at this very cool hotel and stayed up so late each night talking. It was great to hear the legendary Steve Cropper talk about his early days working with Booker T. and the MGs and all the great Stax/Volt recording artists, in particular the songs that came about with Otis Redding and Wilson Pickett. He told us a funny story that when he was working on the tune *Knock on Wood*, all he did was take the intro from *Midnight Hour* and reverse it. Amazing!

*   *   *   *   *

Yet another fun gig I was involved in was a one-off Guitar Greats special at the Capitol Theater in Passaic, New Jersey, on Nov. 20, 1984. I was asked by my old friend John Scher, a great promoter and manager I had known from the ABB days. He had the concept and asked me to be musical director. We put together the core band with Michael Shrieve on drums,

Credit: Chuck Leavell Archive

Guitar Greats: Me looking over at the show's finale with Dickey Betts, Steve Cropper, Brian Setzer and Dave Edmunds (foreground).

Kenny Aaronson on bass, and myself on keys and as MD. The show featured Dave Edmunds, Dickey Betts, Steve Cropper, Brian Setzer, David Gilmour, Link Wray, Toni Iommi, Johnny Winter, Neal

Schon, and Lita Ford and was taped by MTV for broadcast in early 1985.

It was great seeing Setzer again. The first time I ever played with the Stones, back in 1981 at Atlanta's Fox Theater, Setzer's Stray Cats opened the show. He was a pal of Stu's. When he decided to move away from the Stray Cats and strut out on his own first solo album, *The Knife Feels Like Justice*, he called me in to do the keyboard parts, and I was very happy to do so. After the album, we ended up hitting the road for about three months in 1986. It was very good, straight-ahead rock 'n' roll.

* * * * *

Another landmark session in my career was also courtesy of Dave Edmunds. He was producing the soundtrack for the film *Porky's Revenge*. I was over the moon to play with him since he had been one of my heroes for a long time. One of the other acts in the sessions was the Austin, Texas-based Fabulous Thunderbirds, which I'd always liked. Not long after we'd done the music for the movie, I got a call from their manager Mark Proct. He said, "Listen, the guys really liked playing with you on that soundtrack. We're about to do another record and go on tour. Would you like to tag along? We can't pay you what you're used to with the Stones, but ...." He didn't even have to finish his sentence. I said, "You know what, man, I'd really like to do that. Sounds like fun."

It came as no surprise that Dave Edmunds was producing their new album. I was recruited to help with one of the tracks for *Tuff Enuff*, called *Look at That*. The album did very well, with the hit single of the same name as the album charting high. The Stones

My longtime pal and great influence, Dave Edmunds.

were on an extended break, so I hit the road with the T-Birds, having a lot of fun because we were all out there for the music. And having a little extra energy that I didn't have to expend fighting management, agents, and attorneys, as often seems the case in the music business, I was able to really sink my teeth into a correspondence course I'd been taking on forestry. How's that for rock 'n' roll decadence! Here we were touring America as one of the hottest bands of the moment and at the back of the bus Chuck's doing homework. I did get a few unusual glances from lead singer Kim Wilson and guitarist Jimmy Vaughan, but, man, it was a great time all around. I loved that band. We did one tour of Europe, not staying the places I'd become accustomed to with the Stones, but it was a lot of fun. It's easy to lose sight of why you're out there on the road, and it was a good reminder that I'm in it all for the music more than anything. We had a blast, playing about twenty shows or so in Germany, France, and England, and we recorded a follow-up album called *Hot Number*.

One of the most exciting gigs was the Riverfest in Austin, which was always a sort of homecoming for them. We spent quite a bit of time in Austin when we weren't on the road. That's where we'd hang to rehearse, and it seemed like almost every night we headed out to the clubs and jam.

Of course, this was my first time playing with Jimmy's brother Stevie Ray, who often showed up and jammed with the T-Birds. That's where they came up with that routine where Jimmy would stand behind Stevie Ray and they'd play the same guitar.

While I was there, I was approached by Mark Proct about producing Bill Carter's next album, called *Loaded Dice*. "There isn't much of a budget," Proct said, "but I'll pay you what I can." Carter was the Austin native who had written that great tune *Willie the Wimp* that Stevie Ray adopted and was one of his fans' favorites in concert. He also helped write another song that SRV was known for, *Crossfire*.

On the sessions, we had drummer Kenny Aronoff, whom I've always thought was simply amazing. Jimmy Vaughan came in on guitar as well, but the magic was the day Stevie Ray came in. He did a fabulous job. He was a total pro. He came in, set up, and got that incredible SRV sound of his. He absolutely wailed on the song he did. By this time, Stevie had been through rehab and was clean, sober, and clear. He was an absolute joy to work with and readily recognized how much help the Stones had been in the launch of his career. The guy who discovered Stevie, Chesley Millikin, was a close friend of the Stones and former head of Epic Records in London, and it was Chesley who brought in John Hammond, Sr. to produce Stevie and asked Mick Jagger for the favor of sponsoring Stevie's big debut in New York. The rest is history. He was absolutely one of the best guitar players ever, and his loss was yet another in a long list of rock 'n' roll tragedies that robbed us of who knows what musical wonders that might have been.

I stayed with the T-Birds for about a year, until I saw another Stones record on the horizon. Besides, sadly, there was growing discord in the band by this time and Kim Wilson and Jimmy Vaughan were at odds.

* * * * *

Canadian guitarist Colin James was another great, young talent that I had the fortune to work with when he decided to shed his more straight rock image and approach and hit the road with what he called "The Little Big Band."

I was really impressed with Colin, who had early in his career not only caught the ear of Stevie Ray Vaughan, but had opened for Keith Richards on his X-Pensive Winos tour and had become a pal of Keith's. I was called in by my old friend Chris Kimsey. Kimsey and I became very close friends during the recording of the Stones *Undercover* record, the first one I worked on with the band. Since then we've done lots of projects together, and he's always a joy to work with. On this album, Colin and Kimsey decided to record live in the studio a mix of 1940s and 1950s standards, with swinging horns courtesy of Roomful of Blues and me on organ and piano.

It was fast and furious, both in the studio and on the stage. I was so impressed with Colin that when he said he wanted to take the show on the road, I agreed immediately. I had a blast trekking across Canada — even driving the van myself a couple of times, just like the old days. I really had a ball, and I loved that band. I couldn't understand why he never caught on better in the States. Some time after the tour, Colin came down to Charlane and we did a bit of writing together. His Toronto Blue Jays and my Atlanta Braves were playing at the time, though, so we watched a lot of baseball and didn't make much music!

*   *   *   *   *

I was in Los Angeles working with Dave Edmunds when I got a call from a guy out of the blue telling me that he's producing an Atlanta band called Mr. Crowe's Garden, that the band members are big fans, and that they wanted me to play on their album.

The guy was George Drakoulias, who had helped Rick Rubin in the early days of Def Jam and the rise of Public Enemy, Beastie Boys and L. L. Cool J. Drakoulias and Ruben had broken away from Def Jam and launched what became Def American Records, which finally evolved into his current American Records. Drakoulias said he'd take me for lunch and play me a tape. The next day he showed up at the hotel in an old Cadillac convertible. He was a big guy with hair almost down to his knees, and I'm thinking, "What have you gotten yourself into here?" We went to lunch, and in the car he played me this really raw — I mean *really* raw tape — made at a rehearsal with these guys.

It was hard to hear anything on that tape. But the energy came shining through. The musical energy just jumped off the tape. I could tell they had something going and agreed to do the session. It was quite a while later that we actually did the recording back in Atlanta. I was just about to go on tour with the Stones and only had a day and a half to do it. At first, they only wanted me on a couple of tracks. The album was pretty much done, and I was overdubbing.

So I started playing, and it's rockin' — good songs, lots of energy on the tracks — and it was easy for me to do my thing on it. After a couple of tracks, George said, "Well, how about adding some organ on this one?" So I did that. Then he said, "Ah, there's this one more." And I did that. Then he said, "Ooooh, this other one might work." I worked my ass off all day and went back the next day to do even more.

My contract was based on appearing on just a couple of songs, so I had to pull him aside at one point and tell him that we needed to strike a new

Credit: Chuck Leavell Archive

Rich and Chris Robinson with me during sessions for their breakout Black Crowes debut album.

deal. What we did was work out a plan by which I'd get paid a bonus if the LP sold 50,000 copies and another bonus at 100,000 copies and so on. I think we ended at a million. Too bad. The album, *Shake Your Money Maker*, by the band that ended up being called the Black Crowes, sold 5 or 6 million copies!

I can't remember how many tracks I wound up on, but it was a lot — maybe seven or so. I really enjoyed that session. When it's that easy to contribute something, you know it's working. Then after the CD came out, they were going to do a video, and they asked me to do that. I agreed. It was *She Talks to Angels*. This was a live take of the song, and it became another released recording. The Robinson brothers, guitarist Rich and singer Chris, are great guys. Very sweet and terrific writers — even if they borrowed a little from the Faces, the Stones, and other English performers. I remember having my daughter Ashley in the studio with me briefly and Chris was running around playing with her, as if he were an eight-year-old not caring one damn about being on the brink of becoming a rock star.

Shortly before we shot the video, I was talking to a guy named Eddie Harsch, whom I'd met when I was touring with the T-Birds. Eddie was playing with Albert Collins, and we did some shows together. I first heard Eddie at a sound check. He was playing by himself, getting a sound for his keyboards. I heard this fantastic playing and went up to him to introduce myself. We became friends straightaway. So Eddie called me and says, "What about these Crowes' boys?"

And I said, "Well, yeah, I'm doing a video, and they are going on the road soon. They need a keyboard player. I can't do it because of the Stones tour, and you should come down and check it out." He did, and he got the gig the next day. So I put myself out of work! Eddie did a great job with them and I loved all of the stuff they put out before they broke up.

*   *   *   *   *

When I was recording the Black Crowe's record, the engineer was a fellow named Brendan O'Brien. Brendan was a sharp kid who played guitar very well, was an amazing audio engineer, had a bubbly personality, was very professional, and generally made a good impression on me. It didn't take Brendon long to make his mark in rock music history. He eventually got involved with the grunge scene in Seattle, working with Pearl Jam, Stone Temple Pilots, Rage against the Machine, and many other groups. He became a mega-producer in a relatively short time. I watched his rise, but I hadn't heard from him in years, and one day he called me out of the blue. He was in Atlanta and told me that he was working with a band called Train. They were recording there and had a song that needed piano. He told me that the song was one where the piano would have a strong feature and that the record company was really going to push this as a single.

He also told me that there would be an orchestral arrangement done by Paul Buckmaster (arranger extraordinaire, who did many classic string arrangements through the years, including Elton John's *Tumbleweed Connection* record). They wanted to record the tune the next day. Was I available? You bet! I had been a fan of Buckmaster for a long time and knew that he would do a great arrangement, no matter what the song was like. And I had wanted to work with Brendan again.

So the next day I drove up to Atlanta and arrived at the studio. Quick introductions to the band were made, and I made some quick small talk with Brendan about old times and our families. Then to work. They were working on a different tune, and he gave me a tape of the song we were to do: *Drops of Jupiter*. I took the tape to a different room and listened to it, instantly liking the song. I wrote a quick chord chart for it, and about a half hour later the band was ready to take it on. The groove was in the room right away, and we were all feeling great and started doing takes. I think it only took us about three or four takes, and Brendan was happy, as was the band. It was much later when I finally heard the Buckmaster arrangement, and, as I had figured, it knocked me out. The song was a big hit, and I almost got tired of hearing it on the radio! It wound up winning a Grammy for Buckmaster as arranger.

*   *   *   *   *

One of the more unusual sessions I did was for Hank Williams Jr., who was scheduled to do a solo CD and had many of the tracks in the can. It was his first of several comebacks, this one called *Hank Williams Jr. and Friends*, with Charlie Daniels, Toy Caldwell, and others. I was honored to be included, but I didn't meet Hank. He'd taken a break from the sessions to do some hiking and fell nearly 500 feet down a mountain side, splitting his skull and very nearly dying. It took him more than two years to recover. And about another eight years after that I finally met him while working on a show with Dickey Betts that Hank appeared at. He was very gracious, and thanked me for the work I'd done all those years earlier.

* * * * *

I was taking a little time off in 1992 when I got a call about doing a session with the Indigo Girls. I had followed them for several years and loved their strong writing and beautiful harmonies. Peter Collins was the producer, and I was given his number to call. He was very nice and easy going on the phone and seemed excited about the prospect of putting me together with them. But he told me that Amy was not so keen on keyboards in general and that I might have to work a bit to win her over. I took on the challenge and headed to Nashville to record. They played me several songs, one of which really stood out. It was one that Emily had written called *Language of the Kiss*. I took to it immediately and found a comfortable piano part to play. Peter and the Girls liked what I was doing, and I believe I won over Amy on that one. Emily was especially pleased with the part and asked me if I would just play something off the top of my head for the introduction. I did, and they were smiling broadly in the control room after I finished. It was a great feeling and a true honor to work with such talented artists. I wound up on several other tracks on the CD, which they called *Swamp Ophelia*. They asked me if I would be willing to come out and do some shows with them someday, and of course I said yes. Unfortunately, the schedules just haven't worked out for that, but I'm not giving up!

* * * * *

I loved working with my old mate Hutch Hutchinson on a comeback attempt the "Scottish Everly Brothers" — Craig and Charlie Reid, The Proclaimers — made in 2001. The CD was arranged and produced by Chris Kimsey who, of course, has been a part of my career for many years, and I thought it turned out wonderfully well. It had been a long time since I'd had so much fun on a project — I thought the material was so well written that it made my keyboard parts just fall off my fingers and the twin Reid guys were sheer inspiration the whole time we were in the studio. While this effort by the makers of *500 Miles* didn't catch on as well as it should have, it was still a memorable work and a pleasure to record.

* * * * *

During some of the long downtime between Stones projects, I ended up playing on solo albums by Mick, Keith, and Ronnie, which was great. The work with Mick was the most formal and structured, appearing on his *She's the Boss* LP. This was at a time of great dissension in the band. Keith was particularly pissed off that Mick was doing a solo album, and Mick was trying very hard to make a non-Stones sounding album. He brought in Jeff Beck, Pete Townshend, Jan Hammer, Herbie Hancock, Nile Rogers, Steve Ferrone, Anton Fig, and G. E. Smith, among others. One of those others was Bernard Fowler — a kick-ass singer who was later to join the Stones touring band and has been on every tour since. I was happy with the result, but Mick had a rough time with the critics and some Stones fans.

One thing that I thought was cool that came out of the sessions, which were done in Nassau, Bahamas, was that I was able to help hook up Jeff Beck with my old BHLT pal Jimmy Hall. Beck was at the time also working on his first solo album after a long self-imposed exile and was using Nile Rogers as producer. Jeff told me about the record and said that while Rogers was trying to convince him that he could make Jeff the lead singer, he really thought that he needed another vocalist to finish the record. He had worked with Jimmy before, and I suggested that Jimmy would be the cat. They hooked up and hit it off again. I was glad to have helped bring that together.

* * * * *

Later that year I worked with the Stones on the *Dirty Work* LP, but again there was no tour. This time it was Keith who stepped out and did it in a big way. He called and asked if I'd like to join the band he was putting together to help Chuck Berry celebrate his sixtieth birthday. After a series of rehearsals, the show would be put on live and filmed for a concert feature called *Hail! Hail! Rock and Roll*. Keith's idea was a pretty cool gift: whenever Chuck goes out to play he just hires a pickup band in whatever city he's in. Keith said that just once he'd like to give Chuck a really great band to play in front of — including Berry's original piano player, Johnnie Johnson.

"But I want you on organ," Keith said.

He'd also corralled Steve Jordan for drums, NRBQ's Joey Spampinato on bass, Bobby Keys on sax, and guest stars Robert Cray, Linda Ronstadt, Etta James, Julian Lennon, and Eric Clapton.

I soon learned that Keith was not just attempting the impossible, but he was probably going to pull it off. We set up for two weeks of rehearsals — a pretty generous rehearsal time — at Chuck's place outside of St. Louis.

Berry himself rarely showed up for the rehearsals. He was usually off arguing with managers, lawyers, or whomever over his contract. He was always trying to renegotiate his deal with director Taylor Hackford and make a little more coin somehow. Even when he did show up, he was mostly a pain in the ass. You can't take anything way from his legacy, but the man himself is one disagreeable piece of work, which is

The poster for *Hail! Hail! Rock 'N' Roll*.

Credit: Chuck Leavell Archive

pretty obvious from the footage that made it into the final film. The same can be said to testify to the total professional coolness of everybody else, from Keith and Taylor on down.

There's a moment in the film where Berry is seriously provoking Keith, who isn't taking the bait — though you can tell that if this were anyone else on the planet pulling this stunt Keith Richards would have stuffed a Telecaster up his ass ages ago.

Here's the back-story to that fight, which wasn't about amplifier volume or anything else as it appeared on screen: Keith's whole vision was to give Berry a totally professional band with which he could go out on stage and re-create as closely as possible the tunes that made him the icon he is, just like they were done on the records. As we rehearsed, Keith had corrected Berry on a few of the intros and a few of the keys the songs were originally played in, and Berry was getting back at Keith by throwing a tantrum while the cameras were rolling.

Berry had forgotten a lot of what he'd originally done — thrown out the window with years and years of pickup bands and, simply, not caring about anything except the paycheck at the end of the night. He just played whatever he wanted, when he wanted, and the band had to try to keep up; Keith was trying to bring back some musical history and Chuck's total lack of co-operation was incredibly frustrating for all of us.

During the rehearsals, Johnnie Johnson — one of my heroes — paid me one of the highest compliments I have ever had. I watched the piano great as much as I possible so I could soak up anything, and during one of the breaks I was playing a little on my own — just noodling — and he came up to me and said: "Chuck, you remind me of me at your age." Man! This coming from Johnnie Johnson,

Credit: Chuck Leavell Archive

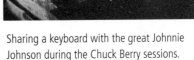

Sharing a keyboard with the great Johnnie Johnson during the Chuck Berry sessions.

the guy who actually came up with that *Johnny B. Goode* riff on piano.

Come show night it was magical. But Berry was still a prick. When it came to introducing Robert Cray's guest spot, Chuck called him "Robert Clay." The producers had to overdub a correction for the film. To bastardize an overused quote: What a piece of work is Chuck Berry, how noble in unreason, how infinite in futilities, in form and moving how repressed and abominable, in action how like a fallen angel, in apprehension how like a dog.

Even during that gig, which was such an act of kindness and reverence on the part of Keith, Berry tried to mess with the band. In the middle of one tune, he leaned over to Keith and told him he wanted to modulate to a different key. Keith just shook his head and said, "No way." Ultimately, the entire band made Chuck look good, despite himself. And Keith deserves all the credit he got. So does Taylor for the film he ended up creating out of the project.

I played with Berry once more right after that at the Felt Forum in New York on the actual day of his sixtieth birthday. It was a very different kind of gig — much more like a regular Chuck Berry gig. John Scher had recruited me, along with Dave Edmunds, Terry Williams, and The Who's John Entwistle on bass. We were Berry's pickup band, and he treated us like it. Again, we rehearsed without Berry, and I warned the band what might happen out on stage and went over all the various keys and changes I guessed Chuck might throw at us.

Dave had never met Berry, and before the show I took him to Chuck's dressing room, knocked on the door, and we walked in when Berry said so. I said, "Mr. Berry, this is my old friend Dave Edmunds. He'll be on guitar tonight, and I wondered if you'd tell him what songs we might do."

Berry kind of snarled back. "We'll be doing Chuck Berry songs."

I said, "Well, I kinda figured that."

Berry turned to Dave and said, "I'll tell you what, can you tell by looking at my hands what chord I'm playing?"

Dave said "Yeah."

"Fine then."

Typical Chuck Berry. For me, I almost found it fun. Berry would launch into a song without telling anyone in the band what it was or turn and say the song title as he started playing, or change keys. I'll tell you, all the cats stepped up to the plate that night, and the gig really rocked hard. It was certainly a challenge, but I was in the company of pros, and there was no way Berry was going to get the best of us!

One thing that most folks in the biz know about Chuck Berry is that he ain't there so much for the rock 'n' roll anymore. He's there for the cash and is very conscious of his contract and how long he's being paid to play. At the end of that night the band was really rockin', and Berry was right in drummer Terry Williams' face, sweating up a storm. Terry was looking at him like, "Go, man! Let's play!" and I thought Berry was enjoying himself. But he then looked down at his watch. He had played what his contract called for and wasn't going to play one note he wasn't getting paid for. He stood back and signaled the song's abrupt end, waved to the crowd and walked off stage.

Like with Keith, the band was up to the task, and we made Berry look good despite himself. I don't mean to take away from a great American rock legend. He's Chuck Berry, and he deserves his place in history for having inspired so many of us and having written and/or recorded an extraordinary body of work — some of the most ground-breaking songs in rock 'n' roll. I know that for myself and for so many other fellow musicians that grew up on Chuck's music, we are all forever grateful for his contribution to the art. It's just a shame that he seems to have such a chip on his shoulder and that he seems to have forgotten, at least to a degree, the essence of why he's so famous. He still rocks, though … when he wants to. Those shows were very important for me, and I'm so grateful I was there. I still adore Chuck Berry, and he has earned a lot of deserved respect, but he's not the easiest cat to work with, I can tell you that!

*   *   *   *   *

About a year later, Keith rang me up again and simply blew my mind. How'd I like to play with Aretha Franklin? What do you say to that? Yes, please! Talk about a living legend, I used to listen to all the great music she made at the legendary Muscle Shoals Sound recording studios in Alabama, and the thought of being able to play with her was very exciting. The deal was that she was going to cover the Stones' classic *Jumping Jack Flash* for inclusion in a movie starring Whoopi Goldberg by the same name. Keith told me that under no circumstances would Aretha fly to a studio in New York or LA and that we had to go to her place in Detroit and record there. Aretha has had a fear of flying for a long time and avoids it at almost any cost. Keith had also been chatting with Jerry Wexler, who gave us a great piece of advice: make her part of the band rather than just have her come in and throw down a vocal. So Keith decided that Aretha would play piano and I'd come in on organ.

What a wonderful day it was! We flew up and all met at the United Sound Studios. One thing that blew my mind was that she smoked Kool cigarettes — rather a lot of them — puffing and singing, puffing and singing her butt off. She liked playing on the black keys, the flats and sharps, which was huge insight into her talent; Aretha, of course, did a lot of the piano tracks on many of her original tunes. As Wexler predicted, she became part of the band and helped organize the arrangement. She was way into it, playing great and singing her ass off. Keith played his cards just right with her, and directed the session brilliantly. It was truly a great experience — her sisters were there singing backup, and everyone was thrilled with the result.

* * * * *

Keith was clearly on a creative roll and went into the studio himself for what would become his first solo album, *Talk Is Cheap* — a great record.

I was in New York at the time working on a Dion album that Dave Edmunds was producing. Working yet again with Edmunds was a joy, and with one of the all-time legends, Dion, made it another landmark for me. The Dion record was called *Yo Frankie*. It put him back on the map, was critically acclaimed, and I think a great effort. The core band for Dion's record was Phil Chen on bass, Terry Williams on drums, Dave on guitar and producing, and me on keys. Interestingly, Bryan Adams produced one track, which I also played on, that included musicians from Bryan's band: drummer Mickey Curry and bass player Dave Taylor. This was a rockin' tune that Bryan co-wrote called *Drive All Night*.

Since I was in Keith's neighborhood while recording the Dion record, I called to say hello. Keith immediately told me that he was doing some sessions and asked if I could make it in for a track. I told him I had the night off from my other sessions and I went over to Jersey to a little studio and cut a song. It was very sweet of him to include me, but that's Keith.

*   *   *   *   *

It was kind of the same feeling when Ronnie Wood rang me up and told me that he was recording a new solo album, *Slide on This*, a few years later. I was so flattered because he already had his old Faces pal Ian MacLagan to do keyboards for him. But it was Woody's way of graciously wanting to include me, so I flew over to his studio in Dublin and worked on some of the tracks. Bernard Fowler was on board, singing his rear end off as usual — and co-writing, arranging, producing the CD, and even doing some of the drum programming. Wayne Sheehy was pumping the drums, and on bass was great Living Color bassist Doug Wimbish. Some of the other guests include U2's The Edge, Joe Elliott, Michael Kamen, and even Charlie Watts.

When the record was done, Woody decided to hit the road. He asked if I'd join him on some of the dates and I did, playing, I think, seven or eight shows in the Northeast and down the east coast, ending up in Atlanta. It was a groove to play with that tight band, and to work with Mac on the keyboards was great. Sheehy came along on drums and Shaun Soloman took over bass duties for the live shows. Our friend, the great Johnny Lee Schell helped out on guitar. We rocked the houses and had tons of fun. Woody stepped up on that tour and proved his mettle as a solo artist and bandleader. Some of the shows made it onto a live disc called *Slide On Live*: *Plugged in and Standing* — where I think not only Woody but Bernard really shone.

* * * * *

I didn't play on Mick Jagger's *Wandering Spirit* CD — with Billy Preston, Benmont Tench, and Matt Clifford he hardly needed me in the studio — but he did call when it came time to promote the record, which is widely seen as his best solo effort yet.

The idea was to do a short tour of the States, playing major cities for maximum exposure. It was a great band, with Jimmy Ripp on guitar, Curt Bisquera on drums, John Pierce on bass, and Frank Simes on second guitar. We rehearsed for two weeks in Los Angles and it went great. To kick things off, we were scheduled to play on *Saturday Night Live*, and during rehearsal week for the show, Mick agreed to participate in a skit in which he imitated Keith. It was hilarious. They rehearsed it, I think, three times before the actual live show, and it got funnier and funnier. The skit was based around their parody of "Point/Counter Point," and while Mick played Keith, Mike Myers played Mick. The premise of the discussion was the police, the "cats in blue." They argued back and forth with hilarious lines. Myers was amazing as Mick, and Mick had Keith down. Smoking a cigarette, he had the "Keith look" going with a bandana on his head and doing Keith's moves to a T. Of course, the killer part of the skit came when Mick's Keith told Myers' Mick: "Mick, you ignorant slut!" We all could have died laughing. The musical segment was just as successful.

Our first show was to be at New York's Webster Hall, followed by the short tour. But for some reason Mick decided, almost at the last minute, that he was going to just do the one show. Too bad — it was a good one. Mick had thrown caution to the wind and had all these naked black men as props in the hall as well as scantily dressed beautiful women groping each other and passersby. The set design was great too, giving the hall a sort of Vaudeville decadent look.

I went up to Mick's dressing room about twenty minutes before the show was to begin to warm up Mick's voice. He had a one-way mirror that looked down over the whole scene. "Do you think," Mick said to me with a smile, "that it's wild enough?"

It went so well that I was terribly disappointed we didn't do more shows. I think they would have all been great.

* * * * *

One of the sadder — but worthy — sessions I've been involved with was a benefit show and CD for my old band mate Jimmy Nalls, who a few years ago learned he has Parkinson's Disease. Jimmy had been there at the start of my professional career — Alex Taylor, Dr. John, and of course was a founding member of Sea Level. From there he'd moved on to a lot of work, among the most significant the band the Nighthawks, which he joined along-side former Wet Willie front man Jimmy Hall, who had been with me in BHLT. He also worked with T. Graham Brown, a well-known country artist, and in earlier years with Paul Stookey of Peter, Paul, and Mary on several of Stookey's solo records.

I played on Jimmy's first solo CD, *Ain't No Stranger* and the benefit show was an effort undertaken to help with Jimmy's mounting medical bills and to raise awareness for the American Parkinson Disease Foundation in the face of his disease.

There was Bluebloods guitarist Mike Henderson, Lee Roy Parnell, T. Graham Brown, ABB guitarist Jack Pearson, Memphis

Horns' Wayne Jackson, Charlie Hayward, me, and others pitching in. It's a fine CD, as well as being a worthy cause. It's sad to see Jimmy's decline, suffering through two brain operations and the loss of his ability to play. I can only hope there's some medical help for him — for everyone with Parkinson's — on the horizon.

* * * * *

In 1997 I got a call from my old friend Stewart Levine, who had produced most of the Sea Level albums years before. I hadn't heard from him in a long time, and it was great to hear his voice. We chatted about old times for a while, then he got to the point: How would I feel about being in the core band for a big show at Wembley stadium in London? The show was called Songs and Visions and had an all-star line up that included Rod Stewart, Chaka Kahn, Steve Winwood, Robert Palmer, Seal, k.d. lang, Mary J. Blige, Jon Bon Jovi, Toni Braxton, and Japanese artist Eikichi Yazawa. Stewart was the musical director and put the band together. I jumped right on that one! To top it off, I got to play with some of my old friends: Nathan East on bass, Tessa Niles and Katie Kissoon on vocals, Lisa Fischer on vocals, as well as Paulino de Costa on percussion (who had played on a couple of Sea Level records). In addition, the other cats in the band included Vinnie Colaiuta on drums (a veteran session player who has worked with Sting extensively), Paul "Wix" Wickens on synthesizer (also a session vet who has been with Paul McCartney for years), a brilliant young Brazilian guitar player named Heitor Pereira, and session guitarist from Los Angeles named Mike Landau.

Jerry Hey, a friend of Levine's and an amazing trumpet player and arranger, put together a horn section of the best players. There was also a twenty-piece orchestra. What a band! We all flew to London for a two-week rehearsal at Olympic Studios. The artists came in one by one over the rehearsal period. The concept was to take songs from forty years of rock 'n' roll — one from each year — and in some cases put the artists together to do duets, trios, and quartets. There was also a tribute to Elvis in the program. The whole thing sold out to 55,000 people and was filmed. It was truly a star-studded affair, and it came off so incredibly well. It was shown a year or so later on the Trio network in the United States and was very well received. Some of the highlights for me were the opening song, *Papa Was a Rolling Stone* with Rod, Chaka, Mary J., and Steve; Seal and Steve doing U2's *Still Haven't Found What I'm Looking For*; Robert Palmer's rendition of Elvis' *All Shook Up*; and even though it may sound a little weird, Jon Bon Jovi doing a great rendition of *Sympathy for the Devil*. Playing in such an incredible band was a highlight in itself, but to work with such well-known and talented artists, even if for just one show, was certainly one of the best times of my career.

* * * * *

In the midst of these plans, schemes, and dreams over the past few years, I came quite by accident to discover that I'd released my first solo CD. I had no intention of it being a record. It started as a Christmas card. I thought, back in 1996, that it would be fun to lay down a few tracks and put them on CDs and cassettes and send them out to friends instead of a conventional Christmas card. I've got a small studio at Charlane, where I did some of the work, and I wrapped it up at my buddy David Clark's studio, which is about fifteen miles away. There was a lot of solo piano, and we employed a few local guys to help out on the tracks. David's a whiz on the computer and whipped up a cover for it. I called it *A Homemade Christmas*, had 1,000 CDs made and 500 cassettes and sent them out.

Friends and family all commented how much they liked it, but I got an even stronger reaction from a very unexpected source: Capricorn Records founder Phil Walden, who'd received a copy of the CD.

After his rise and fall, Walden had made a comeback in the music business and started up Capricorn again, this time out of

Atlanta. He called me and said simply that my little "Christmas card" was so good that I should record a few additional tunes and put it on the market. I was flattered, but I told him it was really a private little recording and that I'd want to go back in and work on some of the existing tracks before even thinking about adding new ones. Phil gave me the green light and I put in a call to my old pal Johnny Sandlin to assemble the players. We met up at Johnny's studio in Huntsville, Alabama — Bill Stewart and Roger Hawkins on drums, David Hood on bass, Kelvin Holly on guitar, Scott Boyer on guitar, and a few others. A few others — what an understatement! I had the famed Muscle Shoals horn section! As the Stones tour resumed, I was able to get Bobby Keys on a tune, as well as Lisa Fischer while we were in Los Angeles on a day off.

In 1999 my first solo CD, *What's In That Bag?* hit the stores. It did quite well for me, but there was one little problem. Capricorn was back in trouble and wound up selling its whole catalogue to Volcano Records. Fortunately, I had put a clause in the contract that if something of that nature were to occur, I could buy it back. It was pretty weird having to buy back my own record, but I did, and it taught me a lesson. Own yourself. So with *Bag* in hand, I started my own label, Evergreen Arts.

Over subsequent Stones tours I've spent a lot of my downtime in my dressing room with a digital piano writing tunes. I was also in the middle of writing my book on forestry, *Forever Green.* So I thought, one day somewhere out there with the Stones, that I should have an album to go with the book: *Forever Blue* — a collection of solo piano tunes and so called mainly because I'm a blues player at heart. I thought it would be an interesting concept — to marry the two — and promote

My longtime pal Paul Hornsby.

them together. I thought it was a good opportunity to make a statement about the resource of wood and doing an album using an instrument that is made of wood.

I called my old pal Paul Hornsby, who has a small studio in Macon called Muscadine. He has a nice piano there, and I thought, it might be a good idea to have somebody on the other side of the glass to critique my efforts and help engineer it. We laid down the tracks over the course of a week or so.

And that was it. Over a very short period of recording I ended up with my first (deliberate!) solo album, an homage to the instrument I love so much. I dedicated the CD to the trees that my grand piano is made from and the craftsmen that shape wood into so many useful and beautiful things.

*   *   *   *   *

I've had a few other plans over the years for solo works and am always scheming and dreaming of even more. I remember sitting in a bar somewhere once with fellow keyboard player Patrick Moraz, and we were drinking and having a great time talking about music. Finally, fuelled and running full out on whiskey wisdom, we decided that we would do an album together. Just us. We decided we'd call the project *It's in Our Hands*. Patrick and I went so far as to drunkenly draw up a contract, which we each signed on a dollar bill! Guess it was the closest piece of paper handy. And maybe, someday, we'll actually do it!

Stones sax man Bobby Keys and I also had a plan to do an album of covers that had, as Southerners, inspired us to become musicians in the first place. The idea was to gather some of the best Southern greats together — artists such as Ray Charles, Gregg Allman, Leon Russell, Willie Nelson, Chris Robinson, and others. We would do a series of shows in the South — Georgia, Texas, the Carolinas, Tennessee, Alabama — and release either a CD or as a video series or both. We came up with a great title for it too, which I'm not going to give away (like the Moraz project ... never say never!).

* * * * *

Don Was, who produced the Stones' *Voodoo Lounge* album, rang me up in early 1997 to invite me in on a solo CD being cut in Los Angeles by Bon Jovi guitarist Richie Sambora. I'd never met Richie and didn't know what to expect of him or the music. But I was quite impressed with everything once I got there. I was very impressed with his voice, which I'd never heard before on a lead vocal because in Bon Jovi it's always Jon singing. The guitar playing was terrific and the songs solid. I enjoyed working with Don again, and he had put together a stellar band to record with. This included my old pals Kenny Aronoff on drums, Hutch Hutchinson on bass, and me and Rami Jaffee (who is in Jakob Dylan's band The Wallflowers) on keys. Various other musicians chimed in on some overdubs — everyone from Greg Phillinganes to Billy Preston. The album was called *Undiscovered Soul*. I thought it was a cool record and was disappointed that it didn't do better for him.

The whole experience was soon cast from my mind, however. I was in Los Angles for only about a week working on the album when I got a call that my mother, already in hospital because of her failing health, had developed pneumonia and the doctor's weren't too optimistic about her chances. Many family members including my sister Judy, her husband Ted, my brother Billy and Pamela, and Rose Lane were spending as much time with her as they could. Thankfully the timing was such that I had nothing after the Sambora CD, so I was able to spend all my time with her as soon as I got back home. We traded duties with Mom for a bit, then when she stabilized to a degree, Judy, Billy, and the others went home while I stayed with her.

The healthcare workers were wonderful and bent the rules for me, letting me sleep in the room with Mom. They

Introducing my Mom to Mick, Keith and the gang.

were so great with her, treating her with the greatest respect and dignity. It's a kindness I'll never forget.

A proud Mom with her happy son.

At first it looked as though she might beat it, and we began considering how to care for her once she left the hospital. No matter what I knew she'd never be able to live unattended again. Rose Lane and I made a quick trip up to Decatur, Alabama, where I was being honored with the state's Music Hall of Fame Musician's Award. We went right back home afterward for what turned out to be Mom's final two days. I stayed with her constantly, alone and helplessly watching her pass away. It was the most powerful experience of my life yet even at the time I was so grateful that she wasn't suffering.

On Jan. 15, 1997, I was talking to her and holding her hands. I bid her good night saying "I love you, Mom." She said, "Good night, darling. I love you, too," and slipped off to sleep. I kept talking to her, telling her how much she was loved by all the children and her grandchildren. She was so tired, but at the same time was trying not to die — for my sake more than her own, perhaps. But she peacefully slept and her breathing slowed and finally, gently, ceased.

She looked so beautiful. So pretty. It was so hard to lose her. I had no shock to get over — but a mountain of grief — so I tried to console myself with the thought that she was finally free, at peace, and united at long last with my father. I thought of all the wonderful things she did for me — and my brother and sister — and how good she was to me throughout my life.

Mom had been a huge inspiration to Billy, Judy, me, her grandchildren, and just about everyone who knew her. She had one of the worst cases of rheumatoid arthritis you can imagine, but she would never complain. When she was in terrible pain, she might say something like, "Well, I've had better days." A few years back, there was even an article in the Tuscaloosa paper about her, about how she kept her faith strong and always looked on the bright side of things, doing as much as she could even with the pain she was in. She had had several operations on her hands, feet, and toes through the year where they would go in and break her bones, then fuse them back together again to try to straighten them out. Usually they would gnarl up again and a couple of years later she would have to go have back for further operations. When she lay dying during the last days, and she was hit by pain, the worst thing I ever heard her say about it was: "Oh, my." Her courage, faith, love, and determination are things of which I'll always be in awe.

I had found huge personal fulfillment and happiness and professional success that put me in league with the best, all no small part due to her guidance, influence and love. I'm glad I got to tell her all this before she left.

Without music, life is a journey through a desert.

———————————————————

Pat Conroy

Unplugged & Beatled

When I was about thirteen I had a brief obsession with the acoustic guitar, learning every folk song I could and soaking up Kingston Trio; Peter, Paul and Mary; and Bob Dylan. Feeding my constant hunger for fresh material was my older sister Judy, who loved to turn me on to the latest groups. One day she came through the door with an album that would change music — and me — forever. It was

the Beatles. There hadn't been anything like the Beatles. At the time, even to me, they sounded a bit wild. But they were fun, and there was magic to the music that I found possessing. I couldn't stop listening to them.

With every record, I'd slow the turntable to 16 RPM, so I could more easily pick out the guitar parts. I was hooked. And like everybody, I

Credit: Chuck Leavell Archive

George Harrison and me in Japan.

soon had a favorite Beatle: George Harrison. Ringo certainly had his fans, while Lennon and McCartney were the brilliant songwriting team with the catchy melodies and stunning harmonies — one the wit and the other the cute face the girls screamed over. But to me the individual with the most interesting, quiet talent was George.

So I was sent reeling back to my childhood when I received a call in the fall of 1984 from my old pal Dave Edmunds asking me to show up at a Los Angeles recording studio to lay down a fairly obscure Bob Dylan tune called *I Don't Want to Do It* with George Harrison. It was the soundtrack for *Porky's Revenge*, and Jeff Beck was on board, as was Carl Perkins, Clarence Clemons, Willie Nelson, the Crawling King Snakes (a one-shot band that included Dave, Robert Plant, and Phil Collins) and, as I mentioned earlier, The Fabulous Thunderbirds.

Dave was producing, and I remember being kind of nervous sitting in the Record Plant studio waiting. I figured George would thunder in with a complete idea of what he wanted to do and how he wanted to do it. After all, the guy was a Beatle! He could do anything! Instead, this gentle, kind man wandered in silently and asked what we thought we should all do. "Let me play it for you," he said, picking up an acoustic guitar, "and tell me how we should do it."

George just wanted to be part of the group. As I got to know him better, he said he enjoyed singing a couple of songs, but that he was just happy to be part of a group and never liked being the center of attention. And it was so true. George was a cat, a player, a part of the team, and he just wanted to be in the band. The recording went smoothly and we were all happy with the results. It all went too fast, in fact, and I was sorry that I didn't get a chance to spend more time with George. He'd done the 1974 solo American tour, which he took a lot of critical heat for because he concentrated on George Harrison songs instead of trying to pretend he was resurrecting the Beatles. After that he retired from the road and concentrated on his philanthropic efforts, his gardening, and a series of solo albums including *Somewhere in England, Cloud Nine*, and the ensemble album *Traveling Wilburys* being among the better received. He didn't get out a lot but was hardly the recluse the press made him out to be. Still, I had little reason to think our paths would cross again.

But I'm learning, in this business, to expect the completely unexpected. One night I wandered into the office at Charlane in late 1990 — fresh off the tractor and still trailing a wake of dust as if I were Pigpen from the *Peanuts* cartoon — to find a message on my answering machine. It was Eric Clapton, calling from Hong Kong, wondering if I'd join him for part of his upcoming series of sold-out concerts at London's famed Royal Albert Hall in the coming year.

Credit: Chuck Leavell Archive

Eric Clapton and me in London during rehearsals for his acclaimed Albert Hall shows.

I'd met Eric a handful of times since joining the Stones, had been to his place in London with Keith and Ronnie, and had enjoyed jamming with him on stage in America. He was chosen by the Stones to be a special guest on several shows in New York and in Los Angeles. They set up his rig next to me, and we had a great musical dialogue on the Stones rendition of *Little Red Rooster*. Man, did he wail on that tune! Since we were set up right next to each other, I was right with him and answered some of his licks occasionally with some Southern blues of my own. We had more than a couple of smiles pass between us, and when I got that message I was in heaven. When the Stones toured Europe and came to London, some of us wound up at his flat playing into all hours of the morning — Keith, Ronnie, me, Allan Rogan, and several other guys. I remember one night we'd stayed up talking about Duane Allman and their time recording Derek and the Dominoes' *Layla and Other Assorted Loved Songs*. One thing that struck me was that Eric is somewhat uncomfortable with being thought of as anything but a guitar player. He was just twenty years old in 1965, having done the John Mayall's *Blues Breakers* album, when "Clapton is God" began appearing spray-painted on London buildings and subway stations, starting first in the city's Islington borough. Following that, audiences began shouting "give God a solo" when he appeared on stage.

Make no mistake: Eric knows he's good. But he doesn't lack for humility and he's incredibly uncomfortable with this "rock god" moniker he's been saddled with for forty years. "I don't understand why anyone should claim anything for me," I remember him saying. "I'm just a guitar player."

As an example, he loved to cite Duane Allman as someone who was just as talented. "Daily, I hear things by other guitarists that surprise the hell out of me," Clapton has said. "And in the United States there are dozens of guys down in the South that have pure genius. I have my own heroes, and I try to think when I am playing, 'How would so-and-so have done this?' It's ridiculous to claim that I am the best guitarist in the world."

Still, who's kidding whom — Eric Clapton is one of the three greats to come out of England in the 1960s, along with fellow Yardbirds guitarists Jeff Beck and Jimmy Page. So when Eric called Charlane like that it was such a surprise that I kept the tape from the answering machine and stashed it away right after listening to it!

So after accepting, I was sent a tape of the band live. I was coming in to replace Allan Clark, who was going to work with Mark Knopfler on a Dire Straits album. Greg Phillinganes, a brilliant keyboard player that had been with Eric for many years was in the band, so I was mostly on organ. I listened to the tape and started working with it straightaway. The band was just amazing, and I couldn't wait to be a part of it. There was Greg, Nathan East on bass, Steve Ferrone on drums, Ray Cooper on percussion, Phil Palmer on guitar, and Tessa Niles and Katie Kissoon on vocals. I was blown away with the talent of all these great players and singers, and a little bit intimidated by them as well. But still, I was chomping at the bit to get started. I worked hard with the tape, trying to get all the parts just right. Finally, the day came to fly over and begin rehearsals. The shows were at the Albert Hall, and Eric was going to do twenty-four of them — six with a quartet, six with the larger band mentioned above but augmented by a horn section, six with special blues guests, and six with full orchestra conducted by Michael Kamen. Quite an undertaking. The whole thing would be recorded and select cuts released as a double CD.

I flew in to the rehearsals feeling good. I had listened repeatedly to the tapes and had learned the parts. The guys seemed impressed upon our first run through. I remember Nate being very complimentary, saying, "Man, you really did your homework. What are we rehearsing for? Let's do a show!" Greg also was great to me, helping me with any parts I wasn't sure of, taking plenty of time to work with me. I was right at home from the beginning and was elated to be in this new and exciting situation. We played a couple of warm-up gigs, and then the Albert Hall shows came.

The first six shows were just Eric, Greg Phillinganes, Steve Ferrone and Nathan East. But I got to be a part of the remaining eighteen performances, which included the six shows with the nine-piece band, six with a full orchestra conducted by Michael Kamen, as well as the six nights of the blues with quite a great feature list including Buddy Guy, Robert Cray, Jimmy Vaughan, Albert Collins, and legendary pianist Johnnie Johnson. Producer Russ Titleman was there to oversee the recordings and to help with the sound. I had most of the tunes down pat by then, but there were still the blues guys to rehearse and the orchestra night for which to prepare. It was a lot to deal with in such a short time, but I didn't care. I was way into it and would do whatever it took to do the gig. The blues stuff was easy, being that I knew most of the tunes and certainly knew the work of the artists we were to play with. The real challenge would be the work with the orchestra and Kamen. This included the *Edge of Darkness*, a piece that was the soundtrack to a popular television show in England and a longer work that Kamen had written for Eric. It is an amazing piece, quite involved and complicated. Unfortunately, for whatever reason, it didn't make it on the CD. For one thing, it was very long and would have required probably another CD to include it. I was helped a great deal by both Greg and Michael since I didn't read music and had a pretty hard time with the score. I made notes myself on all the changes and was finally able to get the pieces down.

The shows were nothing short of amazing. The setting, the Royal Albert Hall, was certainly a big part of what made them so special, but of course with all those great musicians and artists, with me fresh into the band, I was on top of the world. The double CD came out great, but unfortunately it didn't include all the shows. I guess that would have proved to be a daunting task, not to mention how many CDs it might have taken to get the whole thing down. Titleman did an admirable job of choosing the takes and doing the mixes. By the end of the almost two-month experience, I felt right at home with everyone, including Eric. I thought I brought a sort of edginess to the band and felt good about my contribution. But I was also a bit sad to see it come to an end, as Eric had planned to take an extended time off after the shows. No one could have guessed the horrible tragedy that would occur soon after those shows.

It was incredible playing with Eric and all these greats on the Royal Albert stage — probably the best room I've ever played, when it comes down to acoustics and just sheer history and ambience. Eric was about to take a year or so off from touring to rest, relax, and spend some time with his young son Conor. But that plan was short lived, as just a few months later Conor died in a tragic fall from a Manhattan high-rise condo. He was used to leaning on the large glass panels of the condo and looking down at the streets below. Only this time the windows had been cleaned and opened to let in some fresh air. Conor went to lean on the glass, but it wasn't there. A horrible accident — so sad, so terrible. Rose Lane and I sent Eric a letter of condolence, but as a parent myself, I imagine that all words and possible actions would be woefully inadequate — facile gestures no matter how heartfelt. It shook up everyone who knows Eric.

I figured Eric would go into seclusion after the tragedy — especially since before the accident he'd told me he'd planned to take the remainder of the year off. But I suppose he thought that if he took that time off he'd just be hurting himself. He decided he didn't want to stop working and looked to get himself back out on the road so he

The whole George Harrison backup band. From left: Tessa Niles, Eric Clapton, Ray Cooper, Greg Phillinganes, Steve Ferrone, Andy Fairweather-Low, me, George and Nathan East.

wouldn't be sitting at home wallowing in grief. Most unexpectedly, he called George Harrison and told him that they both needed to get out and play. He had tried to get his old pal out on the road many times before, telling him that he was sitting at home while "all the rest of us are out working! Why not you!"

"But I don't even have a band," he told Eric.

"Well, I've got a band," Eric told him, "and you can have it, and what's more, you can have me!"

Whether George sensed that it was something he needed to do for Eric, himself, or both, I don't know; but he agreed. I got another call from Clapton, saying I was needed on the bill with George Harrison.

The band was basically the core from the 24 Nights shows: Eric on lead guitar and vocals; Eric's regular keyboard player, Greg Phillinganes, who chimed in on vocals; Nathan East on bass and background vocals; Steve Ferrone on drums; Ray Cooper on percussion; Tessa Niles and Katie Kissoon on background vocals; and me on keyboards and background vocals. There was one change: the addition of Andy Fairweather-Low, a fabulous guitar player from Wales, who replaced Phil Palmer.

George mailed a tape of select Beatles tunes as well has his own solo recordings to Charlane, so I could do a little homework before the rehearsals started. The easy part was that I had played most of the songs at some point anyway. I had learned them because I liked them to begin with — it was material I had lived with and listened to a zillion times. Still, I didn't know how it was going to all fall into place. As I sat at home and listened to the tapes, I had an idea that I would handle most of the piano, electric piano, and organ parts so that Greg could concentrate on the string, orchestral, and horn sounds.

That held somewhat true, but we ended up having a lot more fun with it and splitting up a lot of the parts. He performed a few piano parts on one or two things and I'd play strings, and vice versa. I think it worked perfectly. We had tremendous fun re-creating some of those sounds. *Piggies* was a great example — I had a blast re-creating that harpsichord sound and playing the part, which was originally done by Chris Thomas. It made me very aware that we were following some great keyboard players; George Martin on the early Beatles material, Billy Preston, Nicky Hopkins and Leon Russell — all of whom I've always been fanatical about.

Credit: Chuck Leavell Archive

Happily flanked by Eric and George.

Once I arrived for the rehearsals in England, it was obvious that George hadn't played live in a long time. He'd done the Wilburys videos and a television special tribute to Carl Perkins, but hadn't appeared on stage with a band of his own since 1974, which meant a lot of technology had passed him by. He was expecting real pianos and real harpsichords and had to be convinced that Greg and I could do it with electronics instead.

Greg was Eric's primary keyboard player and was far more into the programming than I've ever been — a situation that reminded

me of synthesizer wiz Matt Clifford from my second Stones tour —
but I knew a bit about programming and began to work on the
sounds I'd be responsible for, having fun in the process.

We rehearsed at Bray studios, the same place we'd done most of
Eric's rehearsals. We got down to business, playing all those great
songs that George wrote through the years: *My Sweet Lord, I Want To
Tell You, Something, Taxman, Here Comes The Sun, Isn't It a Pity, Set
on You*, and so many others. We were all so into it and so honored to
be playing with him. As the days went on the band really started to
click, and Greg and I were having fun working out our keyboard
duties and backing vocals. We were visited by lots of rock royalty
during the course of the sessions. Ringo stopped by to wish us well.
Steve Winwood, Gary Moore, and others dropped by to offer us
encouragement. Paul McCartney sent best wishes, but couldn't make
it for some reason. The final night we invited a bunch of fellow
musicians, friends, and family in to be the audience for a mock
show. While far from being the tight band we would become after
getting some real shows under our belt, it was still a great night, and
we were well received by all. Being a casual affair with friends and
such made it even more special. We got good and helpful comments
from lots of the musicians and artists that came. One was from Steve
Winwood, who made the suggestion of ending the show with *While
My Guitar Gently Weeps*, with the band still playing and George
taking off his guitar and making his waves of goodbye while the
band carried the song to the end. It was a good suggestion that we
took to heart, and it made for a great way to finish the show.

During our rehearsal period, we were invited several times to
George's famous mansion, Friar Park, Henley-on-Thames, where
he'd lived since the Beatles days. The place is unbelievable — the
most extraordinary estate I've ever seen. Friar Park was so "George."
It truly reflected him. As opulent and magnificent as the house is,
you could tell it truly was a home. You walked in and saw these
beautiful, ornate fixtures and furniture and gorgeous wood crafts-
manship in the walls and mantles as well as the furniture. It had a
studio built into one wing of the house and the most incredible

gardens imaginable. But it was not at all overwhelming, instead feeling quite homey, friendly, and very comfortable. You could sit down and not be intimidated by the vastness of this mega-room Victorian mansion. It was warm and happy, a true family feeling at Friar Park, and the credit for that went to George, his wife Olivia, and their son Dhani. Just one of the heartwarming, sincere surprises was an unbelievable Thanksgiving dinner Olivia prepared for us in honor of the American holiday. It was so touching. And so true to the Harrisons' sense of kindness and giving.

George's love of horticulture was obvious. The grounds were immaculate. There was a Japanese garden, a rose garden, a rock garden, a topiary garden, and more. He was curious about my passion for forestry, and we talked a lot about it. It was a bit foreign to him because he didn't really understand the American South, the pines, and what we were getting into on Charlane; but he was very interested by it, and we had many long talks about our mutual interest and concern for the environment. George loved the outdoors and was a true believer in the value of our Earth and displayed a genuine care about these things. I'm so sorry he never had the chance to see the plantation because I know he would have loved it. He was just so gracious and warm, so engaging. It was refreshing to be around him. I remember these little moments. He would play this silly instrument, which was a combination of a banjo and a ukulele. George Formby, who was an actor back in the 1930s, made movies playing this crazy instrument. He would sing and play, and Beatle George just loved watching those movies. He would pull that funny instrument out, pluck on it, and show us these movies. It was great to watch him because it was sort of the same thing he did with the sitar. He threw himself into it and learned how to master this instrument. For me, it was a joy to see how much pleasure he got out of that. I remember him playing a song that he had written about going to Japan called *The Rising Sun*. I don't think he ever recorded it, and it's unfortunate that we didn't get to play it with him.

He was such a sharing, caring person. His smile and his engaging little chuckle were two of the many little things about

George that made him special. He was an extraordinary human being, and it was an honor, a blessing, and a privilege to have had the opportunity to work with him. Of all the great artists that I have worked with, none was more personable, honorable, likable, and gracious than George Harrison. I was pinching myself every day that I spent with him. George was my hero as a kid, and to be invited to even say "hello" much less play in his band was a special highlight of my career.

When we did the Japan tour, he was the center of attention, and I could sense that he was nervous about that. In the end, even though he was a bit nervous, he stepped up and did a great job. Harkening back to our first session together some six or seven years earlier in Los Angeles, I remembered George saying he most enjoyed a band situation, and I came to understand and appreciate that.

He was also a kid having a good time. He hadn't played live — hadn't been out in the world of touring — in a long while, and he was excited, bubbly, and so sweet. I just can't tell

Credit: Chuck Leavell Archive

George Harrison during one of our first performances in Japan, December 1991.

you what a gentleman and a wonderful man he was to work with. Some artists are aloof. Not George. When we did that tour, most of the shows started and ended pretty early, to accommodate the schedule of public transportation system, which all of the concertgoers would ride.

We'd be done by 10 p.m., back at the hotel, sitting around, wondering what to do, and the phone would ring. It would be George, and he'd say, "I've ordered a bit of food. Would you like to come up and have a bite?" Or "how about coming up for a glass of nice wine?" He didn't drink but was so conscious of making everyone else comfortable. It was all very genuine, and it makes you want to work much harder for someone who treats you like that. He had that kind of personality where there is nothing to hide, very open and honest, which is such a refreshing thing in this business.

He'd sit around and talk, so human, so real. Here he was a Beatle — I don't care who you are: that kind of stardom at the age of twenty has got to affect you — and he was one of the most centered, down-to-earth people I've ever met. He made all of us feel like part of the family. It was an extraordinary kind of thing because he could have very easily hunkered down in his room and hidden away. Instead, he wanted to be part of the team, and he wanted us to realize that. On that level it made for one of the most wonderful, pleasant tours that I've

Credit: Chuck Leavell Archive

Eric and George on stage in Japan.

ever done. There were many special occasions when we were in Japan, and one that stands out was when we gathered for bass player Nathan East's birthday in Osaka. We all ate a wonderful Japanese meal in traditional Japanese style, sitting cross-legged on the floor at a table in a room that had been specially prepared for us. Eric gave Nathan a beautiful Giorgio Armani suit, and George gave him a fabulous leather jacket. It was a fun time, and it was very sweet of them both to put it together for Nate.

One of the best shows on the tour, as I recall, was in Hiroshima. We had a little time off there and I invited the band and crew to join me on a visit to the somber Hiroshima Peace Memorial Museum. A group of us met in the hotel lobby and then left for the downtown memorial, which consists of a large park and several museum buildings, as well as the haunting A-Bomb Dome, the building which remained standing, though heavily damaged, despite being just a few hundred feet from the epicenter of the atomic explosion that destroyed the rest of the city. Once we arrived at the monument, everyone was overcome by the emotion of the horror of what had happened there and we each wandered off on our own. I can think of few experiences as moving.

Our spirits were lifted a few days later when we were leaving Nagoya and a group of Hare Krishna followers had gathered outside the hotel to offer thanks to George in appreciation for all the help he'd given their movement over the years. They had an enormous amount of vegetarian dishes they'd lovingly prepared for George and anyone he wished to share it with. George graciously took the time to chat with them and offer his thanks in return for their acknowledgment.

The Japanese audiences loved us and treated us well. And each night, no matter what on that tour of Japan, there were always two songs that got tremendous reactions from the audience. *Isn't It a Pity* was the first. The lyrics are just a great comment on their own, but in concert the song had just such a wonderful way of building throughout its course and culminating in the crescendo at the end.

More than a decade has passed since my time on stage with George, but I still remember clearly looking out into the audience to see how moved the Japanese crowd was. The other song that had a huge effect on the audience every night was *While My Guitar Gently Weeps*. It was a great Beatles favorite on that Japanese tour, and there were nights where Eric simply tore the place up with his soloing on it.

Credit: © Mark Crossfield

Andy Fairweather-Low and me at a special ESP Guitars clinic in Japan.

Sadly, the experience wasn't all roses. Despite their long friendship and the obvious need for each other at this time, there was a strain between George and Eric's longtime manager, a guy named Roger Forrester. I wasn't privy to the details, but something had happened the night before we were all to travel to Tokyo from London.

They had some kind of row, and the next day the strain became obvious when, quite unexpectedly, Forrester wasn't on the plane to Japan. (After more than thirty years, Eric finally fired Forrester in 1999, and I can't say I shed any tears over him getting the boot. But more on that later.)

It made for a few awkward moments, but largely the conflict stayed off the stage. It was a great tour — far from perfect, however. I remember the first night was not a particularly good show. I think a lot of us had red-light syndrome, knowing the show was being taped and there was a tremendous amount of attention on George's return to live performance.

Only once do I remember the tension spilling over onto the stage: George would sometimes say the wrong thing — not meaning to — and Eric would not take it well. I remember there had been a bit of a feedback that George had been complaining about, and he believed it was coming from the bass amps. One night we finished playing *Isn't It A Pity* and started to leave the stage before the encore, George matter-of-factly told Eric that it was his guitar that was feeding back.

Even if you're George Harrison you don't tell Eric Clapton something like that. "I'm in control of that guitar at all times," Eric snapped at him. "It only feeds back when I want it to."

George certainly meant no harm and just wanted to solve a problem, but he didn't use good judgment or timing on that one. When we went out to play the encore, *My Guitar Gently Weeps*, Eric showed he was pissed off by putting a lot less effort into the tune.

It's the only time I remember the conflict between the superstars and their battling managements affecting the music, but that's not to say that there wasn't tension there concerning the situation. There were some missed opportunities, and people got their toes stepped on a few times, but that's not unusual in this business. It would have been nice if everybody could have just gotten along the whole time and not taken everything so seriously, but it was a very emotional time for George and Eric, I know. In the end these were really minor issues, and small potatoes in the scheme of things. Eric and George resolved their differences and remained close friends up until George's untimely death.

The tour ended brilliantly. On the last night, George's son Dhani and Nick Roylance, the son of Genesis Publishers owner Brian Roylance, who put out the terrific beautiful limited edition book on the tour, came on stage with their guitars at the end of the last number, *Roll over Beethoven*. I will never forget the look on each of their faces — it was very hard for a thirteen-year-old and fourteen-year-old to do in front of 45,000 people, but they stuck it out and earned a great reaction from the Tokyo audience.

Strangely, there was no plan for a party or get-together to commemorate the end of the tour. So I was quite relieved when George called everybody and invited us downstairs to a room he'd arranged in the hotel. We all sat around and ate great food and drank and were having a wonderful time, but no one really stood up and addressed the band and crew. It just seemed to me that something should be said to mark the occasion, so I nervously tapped a knife on my glass and awkwardly stumbled through a few words, saying the tour had been a great success and that I'd personally had a wonderful time and would never forget meeting such a great group of people. That seemed to break the ice and everyone else started taking turns speaking.

One thing about this gig is that when you go on the road with a bunch of strangers for several weeks or months at a time for something so intense as a tour you end up making lifelong friends — musicians, crew members, office staff, whomever — that you know you'll work with again sometime in your future.

That was certainly the case on George's tour with Andy Fairweather-Low, a terrific guitar player whom I'd never worked with before. Andy and I became close friends during that tour and beyond, and I'm grateful for his talent and his friendship. We were kindred spirits thrown into a surreal musical experience together.

"My life changed from the moment I got that call for the George Harrison tour of Japan," Andy recalls. "And you know, it was funny. I've always been such a big fan of Ry Cooder — a very vocal fan —

and George apparently thought that I must be a slide player, too. I'm not! But I came clean with him straightaway. I told him that we should meet anyway, and we did. And we hit it off.

"Being there with Chuck was great because he instantly welcomed me. So did Greg (Phillinganes). They were the two who took

care of me from the minute I walked through the door. I was in such good company. As much as George tried to make us feel comfortable, he was still George Harrison! We were a part of the show, we were there on stage, but with the man who had actually written those songs! It was so great. Besides, Chuck knows a lot about wine

Backstage with Eric Clapton.

— I like to drink it but I don't know anything about it … unless I'm with Chuck!"

Well, I don't claim to be any wine expert, but during the course of rehearsals and the tour, Andy and I did spend a lot of our off time at dinners together having great conversations and, well, the occasional couple of glasses of grape! And to show you what a small world we live in, Andy's now playing guitar with former Stones bassist Bill Wyman and his Rhythm Kings.

I learned so much being on the road with this terrific band. Playing not only with George but Eric was an unforgettable experience. They are all very sophisticated musicians, and Greg Phillinganes showed me voicings on the piano that I had never understood how to get; he and Nate showed me things like special passing chords and other little tricks as well. And just paying attention to Nathan was an eye opener. He'd later explain to me some of the magic of his approach to music: why he might choose to play a particular note — not necessarily the root note of the chord — in a given chord on the bass. I'll always be in awe of his talent.

And speaking of magic: Nate is one of the best magicians you'll ever see! He really does have a fantastic talent for that and is a member of several of the close societies of magicians around the world. He used to keep us all entertained with his tricks. Amazing stuff, some that really left you scratching your head to try and figure out how in the world he did it. Making things disappear and reappear, incredible card tricks, just amazing sleight of hand. It kept us all laughing and was a special part of being in a band with him.

People ask me about Eric often, and often I answer that Eric taught me eloquence in music. Eric is eloquent in his music and in his personality, and I hope a little of that rubbed off on all of us. It was a great lesson to learn.

The special leather-bound, limited edition commemorative of the Japan tour, done by Genesis Publications in England, is quite a remarkable book. Each of us in the band wrote a chapter for the book, and we each got a copy signed by George. In everybody's book, George wrote the same thing. It was a lovely comment that went something like, "How lovely to have worked with you. Love, George. PS. Your chapter was the best." Everybody got the same message — what a wonderful thing, it was brilliant! I can just imagine him chuckling when he was writing those comments. He had this great chuckle. He would talk, and when something would strike him as funny, he had this great little chuckle, and I'll always remember that.

Ironically, George himself wrote in the book that he was nervous about going on tour. "I was a little concerned about my throat, because as a child I always used to get throat trouble; and as recently as the October before we went on tour, a doctor told me always to be aware of the fact that my chest and throat are the most vulnerable parts of my body." Cruelly, it was throat cancer that ended up taking his life.

Certainly, his music and the songs are timeless, precious, and will live forever. I think beyond that was his expression of love for humanity. I have heard from various people that his last words were something like: "The important thing is to find God, and love one another. Everything else can wait." I think it is a testimony to him

Credit: Chuck Leavell Archive

that beyond all of his contributions to music, he was a person who was in search of love, and he gave that to all of us. He showed all of us how important it is to remember that God is love, and he set an example of that. Just consider the Concert for Bangladesh; George was the first big-name musician to reach out in a public way to try and help a cause that was clearly just. He did it unabashedly and unashamedly. George just stepped right up

Waving to an appreciative Japapnese crowd after a gracious introduction by George Harrison.

and said, "Someone needs to do this, and I'm going to be the one," and he saved a lot of lives with that concert. That was what George Harrison was all about, loving his fellow man.

When the Japan dates were done we begged George to carry it over to the States, but it just never happened. I think the 1974 experience was too sore a memory for him. Besides, as he told me, he witnessed outdoor concert sites after he'd played and saw what disaster and trash followed in the wake of one of his shows (any big rock show, in fact), and he simply didn't want to be the cause of that. How curious and selfless that this was George's first thought — rather than the imagining how much money he could rake in or how much a blockbuster American tour might stroke his ego. He didn't care about that.

Andy says that he believes George would have come around and gone back on the road eventually in the years that followed, except that too many other things got in the way — the *Beatles Anthology* book, *The Beatles 1* CD project, and the recording of what would turn out to be George's final solo CD, which was released posthumously.

I would have loved to go back on the road — or work in any way with George — but even though the tour ended in Japan, my own career took an exciting turn. Just before we finished the Japan shows, Greg went to Eric and told him that once the tour was over he wanted to return to the United States and pursue some of his own projects. Eric came to me and told me Greg was leaving and offered me the new gig as his piano player. "I want to continue working after this tour with George," he said. "Do you want to handle the keyboards on your own or do you think we should get someone else in?"

I said, "Eric, let me sleep on that." The next day I went to him and said, "You know, I think I'd be happy to try this myself. It would give me some room to stretch and contribute more."

Eric agreed.

Our first stop, however, was the studio, where Eric recorded songs for the soundtrack of the drug-crime movie *Rush*, which sported a great cameo by none other than Gregg Allman. We recorded the "incidental" music — the "mood" themes that you hear behind the scenes — as well as some more mainstream songs. One of the songs Eric included was a beautiful tribute he'd written to his late son, Conor, called *Tears in Heaven*. I didn't play on the studio version, but thought it was incredible. The movie did fair at the box office and our CD did well too. I thought Gregg did a wonderful job in the film. He played the part of a club owner who was

Credit: Chuck Leavell Archive

Me, Andy Fairweather-Low and Eric Clapton during the taping of the *Unplugged* special.

mysterious and connected in drug activity. He played his character just right and received good reviews for his performance. It was pretty cool seeing my old pal up there on the screen doing such a great job!

We then started rehearsals for Eric's next project, which turned out to be the *Unplugged* CD and video, which we recorded in front of about 300 people, 90 percent of whom were lucky fans who had won tickets in a BBC 1 radio competition. It was staged at Bray Studios in Berkshire outside of London on the evening of Jan. 16, 1992. Eric had told me he planned to do it, and I had seen a few of the MTV *Unplugged* shows. Most folks know that the methodology is to play an acoustic set, with no electronic "tricks." Just man and the elements — acoustic instruments. This was the first live performance that I did with Eric as the sole keyboard player. I had spent over a year with him not being able to really step out and do my thing. Even though Greg had been really good to me, in the earlier situation he had most all the solos and main parts, and I was support. This was my chance to finally step out. Man, was that like letting the tiger out of the cage! I was finally able to stretch with the band and with Eric. We had rehearsed for only three days — not very long to put together a whole different set of music — we went through songs in Eric's regular set plus something like fourteen or fifteen tunes in different acoustic arrangements — *Layla*, for instance, being the most obvious and now famous of the alternate arrangements. I couldn't wait to play! What I wanted to bring to the band was a kind of counterpoint and a bit of a tougher edge — my Southern touch, if you will. Because those other guys are so strong, so schooled, and so proficient on their instruments, they could play rings around me, but I think I balanced it by bringing a certain raw, tougher, and rougher approach. And to my mind, that blend would work if I just had the chance to chip in there. All of those people are just extraordinary players and singers, and I couldn't believe I had the good fortune to be playing in that band.

The rehearsals flew by quickly, and the next thing we knew we were about to go in front of the small audience and the cameras. Eric was more nervous than I'd ever seen him. I could understand why. It was a pretty risky thing to do to break down his band into this setting, and after losing Greg he probably wasn't sure about me as the only keyboard player. We didn't have much rehearsal time. He had thrown us a lot of new material in a very short time. There were big cameras in our faces. I can remember him fidgeting a bit before the show, just little nervous movements and chatty talk trying to calm down and get ready for the big moment. Eric has always been into fashion, and at the time had a deal with Armani. We were all dressed up in these beautiful, if somewhat conservative, suits, and he was checking everyone out, brushing off jackets and such. All of this was his way to try and get rid of some nervous energy, I thought. Finally, the moment came and the floor manager put us in place. The audience had been waiting for a while, and now they were ready to hear some Eric Clapton. They shrieked in excitement when they saw him and the rest of us come out. The director gave us the count-down, and we were on.

Eric started the show with a new instrumental called *Signe*, which was a nickname he had for Conor. It was a good warm up, and the fingers loosened. Next came a couple of blues tunes, *Before You Accuse Me* and *Hey, Hey*. Everyone was into it by then, and Eric was much more relaxed after playing a few tunes. The sound was good, and the band was loose and comfortable. From there we did some more intimate new songs, *Circus Has Left Town*, another one about Conor, and *My Father's Eyes*, followed by *Lonely Stranger*. Eric didn't include *My Father's Eyes* on the CD for some reason, and a couple of years later he released a much different version of it on his *Pilgram* record. Personally, I much preferred the *Unplugged* treatment. It was much more heartfelt, I thought. Anyway, the next tune was the beautiful *Tears in Heaven*. This version was to become the general favorite over the earlier recorded studio version, which made me proud because I am on this one. All of these songs were very touching, as they all had some relation to Conor or some other con-nection to Eric's life. Then the new version of *Layla* came. Before he started it, he asked the audience to "spot this one." Even with the radically different treatment, doing it in a 3/4 waltz-time feel, it didn't take them long to catch on. They all loved it, and it became a hit for Eric yet again as a single.

From there we did some blues tunes, one of which had us all laughing along with the audience. On *San Francisco Bay Blues* we all pulled out kazoos at the end, and it was hilarious and fun. We moved through *Nobody Knows You ...* and *Alberta, Alberta*, both of which offered me some nice solo room. Then there was a technical breakdown, and we had to stop for a few minutes. It felt quite awkward.

We were just sort of sitting there with our hands tied until Eric broke loose on and impromptu version of *Rollin' and Tumblin'*. It broke the doldrums of the breakdown, and it was just so cool that he thought to do it. We all jumped in and whipped it up, and the audience went wild.

The set ended and we had played everything Eric had on his list. But the audience still wanted more. He did a quick unrehearsed *Worried Life Blues* to appease them, but still they weren't satisfied. They were loving every moment and weren't about to let him stop. Eric didn't quite know what to do. He sort of scratched his head and looked around. For some reason he looked over at me and asked, "What can we do?"

Heading into my solo during Unplugged's *Old Love* (above) and Andy and Eric's reaction as I really let loose (below).

We had rehearsed *Old Love*, a great slow blues number that Eric had co-written with Robert Cray, but he decided he didn't want it in the set. But I thought it had sounded great, plus it had a perfect slot for a piano solo, and I was dying to do it. So I leaned over to him and said "Eric ... do *Old Love*." He agreed and called the tune. Man, I was wound up like a spring laying in wait for that solo and when it came, it was the huge release I'd been waiting for, and I cut loose. It felt so good to get that out, I just can't tell you. I had to laugh the first time I saw the *Unplugged* footage and noticed Nathan, Eric, and Andy all staring at me as I'm pounding the keys ... sitting down, standing up, sitting down ... and Andy making a facial gesture toward Eric like, "Jeez, who is that guy? — Chuck's really goin' for it!" I am so proud of everyone's playing on *Unplugged*, but that was a career highlight.

"That was an *incredible* moment!" Andy recently said. "Chuck just made magic. We were all blown away by him. It was so nice playing in such a small space to just a few hundred people like that. Playing like that gets the music to the people and you get their reaction back right away. Going acoustic is so great; there's nothing to get in the way of the instruments."

Several years later I heard this great story that related to one of the songs on the record. As you may know, after the song *Alberta*, Eric calls out my name, in his English accent, "Chaulk La-Velle!" Now, I have this friend that works in the forestry industry, and she told me, "I love that *Unplugged* record."

"Well, thanks," I said.

"My little boy, who is about six years old, just loves that part where he calls out your name."

"Why in the world would your son get excited about hearing 'Chaulk LaVelle," I asked. And she said, "Because he thinks Eric is saying 'chocolate milk!'" I nearly died laughing!

Anyway, after the *Unplugged* taping we had a couple of days off, then went back and rehearsed the regular set, and I had to adapt a lot of what I had done before with him, as Greg had done most of the major stuff before. But I did my homework and pulled it together for the tour. Along the way, Eric said, "So who's gonna sing those parts that Greg sang?" I said, "Well, I'd like to give it a go." He put me right on the spot then and there, and said, "OK, let's hear it." So I sang the part in *White Room* that Jack Bruce originally did, and Eric said, "You've got the gig!" That made me feel really good, as I hadn't really had a chance to sing much since the Sea Level days.

Well, the true *Unplugged* was just one show, but we did a tour of Europe and America afterward that was designed around the release of it, and I think it was one of the best tours I've ever done. Eric was good to me and good for me. I can't say the same for his manager. *Unplugged*, would be released as a CD, we were told, and we made a deal for the band's involvement. While I thought it was much less than we should have gotten, I agreed to it and that was that. When the issue of a video came up, the band was told that there wasn't much hope that there would be a hot video out of it, but that it probably would be released. I said to his manager Roger Forrester, "Well, that's fine. But if it does do well, can we discuss some further compensation from it?"

"Sure, if anything else happens with it," I remember Forrester telling me "you'll be looked after."

"Well, fair enough then," I said, and I did what my better judgment told me not to do. I signed the contract without that being spelled out.

As we all know, it was the biggest hit in MTV's *Unplugged* series and soon after released on CD, going on to earn Eric (quite rightly) a fist full of Grammy Awards and by some estimations nearly $100 million in royalties and was a huge hit on video. In fact, it was the biggest-selling music video of the time. After it was obvious how successful it was becoming, I sent a fax to Forrester reminding him of his verbal commitment to revisit the issue. In return, I got a short and curt reply saying how lucky I was even to be there, that I had very little part in it, and that I should be grateful even to be in a band with Eric. OK, I was an idiot for not getting it in writing. I should have known better and I accept that. But I'll tell you, where I come from, a man's word is his bond. And I was really disappointed in this situation. All I can say is that it made me feel really good about having paid back those bills on the last Sea Level tour. At least I stood up to my word and didn't walk away from my promises. In any case, it's history now, and I've moved way beyond it. I can't and won't speak for anyone else, but Forrester's idea of the band being "taken care of" for the video/DVD release didn't quite measure up to what I'd imagined. None of the supporting band got an extra penny. But that was business and had nothing to do with Eric or the honor it was to share the stage with him and all those great players. Live and learn, Chuck, live and learn.

The tour went on through Europe and to America. We played tons of shows, and the band, at least in my opinion, just got better and better. We played about a dozen shows with Elton John, both in Europe and the United States. We'd swap headlining, and usually Eric and Elton would have some wonderful jams at the end. One of the magical shows was in my backyard in Atlanta. It felt so good to come back to Georgia with a different situation than the Stones. We played the now-defunct Omni, which was a large indoor arena that held a little over 20,000 people. It was sold out weeks in advance. The show absolutely smoked, and the hometown crowd made me feel like a million dollars, even if I wasn't earning anywhere near it! We did some stadium shows, like the ones with Elton, but mostly large arenas and "sheds," the indoor-outdoor venues like the Alpine Valley Amphitheater in Wisconsin, where Stevie Ray Vaughan played his last show. It was all wonderful, and I felt like I was part of another family. We traveled mostly in a G4 private airplane with just the band, Eric, tour manager Peter Jackson, and a couple of others. Sometimes Forrester would join us, but mostly it was a small group, and we were all pretty close. I liked everyone in the band and was comfortable in this new setting. It was much more intimate than the Stones situation, which is usually at least a 727 or larger aircraft with sometimes more than fifty or sixty people onboard.

One very special person in the band was Ray Cooper. Ray is not only an amazing and talented percussionist, but also an actor, having made it into several movies over the years, including *Popeye* with Robin Williams, the quirky *Brazil*, and others. Ray is the nicest guy. On the stage he would take on this whole different persona, a sort of madman on the percussion, especially when he did his nightly solo. It was always great musically and also very entertaining to watch.

Off the stage he is very quiet and polite, almost to a fault. Nate and I used to joke that if you stepped on his foot, he'd be the one to say "Oh, so sorry, mate!" One thing he did that drove me crazy was that he would try to pay the tab for drinks or a meal. It could be that he wasn't even in the dinner party, but maybe he saw us in there eating, and he'd go to the waiter and tell him to give him the tab. Sometimes a bottle of fine wine or champagne would just show up at our table, courtesy of Ray. Or if he saw us in the bar, he'd sneak the tab. It got to be almost ridiculous, and we'd even get mad at him for it, but it was just his wonderful way of trying to be nice and to be a friend. We had many long hours of conversation and fun together, not to mention the playing. But really, the whole band was like that. Nate, Andy, Ray, Steve, Tessa, Katie, and Greg, who was in the band when I joined, are all special and talented folks. I count my blessings that I was able to spend a couple of years with them. Eric was always great, too, if a bit aloof. He didn't join in on much of the social hangs, as he's very committed to his addiction recovery. But that doesn't mean he was a recluse. He was always cordial and fun to be with. One of his special and weird talents is the table game of Foosball. He's really amazing at it, and so is Nate. I tried to get good at it, but it was no use for me. They are in a different league. I'd get beat solid every time, and no matter how hard I tried I just couldn't compete with them. In any case, Eric was good to me, and I always felt at home with him. I have the utmost admiration for his strength and commitment to his own recovery and to help others. He says it saved his life, and I'm sure it did. It's common knowledge that he's done a great deal for others in this situation, both in a private and a public way. His Crossroads addiction and recovery facility in Antigua is one of the best in the world and boasts a high success rate. I even know some people from around my part of the world that have gone there and changed their lives. He is to be congratulated and revered for this great work.

Finally, the tour came to an end. It was very strange because Eric didn't say anything about the future to the band. We all wondered what he might do next, but there was no clue coming from him until he made a rather weird remark on the last night we were together. There was a little end of tour get-together going on. While we were on our way to the social, he was asking me what I was going to do.

"Go home, first," I said. "But then Rose Lane's birthday is coming up and we're getting a group together to go to Costa Rica for a week or so."

"Ah, great. Costa Rica, that's wonderful," he said. Then came some silence, and finally he said something like, "Well, it's sad, but it must be done." At the time I had no idea what he was talking about, but what he meant was that he was breaking up the band. He had not said a word to anyone about this, and we sort of assumed that there would be a break and then perhaps we'd carry on with a record or another tour sometime in the future. I think Eric has a hard time facing things like this, and he just didn't want to say it directly. Anyway, in the end I just didn't hear anything from him. Several months later I heard that he was going into the studio with another set of musicians and was planning a tour. Some of the band remained. Andy and Nate worked with him for years afterwards and sometimes do still, and I think Tessa and Katie did some work with him occasionally. But for me it was the last time. Of course, I never felt that I'd be in Eric's band for some indefinite period, and I was aware that he does like change. That's even evident in the changes in his looks through the years. It's also evident in his previous changes in his bands. But this band had been together a long time. Maybe that's why he felt he needed a change. In any case, the fact that there would likely be another Stones record and tour before long or some other session work kept me from worrying too much about it. I did feel like we had something very special and that we'd work together again. But we haven't, for whatever reason. He's gone on to make some fine recordings and done some great tours in recent years, and I applaud his works and fact that he still explores his talents in so many different ways. But somewhere deep down I'm a little hurt that he's never called me in to play with him again. But we're both still young!

In April of that year, however, George Harrison again called on us to back him up for what turned out to be the last time he ever performed in the UK, a benefit in support of the Natural Law party's election campaign. Eric and Nathan East couldn't make it, so the team was made up of George, Mike Campbell from Tom Petty's Heartbreakers on guitar, Andy Fairweather-Low on guitar, Will Lee on bass, Steve Ferrone on drums, me and Greg Phillinganes on keyboards, Ray Cooper on percussion, and Katie Kissoon and Tessa Niles on background vocals. Special guests included Ringo Starr, Gary Moore, Joe Walsh, and George's son Dhani.

It was certainly one of the most unusual shows I've ever done. You can imagine what a show that is produced and run by an entity like the Natural Law Party might be like. There were a couple of speeches from their representatives about their philosophy and such, and some if it got a bit far out there, but when it came down to the music, it was just great. Joe Walsh rocked the house with his classic *Rocky Mountain Way* and a couple of others. Gary Moore smoked his guitar until it almost burned on some blues, and George brought down the house with several of his tunes from solo albums and a few Beatles songs. It was great to get us back together for this event, and it sure was a joy to play with him again. It was a shame not to have Eric there, but we had a great time with all the talent that we had on stage. We also got to visit George and his family at Friar Park again, which made the trip even more special.

Through the years I'd be pleased to see George and speak briefly backstage at Stones shows. Without fail, Rose Lane and I also always got elaborate, handmade Christmas cards from him, Olivia, and Dhani. Each is a work of art, a unique little thing of beauty to be treasured. Just like George.

God gave us Music
that we might pray without words.

Unknown

Epilogue

If the Rolling Stones tour again, I'd be honored to be asked to participate — just like I'd be honored if Eric Clapton or the Allman Brothers rang up with an offer to play some music. I might even accept. I've had a career of incredible highs and in the scheme of things, relatively few lows. The Stones gig I got in part because of my involvement in the Allman Brothers Band. The Stones led to Eric Clapton and George Harrison. So much of my session work is due to past relationships. I've enjoyed just about every single moment. It's been more than interesting and fun to watch it all unfold, and to have been in this movie called Life.

Dickey Betts' tune *Jessica* was huge for me, and I never get tired of playing it. Eric Clapton's *Unplugged* was another landmark moment for me, especially my solo on *Old Love*. I loved doing the Black Crowes album, working with the T-Birds, Sea Level, Indigo Girls, Blues Traveler, Gov't Mule, Train, and all the others.

And my time with the Stones — half my career now and half theirs — has never *not* been an education. I learned a lot about the "big picture" from being with the Stones. I've learned a great deal from watching Mick and Keith run the office — the way they run everything. About how to handle all kinds of issues from the music to the press, promotions, image — all of that. They are masters at the

Randall Bramblett, Phil Walden and me at the 2004 reception for my Atlanta Heroes Award.

music and at running a huge business. It has been a very interesting thing to observe and learn from.

Any plans for me to embark on a true solo career seem to have taken a backseat to other opportunities and responsibilities, whether with the Stones, the plantation, or my family, which ultimately is my number one priority. But I've managed to stick a small solo career in the mix, and I'm grateful for that.

Sometimes it took a backseat simply because I was on the road making money to support my family. Sometimes this meant I wasn't always the husband or father I wanted to be — and I regret that I had to spend so much time being a partner and raising daughters from the other end of a telephone line.

I was lucky that I had an understanding and loving wife and that we had such great kids. They went through all the trials and troubles that a lot of teenagers go through, often without a dad right there to help. They came through it all with flying colors, and Rose Lane and I are truly grateful. We're blessed that Amy and Ashley are both

The greatest pride of my life: My family … Son-in-law Steve, Rose Lane, me, Amy, Rose Lane's Mom Rosaline and Ashley.

wonderful human beings. They turned out great and I couldn't be more proud of them. They're both happy, healthy, intelligent young women, and enjoying the roads that life is taking them down. You don't get more fortunate than.

My absences have, at times, taken a toll on my marriage. Rose Lane and I have been through some tough times in our relationship. While the only perspective I have is that part of those problems were caused by my chosen profession, I do also have to remember this: No marriage is perfect. I don't know a single couple that goes through this life without some problems, tension, misunderstanding, mistrust, and misgivings. I think Rosie and I are also fortunate that we had parents who showed us how important marriage and family are.

My folks were wonderful role models for Judy, Billy, and me, as were Rose Lane and Alton's parents. We learned a lot from growing up in households that taught us things like dedication, determination, honor, strength, and courage. Our families were understanding and forgiving, and they gave us a whole lot of love. We also had extended family support from our brothers, my sister, our aunts, uncles, and cousins. We learned the value of strong family ties. The point is that we've come out the other side better people, and our relationship is better and stronger now than it ever has been. All that we've been through both together and as individuals is beginning to pay off. Rosie's afforded the luxury now to dedicate more of her time to her spectacular artwork and getting to explore her own creative endeavors. She's great to me. Better than I deserve.

Every day that we spend at Charlane is a blessing, and we're fortunate to have been able to work on it, nurture it, cultivate it, learn from it, and to strive to make it healthier and better. I'll always have considerable work to do on the forestry side of the family business. In fact, I'd like to do more. I love being in the woods, I love the hard work, and I love the way it makes me feel at the end of the day. I love the smells of the outdoors, the feel of the wind and sun on my face, and the satisfaction of seeing small seedlings grow into stately trees. I love the sound of the wind in the pines, seeing deer running in the woods, watching fox squirrels scampering up a tree, hearing wild turkeys gobbling or an owl hoot, or experiencing the thrill and beauty of a covey rise at sunset. I love the way it feels to be up on my horse Lucky and the way it feels to be on my John Deere 4020. I enjoy spending more time at home and giving speeches and being an active advocate for family forests and the environment. I get a kick out of working with legislators, governors, senators, congressmen and other politicians. I'm not certain where this area of my life will lead me.

But, you see, I also love the way it feels when I have recorded a great song or when I have written a piece of music that makes me feel like I have said something worthwhile. I love the sound of 80,000 screaming fans and the sound of a small appreciative club audience. I love the touch of piano keys under my fingers. I love to hear my voice with others creating harmony. I love the excitement that flows through me when an arrangement idea hits me like a hammer. I love hearing a fellow musician do something amazing that makes me want to talk back musically. I love to lock into a groove with the bass and drums and swing for as long as we can all stand it.

And I love to kiss my wife. I love the way I feel when I hold her close. I loved when I held my daughters in my arms for the first time. I loved seeing Amy and Ashley play when they were little. I loved watching them when they were growing up, seeing them in their Easter white with all the bows and laces. I loved them as young adults, finding their way and exploring life. I loved seeing Amy as we walked down the isle together and I handed her off to Steve. I loved watching Ashley as she walked up to receive her Boston University degree with honors. I love seeing them now as often as they can come back home or as often as Rosie and I can go see them. I love it when we all get in a huddle and hug. I really love that.

It's amazing to me that I've been so fortunate to do these things, to have had all these experiences. Life has been much better to me than I probably deserve. It's been one heck of a ride so far, and I can't wait to see what the other half brings!

We all have dreams, and certainly I have all kinds of ideas and dreams that I'd love to have see the light of day before the curtain falls. There are scores of artists I'd love to work with for the first time and scores of artists I'd like to work with for the second, third, or hundredth time. There are fields to plough and trees to nurture and many more family times to enjoy.

Only time — and fate — will tell what lies ahead. So long as my life is filled with my family, my trees, and some keys, I will never think of myself just lucky, happy, or content. I'll consider myself blessed as I'm caught, happily, between rock and a home place.

*Music is a higher revelation
than all wisdom and philosophy.
Music is the electrical soil
in which the spirit lives,
thinks and invents.*

Ludwig van Beethoven

Things I Think You Should Hear

Everybody's taste is different, of course. Hey, look at *Exile on Main Street*, which most Rolling Stones fans generally consider the band's double-album a career masterpiece. Mick Jagger doesn't think it's a "classic" album, though he admits it might have a couple of good tunes on it! If you manage to find a copy of John Lennon's final print interview with *Playboy*, he runs through every Beatles song and trashes a lot of his own songs like *And Your Bird Can Sing*, *Mean Mr. Mustard*, *Sun King*, *Dig a Pony*, and *Good Morning* as "throwaways," calling each one "another piece of garbage."

So that's how extreme and subjective the whole idea of picks and pans can be. I've mentioned most of my early influences and artists for whom I have great admiration. But for what it's worth — and for the few pages of paper it will take up (wood is a renewable resource, if I neglected to mention that somewhere here!) — here's my idea of some music you need to hear. In one way or at one time or another, each had some inspiration for me or influence on me and may, if nothing else, tell you just a little more about Chuck Leavell.

Check out some early Ray Charles, Little Richard, Jerry Lee Lewis, Bill Evans, Nicky Hopkins, Leon Russell, Billy Preston. If you see any one of their names on a CD, check it out. I've found Earl Hines, Duke Ellington, Count Basie, Thelonious Monk, McCoy Tyner, Nat "King" Cole, Abdula Ibrahim, Ramsey Lewis, Charles

Mingus, Oscar Peterson and Art Tatum to be hugely influential. For Hammond B3, there's Jimmy Smith, Jimmy McGriff, Brother Jack McDuff, Groove Holmes, Booker T. Jones (Booker T. and the MG's), and Joey DeFranchesco. Of course, these guys are all piano and organ players, but you'd also want to hear Miles Davis, John Coletrane, Django Reinhardt, Eddie Lang and Joe Venuti, Charlie Parker, Cannonball Adderley, Frank Sinatra, Tony Bennett, Chet Baker, Stan Getz, Tony Williams, Elvin Jones, and the like. I'd also add Weather Report, The Crusaders, Return to Forever, and Mahavishnu Orchestra to the list. It's not infrequent that I stroll down to our "pondo" with a few Debussy, Paganini, Mozart, Shubert, Scriabin, Bach, Beethoven or — obviously — Chopin CDs. But probably no one has affected me and my playing more than Keith Jarrett. I'll never be in the league of any of these cats, but listening to them — even now, at my age and having accomplished what I have — has a rejuvenating and inspiring effect.

Ian Stewart taught me about the boogie-woogie greats like Albert Ammons, Meade Lux Lewis, Montana Taylor, James P. Johnson, and Pete Johnson. Take a page from Stu and check them out. For more modern boogie guys, Bob Seeley, Axel Zwingenberger, Carl "Sonny" Leyland, and Rudy "Blue Shoes" Wyatt are names to remember. Boogie-woogie is a real art form, and it's not easy to play, especially when those left-hand figures get complicated — but I love that stuff! Don't forget that even Led Zeppelin paid tribute to Stu's talent with their great track *Boogie with Stu*.

If you were to walk into a record store tomorrow, I'd tell you to buy any early Ella Fitzgerald and Keith Jarrett's *Koln Concerts* and *Standards,* volume 2. I'd also tell you to find *Crystal Silence* by Chick Corea and Gary Burton.

Joni Mitchell is someone who I've listened to through the years and who has always amazed me with her powerful, colorful lyrics, innovative tunings, unique chord progressions, and arrangements, not to mention that fabulous voice. I'm always moved. My good friend Randall Bramblett is my favorite Southern singer/songwriter. If you've never heard him, go find one of his CDs.

And I'd tell you that if you're sifting through the bins in the record store and see the names Little Walter, Howlin' Wolf, Muddy Waters, Pinetop Perkins, Memphis Slim, Otis Span, Little Milton, B. B. King, Freddie King, Albert King, Buddy Guy, Willie Dixon, or John Lee Hooker, buy it! As a matter of fact, I'd say all the "Littles, Kings, Slims, Fats, Blinds, and Bigs" are good bets.

Bob Marley was certainly a great one, and there are many other wonderful reggae artists like Toots and The Maytalls, Peter Tosh and more.

I still stop the radio dial if I stumble across some of the old rock or R&B stuff — Sam and Dave, Otis Redding, Aretha Franklin, Wilson Pickett, Joe Tex, King Curtis, Johnny Taylor, Clarence Carter, Sam Cooke, and James Brown. Even though as I've stated earlier in this book about how hard Chuck Berry is to work with, I still have to say he's a classic and must be mentioned for his great songs and guitar playing. The classic Motown artists like Stevie Wonder, The Temptations, The Four Tops, and The Supremes. Let's pay homage to the great rhythm section that backed them up on those records, know as the "Funk Brothers" — Richard "Pistol" Allen, Jack "Black Jack" Ashford, Robert White, Uriel Jones, James Jamerson, Earl Van Dyke, Joe Hunter, Joe Messina, Eddie "Chank" Willis, Benny Benjamin, and all the other great Motown session players. And, I have to admit, I never turn off a Beatles song, a Dylan tune, a Van Morrison cut, or a Stones track if it comes across the radio. The same for some of the Allman Brothers Band or Gov't Mule. Then there is Crosby, Stills, and Nash (and sometimes Young); The Beach Boys; Simon and Garfunkel; Joe Cocker (*Mad Dogs and Englishmen* is one I still pull out every now and then, a great live rock record); Led Zeppelin; The Who; Jimi Hendrix; Traffic; Steve Winwood; and other great 1960s bands.

For early R&B, Little Willie John, Earl Bostic, Bill Doggett, Jackie Wilson, The Dominoes, and The Platters are good studies.

Country's important too, and even if some of the modern country has become a bit corporate and plastic, there is a lot of good stuff out there. Like Clint Black, Lee Roy Parnell, Travis Tritt,

Alison Krauss, Vince Gill, Randy Scruggs (OK — disclaimer, I was proud to have worked with Roseanne Cash and him on a CD.), Lee Ann Womack, and Montgomery-Gentry Band (I got to work with both those artists, too!). You can't go wrong with Hank Williams, Chet Atkins, Floyd Cramer, Jimmy Rogers, Johnny Cash, Ralph Stanley, Bill Monroe, Patsy Cline, Willie, Waylon, Reba, Winnona, or Trisha Yearwood.

I can't say I'm an expert on rap or hip-hop — though I thought some of the early stuff like Arrested Development was innovative and had relevant social commentary. Lauryn Hill I sometimes find interesting, and I love Outkast. But some rap, well, I loved Keith's quote about the violence that seems to be its foundation: "We never had the Temptations killing the Four Tops."

I like Faith Hill, Sara McLaughlin and Macy Gray … and Sheryl Crow will always have a special place for me — we've been friends for many years and she's opened for the Stones on numerous occasions and I'm never disappointed or fail to be moved when she performs.

I have to mention the New Orleans piano masters: Dr. John, Professor Longhair, James Booker, Eddie Bo, Henry Butler, and Allan Toussaint.

There are so many others I could name, some that are famous and many that are obscure, but maybe this will give you an idea of where I'm coming from. Part of the canvas for your listening pleasure is based on who you are and if you have an interest or particular talent for a certain instrument, which is why, as I say, it's all subjective and one of the only things in life where no one is wrong!

Finally, I guess there's just one final thing to say: Elvis.

Chuck Leavell: Discography

1970 Sundown — *Sundown*

1970 Freddie North — *Friend Mankind*

1971 John Buck Wilkin — *In Search of Food, Clothing, Shelter and Sex*

1971 Cowboy — *5'll Get You Ten*

1972 Marlin Greene — *Tiptoe Past the Dragon*

1972 Sailcat — *Motorcycle Mama*

1972 Alex Taylor — *Dinnertime*

1972 Various Artists — *Ann Arbor Blues and Jazz Festival*

1972 Various Artists — *Burbank Downtown Strutters*

1972 Whiskey Howl — *Whiskey Howl*

1973 Allman Brothers Band — *Brothers and Sisters*

1973 Cowboy — *Why Quit When You're Losing*

1973 Gregg Allman — *Laid Back*

1973 Livingston Taylor — *Over the Rainbow*

1974 Don McLean — *Playin' Favourites*

1974 Gregg Allman — *Gregg Allman Tour*

1974 Dickey Betts — *Highway Call*

1974 Martin Mull — *Normal*

1974 Kitty Wells — *Forever Young*

1974 Various Artists — *Peaches Pick of the Crop*

1975 Allman Brothers Band — *Win, Lose, or Draw*

1975 Bonnie Bramlett — *It's Time*

1975 Randall Bramlett — *That Other Mile*

1975 Bobby Whitlock — *One of a Kind*

1975 Cowboy — *Boyer and Talton*

1975   Doris Duke — *Legend in Her Own Time*

1975   Hydra — *Land of Money*

1975   Marshall Tucker Band — *Searchin' for a Rainbow*

1975   Marcia Waldoft — *Memoranda*

1975   Pete Carr — *Not a Word on It*

1975   Various Artists — *Volunteer Jam*

1976   Allman Brothers Band — *The Road Goes On Forever*

1976   Allman Brothers Band — *Wipe the Windows, Check the Oil, Dollar Gas*

1976   Bonnie Bramlett — *Lady's Choice*

1976   Charlie Daniels — *Volunteer Jam*

1976   Randall Bramlett — *Light of the Night*

1976   Mickey Carroll — *Mickey Carroll*

1976   Cowboy — *5'll Get You Ten*

1976   Hank Williams Jr. — *Hank Williams Jr. & Friends*

1976   Johnny Rivers — *Wild Night*

1976   Billy Joe Shaver — *When I Get My Wings*

1976   Talton/Stewart/Sandlin — *Happy to Be Alive*

1976   Bobby Whitlock — *Rock Your Sox Off*

1977   Marshall Tucker Band — *Carolina Dreams*

1977   Sea Level — *Best of Sea Level*

1977   Sea Level — *Sea Level*

1977   Tim Weisberg — *Tim Weisberg Band*

1978   Duke Jupiter — *Sweet Checks*

1978   Katy Moffatt — *Kissin' in the California Sun*

1978   Randy Richards — *If You've Ever Loved*

1978   Sea Level — *Cats on the Coast*

1978   Sea Level — *On the Edge*

1978   Sea Level — *Special Limited Edition Pressing*

1978   Various Artists — *Hotels, Motels Road Shows*

1978   Various Artists — *The South's Greatest Hits Volume II*

1978   Various Artists — *Volunteer Jams Volumes III and IV*

1978   Tim Weisberg Band — *Rotations*

1979   Cooper Brothers — *Pitfalls of the Ballroom*

1979   Livingston Taylor — *Echoes*

1979   Marshall Tucker Band — *Running Like the Wind*

1979   The Rockets — *Rockets (Turn Up the Radio)* (US)

1979   Sea Level — *Long Walk on a Short Pier*

1980   Aretha Franklin — *Aretha*

1980   Sea Level — *Ball Room*

1981   Allman Brothers Band — *Best of the Allman Brothers*

1981   The Normaltown Flyers — *Normaltown Flyers*

1981   The Dice — *Dice*

1981   Rick Christian — *Sweet Young Thing*

1983   Rolling Stones — *Undercover*

1985   Mick Jagger — *She's the Boss*

1985   Original Soundtrack — *Porky's Revenge*

1986   Brian Setzer — *Knife Feels Like Justice*

1986   The Fabulous Thunderbirds — *Tuff Enuff*

1986   Rolling Stones — *Dirty Work*

1987   Chuck Berry — *Hail! Hail! Rock 'N' Roll*

1987   The Fabulous Thunderbirds — *Hot Number*

1987   The Tim Weisberg Band — *Rotations*

1988   Aretha Franklin — *Aretha* (Import)

1988   Bill Carter — *Loaded Dice*

1988   Keith Richards — *Talk is Cheap*

1988   Fabio Treves — *Sunday Blues*

1989   Allman Brothers Band — *Dreams*

1989   Dion — *Yo Frankie*

1989   The Golden Palominos — *Dead Horse*

1989   Grapes of Wrath — *Now & Again*

1989   Joe Henry — *Murder and Crows*

1989   Missouri — *Welcome to Missouri*

1989   Rolling Stones — *Steel Wheels*

1990   The Black Crowes — *Shake Your Money Maker*

1990   Dave Edmunds — *Closer to the Flame*

1990   John Hiatt — *Stolen Moments*

1990   Original Soundtrack — *Sundown*

1990   Rolling Stones — *The Rolling Stones: The CBS Collection*

1990   Rolling Stones — *The Rolling Stones Collection*

1990   Sea Level — *Best of Sea Level*

1990   Russ Taff — *Way Home*

1991   Allgood — *Ride the Bee*

1991   Allman Brothers Band — *The Decade of Hits*

1991   Allman Brothers Band — *Ramblin' Man*

1991   Scott Boyer — *All My Friends*

1991   Larry Carlton — *Renegade Gentleman*

1991   Eric Clapton — *24 Nights*

1991   Col. Bruce Hampton & the Aquarium Rescue Unit —
       Col. Bruce Hampton & the Aquarium Rescue Unit

1991   The Normaltown Flyers — *Normaltown Flyers*

1991   Rolling Stones — *Flashpoint Collectibles*

1991   Rolling Stones — *Flashpoint*

1992   Eric Clapton — *Unplugged*

1992   Eric Clapton — *Rush Soundtrack*

1992   Tinsley Ellis — *Trouble Time*

1992   George Harrison — *Live in Japan*

1992   Charles Mingus — *Weird Nightmare*

1992   Tom Principato — *Tip of the Iceberg*

1992   Ron Wood — *Slide On This*

1992   Various Artists — *Rock of the 70's, Vol.3*

1992   Various Artists — *Rock of the 70's, Vol. 4*

1992   Various Artists — *Weird Nightmare: Meditations on Mingus*

1993   Brother Cane — *Brother Cane*

1993   Brother Cane — *Hard Act to Follow*

1993   Col. Bruce Hampton & the Aquarium Rescue Unit —
       Mirrors of Embarrassment

1993   Cowboy — *Different Time: The Best of Cowboy*

1993   Warren Haynes — *Tales of Ordinary Madness*

1993   Jenni Muldaur — *Jenni Muldaur*

1993   Colin James — *Colin James & the Little Big Band*

1993   Rolling Stones — *Jump Back: The Best of the Rolling Stones 1971-1993*

1994   Allgood — *Ride the Bee*

1994   Allman Brothers Band — *Legendary Hits*

1994   Tinsley Ellis — *Storm Warning*

1994   Aretha Franklin — *Greatest Hits (1980-1994)*

1994   Indigo Girls — *Swamp Ophelia*

1994   Rolling Stones — *Voodoo Lounge*

1994   Ron Wood — *Slide On Live: Plugged In and Standing*

1994   Billy Joe Shaver — *Honky Tonk Heroes*

1994   Blues Traveler — *Four*

1995   Jennifer Holliday — *On & On*

1995   Indigo Girls — *4.5: The Best of the Indigo Girls*

1995   Marshall Tucker Band — *Best of the Marshall Tucker Band: Capricorn Years*

1995   Original Soundtrack — *Boys on the Side*

1995   Rolling Stones — *Stripped*

1995   Various Artists — *Move to Groove: Best of 1970s Jazz Funk*

1995   Gov't Mule — *Live At Roseland Ballroom*

1996   Iris Dement — *Way I Should*

1996   Johnny Hallyday — *Rough Town*

1996   Johnny Jenkins — *Blessed Blues*

1996   Various Artists — *Celebration of Blues: The Great Guitarists, Vol. 3*

1996   Various Artists — *Celebration of Blues:
       The Great Guitarists, Vol. 3/Women in Blues*

1996   Various Artists — *Celebration of Blues: The New Breed/Acoustic Blues*

1996   Various Artists — *Celebration of Blues: The New Breed*

1996   Various Artists — *Steinway to Heaven*

1998   Allman Brothers Band — *All Live*

1998   The Black Crowes — *Shu'Nuff*

1998   Chuck Leavell — *What's In That Bag?*

1998   Gov't Mule — *Dose*

1998   Martin Mull — *Mulling It Over: A Musical Oeuvre*

1998   Tom Principato — *Really Blue*

1998   Rolling Stones — *No Security*

1998   Rolling Stones — *No Security* (Japan Bonus Track)

1998   Rolling Stones — *Poland, 1998*

1998   Richie Sambora — *Undiscovered Soul* (US)

1998   Randy Scruggs — *Crown of Jewels*

1998   Livingston Taylor — *Carolina Day: The Collection (1970-80)*

1998   Various Artists — *Celebrate the Season: T.J. Martell Christmas Album*

1999   Eric Clapton — *Clapton Chronicles: The Best of Eric Clapton*

1999   Gov't Mule — *Live with a Little Help from Our Friends*

1999   Jimmy Nalls — *Ain't No Stranger*

1999   Linda Ronstadt — *Linda Ronstadt Box Set*

1999   Rolling Stones — *Bridges to Babylon* (Japan Bonus Track)

2000   Allman Brothers Band — 20th Century Masters —
       The Millennium Collection: The Allman Brothers Band

2000   American Diesel Machine — *American Diesel Machine*

2000   Richard Ashcroft — *Alone with Everybody*

2000   Richard Ashcroft — *Alone with Everybody* (Japan)

2000   Eric Clapton — *Best of Eric Clapton* (Import Bonus Tracks)

2000   Eric Clapton — *Clapton Chronicles: The Best of Eric Clapton* (Australia)

2000   Indigo Girls — *Retrospective*

2000   Richie Sambora — *Undiscovered Soul* (Imported Bonus Tracks)

2000   Hank Williams, Jr. — *Hank Williams Jr. & Friends*

2001   Allman Brothers Band — *Road Goes on Forever* (Expanded)

2001   Brand New Immortals — *Tragic Show*

2001   Chuck Leavell — *Forever Blue: Solo Piano*

2001   Count M'butu Orchestra — *See the Sun*

2001   Eric Clapton — *Clapton Chronicles: The Best of Eric Clapton Unplugged*

2001   Gov't Mule — *Deep End, Vol.1*

2001   The Proclaimers — *Persevere*

2001   Train — *Drops of Jupiter*

2002   Eric Jerardi — *Virtual Virtue*

2002   Gregg Allman — *20th Century Masters — The Millennium Collection: Gregg Allman*

2002   Gov't Mule — *Deep End, Vol. 2*

2002   Gov't Mule — *Live with a Little Help from Our Friends, Vol. 2*

2002   Jerry Joseph/The Jack Mormons — *Conscious Contact*

2002   Lee Ann Womack — *Something Worth Leaving Behind*

2002   Lee Ann Womack — *Something Worth Leaving Behind* (UK Bonus Track)

2002   Montgomery Gentry — *My Town*

2002   The Proclaimers — *Best of the Proclaimers*

2002   Richard Ashcroft — *Human Conditions*

2002   Rolling Stones — *Forty Licks*

2002   Rolling Stones — *Forty Licks* (Collectors Edition)

2002   Ron Wood — *Live at Electric Ladyland*

2002   Blues Traveler — *Travelogue: Blues Traveler Classics*

2002   Widespread Panic — *Live in the Classic City*

2003   The Allman Brothers Band — *Martin Scorsese Presents the Blues: The Allman Brothers*

2003   Danny Barnes — *Dirt on the Angel*

2003   E.G. Kight — *Southern Comfort*

2003   Feathermerchants — *Unarmed Against the Dark*

2003   Jimmie Vaughan — *Essential Jimmie Vaughan*

2003   Kate Taylor — *Beautiful Road*

2003   The Marshall Tucker Band — *Stompin' Room Only* (Bonus Tracks)

2003   Richard Ashcroft — *Human Conditions* (Bonus Track)

2003   Richard Ashcroft — *Human Conditions* (Canada Bonus Track)

2004   The Allman Brothers Band — *Stand Bank: The Anthology*

2004   George Harrison — *Dark Horse Years 1976-1992*

2004 James Otto — *Days of Our Lives*

2004 Marshall Tucker Band — *Carolina Dreams* (Bonus Track)

2004 Marshall Tucker Band — *Searchin' for a Rainbow* (Bonus Tracks)

2004 Original Soundtrack — *Porky's Revenge!* (Expanded)

2004 Rolling Stones — *Jump Back: The Best of the Rolling Stones 1971 – 1993* (Remastered)

2004/2005 Releases Scheduled

Rolling Stones — *Licks Live*

Chuck Leavell — *Southscape*

John Herman — *Just Ain't Right*

Michael Lee Ferkins — *Mood Swing*

Plus appearances on new CDs by:

Lee Ann Womack

Sevenmore

Index

John Lennon was shot to death [feeling a ...]
[yes]terday in New York. The world is [Bill Wym...]
[in] shock. Probably the most influential [me to stay]
[so]ngwriter of the past fifteen years, [...] [It wa...]
[...] as "[...]" to a generation. I feel so [...] horrible
[...] loss. Mark David Chapman. God have [...]va Princess
[...] Fayed along
[...] He knew not what [...] a car cra[sh]
[...]s on mo[...]
in a tun[...]

OOLS OUT   8-16-78 [...]

[Mick's re...]
[...]e finished the record. Got [...] to working on [...]
Monday morning at 7:30 AM. [...] about the acci[...]
[s]uicide flight. Been taking [...] was gravely inju[...]
business around [...] [...] the time I got [...] [s]ell
[...] still the case. But [...]
hotel to go to [...]
[...]een in my roo[...]
5-6-78   [...]d. Of course [...]
[...] story. People
[...] myself... it's [...]

I just woke up from a nap on
bus. We're at some college (SUNY, I think)
[u]pper state N.Y. That's all I know about   [...] on
[wher]e we are. Guess what... the truck broke   seminar
[dow]n again. HELP!! Man, I wish we could run   [pr]oduct a[t]
[tha]t damn thing into the river. But we're   [...] my [...]
[...] please. They've sent a wrecker   [l]astin[g] [...]